THE TEN HOURS PARSON

GEORGE STRINGER BULL

THE TEN HOURS PARSON

*Christian Social Action in the
Eighteen-Thirties*

By

J. C. GILL

LONDON

S·P·C·K

1959

First published in 1959
by S.P.C.K.
Holy Trinity Church
Marylebone Road
London N.W.1
Made and printed in Great Britain by
William Clowes and Sons, Limited
London and Beccles

FOR

E. L. and C. J.
STRANKS

ACKNOWLEDGEMENTS

LACK OF space prevents my going into detail, but I am in debt to many people for help or encouragement. Some of the information gathered does not find a place in this book, but I hope to use it in a biography of Bull, to follow this shortly. I must place on record my thanks to many people who have helped me in varying degrees.

First, I am greatly indebted to Mrs Yelloly, Wood End, Carleton, Carlisle, and her family. I shall have more to say of them when I introduce Bull's biography. Mrs Yelloly is the granddaughter of George Bull's brother, Edward. Her interest in what I have been doing has been encouraging and her help valuable. Her mother, the late Mrs F. P. Bull, kindly supplied a photograph of the water-colour of old Pentlow Rectory. I am sorry that she did not live to see the book, in which she was very interested.

After I had been working for some time, I came across Professor Driver's *Tory-Radical*. No writer on this period will be able to ignore that excellent book. I had the advantage of sources not open to its author: the Balme Letters have become available since it was written. An interesting link with the Christian social movement of our own day is to be found in the fact that Matthew Balme was the great-uncle of Mr T. M. Heron, whose name is known to all who have kept abreast with the movement. His family gave the Collection to the Bradford Libraries Committee.

I have benefited from the friendship of Dr J. T. Ward, formerly of Magdalene College, Cambridge, now of Queen's College, Dundee. Correspondence and conversation with him have been helpful. He is a generous fellow-student. I look forward to his comprehensive work on the Factory Movement and his "Life" of W. B. Ferrand.

I am in debt to various clergymen who answered my letters, helping me to confirm or disprove theories or ideas about Bull's movements and those of other clergymen connected with him. I have to thank: The Venerable B. C. Snell (then at Tattingstone), The Reverends L. Folkard (Pentlow), F. W. J. Reynolds (Stanway), R. A. Maddocks (Hanging Heaton), J. Lennox (Woodhouse), and E. H. P. Norton (Almesley). Dr J. S. Purvis, Canon of York and Diocesan Archivist, answered a number of my queries and gave me access to the records at the Borthwick Institute. The Diocesan Registrars of Ripon and Chester were helpful also.

Most of all, I must pay tribute to the interest and help of many Librarians. The City Librarians of Bradford and Birmingham, the Borough Librarians of Dewsbury, Halifax, and Huddersfield, were very kind. My friend the Borough Librarian of Burnley, Mr Caul, has gone to much trouble for me. The staffs of all these libraries, as well as of Manchester and Leeds, have all helped me to feel that librarians have high professional standards and live up to them. No trouble has been too great for them. But of all of them, I must acknowledge the co-operation of Mr Macdonald, the Reference Librarian at Bradford, of Mr H. J. P. Pafford, the Goldsmith's Librarian at London University, and of Miss Canney and Miss Spurrell, two of the latter's assistants. Access to the Oastler Collection was essential to me. Mr Pafford gave me access and the two young ladies saw to it that I missed no part of it. Through them I was able to trace material in the Columbia University Library, and Miss Mary Rita Burns and Miss Alice H. Bonsall there showed the same interest as all other librarians. I cannot overlook Mr Frank Beckwith, of the Leeds Library, who allowed me access to relevant copies of *The Leeds Intelligencer*. He is himself well-versed in this phase of social history, as befits the Secretary of the Library of which Michael Sadler was Chairman. I am also indebted to the Librarian of the Church Missionary Society, and to the officials of the National Portrait Gallery who supplied me with reproductions of portraits.

My friends the Reverend George Suthers read the first rough draft, the Reverend Harry Isherwood the last one, and the Reverend Alan Clark portions of both. They have all been helpful and encouraging.

Two young ladies helped me with typing. Mrs Rosemary Larter typed the first draft and Mrs Joyce Blackledge typed some revisions for me. Another Burnley friend, Mr E. N. Egar, whose work takes him to many places to which I had to go, enabled me to spend an hour or two in them when I could not have gone without the transport which he provided. As a parish priest with diocesan and central commitments, I could not have found the time to do this work so quickly without this practical service.

Like many other writers, I am deeply indebted to the S.P.C.K. for valuable advice, and I am particularly grateful to them for the suggestion that I should use the material available in this way. In saying that I have followed their advice, I do not lay at their door any blame for the faults in this book. Their suggestions caused me to improve it.

I hope that all these people will accept my acknowledgements as an expression of my warm thanks. Others will find their help was relevant to matters dealt with in the biographical work.   J. C. G.

Acknowledgements are due for permission to include quotations from the following works :

Lord David Cecil : *Melbourne* (Constable and Co., Ltd)

C. Driver : *Tory-Radical* (Oxford University Press, Inc.)

E. Hodder : *The Life and Work of the Seventh Earl of Shaftesbury* (Cassel and Co., Ltd)

A. C. Johnson : *Viscount Halifax* (Robert Hale, Ltd)

G. M. Trevelyan : *History of England* and *English Social History* (Longmans, Green and Co., Ltd)

CONTENTS

ILLUSTRATIONS

PREFACE

SOME SIX years ago my friend Canon Stranks, now Archdeacon of Auckland, was talking to me of his biography of Dean Hook, which he had just completed. Our conversation turned to the Ten Hours agitation. He said, "There is room for a 'Life' of Parson Bull, you know", and suggested that I ought to write it.

I was born in Bowling and knew of Bull as a legendary figure, and I knew that his name appears in some of the older books about Bradford and in others about English social history. It had never occurred to me that no one had thought of writing his biography. My friend added, "You have always been more interested in this social stuff than I have." I took up the task and found myself enthralled by it. I must therefore make my first act of acknowledgement one of gratitude to him for suggesting that I should undertake it. I am glad that he and his lady have allowed me to inscribe this book to them.

When it was finished, although I had telescoped some parts, it was too long for publication, and the publishers suggested that I should extract the material dealing with the two great controversies in which Bull was involved and write a book which would put on record the Church's part in the social history of that period. That is what I have tried to do here. I should like to make it clear that I did not begin this task with any thought of special pleading. I found that Bull's life during those years was dominated by these two controversies, although he was active in other fields. I could not help finding out how active were the parsons and their associates. I have stood on the hustings to propagate the Christian Faith in places so far apart as Portsmouth and Glasgow Green—as well as many places between—and faced heckling by the Church's enemies. I often wished that there was less for which apology had to be made or extenuation pleaded. I have myself been surprised to find how closely the Church was associated with the two great movements of the eighteen-thirties.

As I gathered material, the force of much of Coleridge's writing struck me afresh. When Bull began his ministry, Coleridge was deploring the departure from Christian social tradition. In our own day, Dr Demant has looked backward and shown that Capitalism "kicked away the ladder by which it had climbed". He says that "the nerve of Capitalism is the predominance of market relationships over a greater part of the social field". This has seemed to me to be borne out by the writings and speeches of the period with which this book deals.

I began with a desire to give his due to a man who had done notable work. As I came to know him better, I found it to be a greater work than I had realized. The views he held have become unfashionable, seeming to be irrelevant. I have no hope that my account of his work will change this. I cannot help wondering, however, what problems would never have arisen had the factory reformers managed to keep alive the tradition they sought to preserve. Would the Labour Party have come into being? What would have been the pattern of our trading and economic life? Would work have united men instead of dividing them? These and other questions occur as one looks back to the intervening period. Bull and his friends were concerned with the immediate effects of the system which they criticized, but they looked closely enough to be able to criticize the assumptions of those who sponsored it. It is my belief that later developments have proved them to be right, in spite of the ameliorative effects of legislation and social services.

I

CURATE OF BYERLEY

WHILE IT is true that to most of us has been imparted a one-sided and misleading version of many aspects of the history of our own country, of no period is this more true than of the early days of the nineteenth century, when a battle of ideas was being fought. The teaching of Adam Smith was being developed and, in some respects, distorted, Ricardo and Malthus were exercising great influence, and the application of their teaching to social and industrial life was regarded as the working out of the natural law. As the apostles of Liberalism gained influence, capturing the organs of propaganda and the seats of learning, they succeeded in changing many of the assumptions hitherto held without question. The assumptions held unconsciously by the community in which we live are the most potent factors in our education, and the change of outlook brought about by the political economists during the third and fourth decades of last century enabled the Liberal historian to impart a one-sided view of the social history of England.

In consequence of their success, it is widely assumed that the political reformers of the early nineteenth century were also the social reformers who sought to better the lot of the working population. Social historians have overlooked the contrary evidence—if, indeed, they have not concealed it—and their successors have copied their mistakes. During the eighteen-thirties, there were two important social issues about which there was deep division; they were: the limitation by legislation of the hours of child labour in textile factories, and the reform of the Poor Law. The division sprang from different modes of thought and from the acceptance of different ways of life. Those who led the movement to secure factory legislation, and who were to be found amongst the opponents of the Poor Law Amendment of 1834, took up their position because they were opposed to the political economists and to the greater part of their teaching. They have largely been forgotten because they lost the battle of ideas. What they accomplished has been accredited to their opponents because the history of those days has largely been recalled and interpreted by the successors of their opponents.

The factory movement was first built up under the leadership of four men, although of course, it is true that they had support from men whose names figure in social history in other connections. These four men were: Michael Thomas Sadler, John Wood, Richard Oastler, and George Stringer Bull. Sadler was the Parliamentary leader, the first Member of Parliament to introduce the Ten Hours Bill into Parliament. Yet his name is known to our generation mainly because of the tradition for public service maintained by succeeding generations of Sadlers. Few people know of his work as a factory reformer. Wood was a Bradford manufacturer, Tory and Churchman, a man of good works and varied interests. Oastler was a Tory, a Churchman cradled in Methodism, agent of the Fixby estate of Thomas Thornhill. As Thornhill did not live on his Yorkshire estate, Oastler had much of the influence that would have been his master's. Bull, the fourth member of the quartet, was an Evangelical clergyman who worked in Bowling and Bradford for fourteen crucial years.

Each of these men made his own particular contribution to the movement. Through them, the support of other people and groups was won. Bull is of particular interest because he was the kingpin, as it were, of the Church's connection with the movement. It is in searching out his part in the campaign that the extent of the Church's support for it becomes evident. Others, holding high ecclesiastical office, played their part, but by common consent he was the cleric most active and influential in the movement.

He was the sixth son of John and Mary Bull and was born on 12 July 1799 at Stanway, Essex. The following year, John became curate to his father, who was Rector of Pentlow in the same county. The benefice has been held by several generations of the family and indeed is still in the gift of John's great-grandchildren. George spent his early boyhood there, but a spirit of adventure or restlessness caused him to join the Navy when he was ten years of age. (Budding officers went to sea at an early age in those days.) The same adventurous spirit, coupled with a developing sense of vocation, led him to share in an early Church Missionary Society venture in Sierra Leone. These experiences have their place in a biography of Bull, but their mention here is justified by subsequent references made to them and because they help us to know something of his early life and training.

His work in Sierra Leone was cut short by a bout of the fever which earned for Sierra Leone such a bad name. After studying at home—the family had by this time moved to Tattingstone in Suffolk—he was ordained to the diaconate by the Bishop of Chester (for the Archbishop of York). The ordination took place in the parish church of Saint James, Piccadilly, on 23 March 1823, and that to the priesthood at Bishopthorpe sixteen months later. He was licensed to the curacy of Hessle, near Hull, where Edmund Garwood, a family friend, was the Vicar. Shortly before he left there, he married Mary Coulson, the daughter of a Hull merchant.

Although he lacked academic training, Bull had a flair for teaching. Letters written to his home during his service in the Navy show him to have been a good penman and a ready writer. He went to Sierra Leone as a missionary schoolmaster, and during his stay at Tattingstone earned a local reputation as a teacher. The Evangelical Revival had quickened the conscience of many people, and was stimulating the demand for the emancipation of slaves, for evangelism, and for education. Bull's gift for teaching was an asset to him throughout his ministry, and in his first curacy he combined his pastoral work with pioneering work in education. It was this work that led to a momentous meeting. During the summer of 1824, he attended a Hull conference on Sunday School work. Although the plight of Yorkshire factory children had not at that time become a live issue, Sadler was even then concerned about them. He spoke to Bull about the difficulty of teaching children overworked in unhealthy conditions as these children were. At a time when education was beginning to be the concern of Churchmen and Dissenters—as well as of other voluntary bodies—hindrances in the way of children acquiring the rudimentary education available were an offence in the eyes of those who were struggling to impart it. This conversation with Sadler was Bull's first knowledge of this social evil, the remedying of which was to take up so much of his energy. That lay in the future, however, for it was not an issue that came close to him at Hessle, a country town with largely rural trades. The immediate result of this meeting was the beginning of a friendship between the two men which lasted until Sadler's death and which grew with the passing of the years. During their later association, Sadler had cause to value Bull's stout championship, and Bull's regard for Sadler was often made evident, not least when he named one of his sons after him.

During the second half of 1825, Bull began to work at Hanging Heaton, in the ancient parish of Dewsbury, to which parish he was licensed at the end of the year, when the Archbishop of York consecrated the new church at Hanging Heaton. Although in the parish of Dewsbury, the village had a community life of its own, and the curate had a considerable measure of independence. While Bull's first task was to finish and furnish the church building, to build the school, and to build up a worshipping community there, he was active in other fields. He was one of the leaders of the temperance movement which grew up to persuade the working population to resist the temptations to drink excessively, he was a leading speaker in the missionary cause, his vigorous support of the movement for the emancipation of the slaves was never forgotten during his Yorkshire ministry, and his work for education was unceasing. These activities earned him a wide reputation in the West Riding and he had not been at Hanging Heaton very long before he was invited to take charge of the church at Byerley, where he had greater scope and where he did his greatest work.

His stay at Hanging Heaton enabled him to have a first-hand knowledge of the problem to which Sadler had referred. Dewsbury is the centre of the Heavy Woollen district, an area specializing in the making of shoddy goods. The term "shoddy" has come to mean "second-rate", poor in quality, stuff not made to last, but this is a misleading use of the word. In Lancashire and the parts of Yorkshire where shoddy goods are made, the word has a more precise meaning. In Lancashire, the cloth is woven from yarn spun from cotton waste, while in Yorkshire it is mainly woven from the fibre of rags which have been unpicked, mixed with virgin wool. Some of the goods made in the Heavy Woollen district are of first-class quality.[1] In the early nineteenth century, of course, this trade was in its infancy, but already Dewsbury and its neighbouring villages were being industrialized. Bull, therefore, gained his first experience of the new industrialism. He began to understand what Sadler had in mind when he had dis-

[1] A novel giving local colour of this area is *Value for Money*, by Derrick Boothroyd.

cussed the difficulties in the way of the education of factory children. Later, when giving evidence before a Parliamentary Committee inquiring into factory conditions and their effects, he told of the shock the experience had been to him. There was as yet no sign of any organized agitation to improve the shocking conditions, and he was new to the district, unknown, and gaining only an onlooker's impressions. Bull became a well-known, well-liked, but much hated man in the West Riding, and while it is true that his main work in Yorkshire was done during the eighteen-thirties, his own testimony told of the intense unhappiness which he felt when he first saw the conditions of life endured by the factory workers, especially by the factory children. Although four years were to pass before he became active in this cause, his allegiance to it was being won during those years.

Ten years earlier, it had seemed possible that the ideas of Robert Owen might provide the solution to the problems raised by the new industrialism. He could provide evidence that he was no mere dreamer by the success of his own venture at New Lanark. He anticipated the later model village of enlightened industrialists, and his idea of "villages of co-operation" was in some senses better than the paternalism of some of the later experiments. Owen, however, was forced to recognize that the working classes needed a good deal of education before the affairs of the village community could be entrusted to them, so that even New Lanark did not constitute an ideal illustration of what he hoped to achieve. He did not win the help of those people whose help he needed. When the rich and powerful were giving to him help and encouragement and showing interest in his experiments, it seemed that his proposals would soon become practical politics. But his attack on the monetary system lost him some support, his attack on the profit motive and on the competitive nature of industrialism earned for him the enmity of traders and industrialists, while his attack on religion made it difficult for Churchmen and Dissenters to support him. References to him in speeches and writings of some eminent Churchmen betray their interest in his ideas and their regret that he should so misrepresent religious teaching and institutions that he set a gulf between himself and some of his well-wishers.

When Bull first came into contact with the new industrialism, however, Owenism was rather less to the fore than it had been. Owen realized that neither rulers nor potential rulers were likely to form a policy based upon his ideas, and he went to spend some time in America in the hope that a new nation with a republican constitution, and without (as he thought) the class traditions of this country, might prove more receptive.

With the temporary decline of Owenism, though not as a result of it, had come a revival of trade unions. The repressive measures enacted during the French war had been accepted by many people as necessary, although Radicals hated even the memory of Pitt on account of them. The unrest that followed Waterloo and culminated in Peterloo—when the magistrates of Manchester read the Riot Act and ordered the yeomanry to charge demonstrators at Saint Peter's Fields—had led to further repressive measures. The Six Acts, besides prohibiting the bearing of arms, private drilling and the holding of certain kinds of meeting, had muzzled the cheap press. Attempts to silence the Radicals continued for some fifteen or twenty years, but by 1824 the Government had been persuaded to repeal Pitt's Combination Act and to legalize trade unions. Francis Place, outside Parliament, and Joseph Hume, inside Parliament, were the prime movers in this, although even their careful selection of witnesses to give evidence before the Parliamentary Committee and their assiduous lobbying would have been inadequate without a considerable body of support ready to be mobilized. It came from the better type of employer, the steady, thoughtful, type of worker with gifts of leadership, and members of the ruling classes not averse to any move that would halt the growth in power of the new industrialists. Some support came from Ricardo and those who shared his outlook, as indeed Place himself did. They believed that trade unions could not affect the working of the laws of political economy but could be a means of enabling the workers to learn how inexorable is the working of those laws. After the passing of the Acts of 1824 and 1825, the nature of trade unionism began to change. Unions were no longer underground movements, subversive, and disguised as friendly societies. They became legalized bodies with growing power, though this power shrank in times of bad trade. In spite of some adverse legal judgements when trade unionists were charged on some technicality, the unions slowly developed. Bull's short ministry at Hanging Heaton coincided with the beginning of this rebirth. During 1824 and 1825 there was a boom, and wages took an upward turn, although they were still pitifully low. At the end of 1825 wages fell again. With these variations in trade came similar ups and downs in the fortunes of the trade unions, but the movement slowly developed and was destined to play a major part in the social history of the country. Some years were to pass, however, before the workers could combine with sufficient strength to influence the course of events in the industrial world. The first improvements were effected by the weight of a public opinion aroused and educated by others, although trade union leaders often lent their weight to those causes.

Many people, especially Radicals, attached little importance either to Owen's proposals or to the campaign for industrial action. They pinned their faith on the idea of political reform, which they believed would enable all social and economic problems to be solved. Even Place and Hume were amongst them. With the fear of Jacobinism passing, the Reform movement grew in strength. Slumps and depressions increased the demand for reform. Workers were led to believe that reform would improve their lot. There was much violence, especially in the country places, and the responsibility for this must be laid at the door of politicians whose interests were served by those unfortunate people who clamoured to exchange one set of oppressors for another. Indeed, the proposed reforms were not designed to give the oppressed the right even to choose their oppressors.

Bull was no supporter of the Reform movement. He was a Tory. He did not trust those who sought to gain political power. Not all opponents of parliamentary reform were obscurantists and reactionaries. Some Parliamentary leaders—Canning and Huskisson, for example—were sympathetic towards the aspirations of the industrial workers. Many who lived in the industrial areas—Sadler the politician, and Bull the parson, for example—knew only too well the type of person which would secure election to Parliament if the reform proposals were carried through. The record of the bishops during the reform debates has been made much of by anti-clericalists. It may be true that they opposed the Reform Bill because of narrow party considerations—and no doubt the fear of disestablishment had much to do with their opposition—but there was good ground for the belief that the lot of workers would not be bettered by Parliamentary reform. If the right to elect Parliament was accorded to those whose outlook led them to regard the poverty of the industrious classes as being in the nature of things, the outlook for the workers was grim. Men whose interests were served by the sacrifice of politics to industrialism and commercialism were not the ideal judges of the issues confronting the nation.

In our own day, we attach much importance to the power of the ballot-box. We are inclined to think that no country can be truly democratic unless it enjoys our own system of Parliamentary government. We believe that we exercise pressure on our Members because they will sooner or later solicit our votes, giving us the opportunity of expressing our views on the major political issues of the day. A person who does not vote is regarded as a bad citizen, indifferent to the issues of the day, although in fact he might refrain from voting precisely because he is alive to them. Actually, of course, there is usually no fundamental difference between the candidates, and voters are left with the option of choosing which colour they prefer, providing they choose black. For party politics would be impracticable if there were no agreement on fundamental issues. In Bull's day, the real battle was to determine which set of ideas should order the nation's life and dominate the political scene.

Even to-day, it would be interesting to reflect upon the source of the demand for particular legislative acts. Do the political parties create a demand for them or does it first appear in some movement outside Parliament? It is certain that at the beginning of the nineteenth century changes were made as the result of public pressure rather than by the willing choice of rulers, unless the changes benefited the rulers. Without doubt, the first of the mass movements which set the pattern for subsequent campaigns was that which led to the emancipation of the slaves and ultimately to the ending of slavery. The act of 1807 had made it illegal for a British subject to engage in the slave trade. But there remained 750,000 slaves in the British Empire, and the abolitionists were determined to free them. The missionary societies were in the forefront of the campaign. Men of goodwill and men whose motives were mixed gave active support. Missionary zeal was one of the first results of the Evangelical Revival; Churchman, Dissenter, and Methodist vied with each other in this. Missionaries in slave-owning colonies kept their societies informed of the treatment meted out to some of the unfortunate enslaved people. Some of them, linked with members of home congregations by friendship or kinship, kept their friends informed of their difficulties and of the opposition with which they had to contend. Even if slaves were well-treated, their enslavement was an offence to the newly awakened conscience of the abolitionists.

They sought to quicken the conscience of the nation. Sermons, letters read in churches, broadsheets, meetings in public halls, in schools and chapels, meetings on the hustings, every possible means of arousing public opinion was used very effectively. In 1823, Fowell Buxton introduced a motion into the House of Commons which called for the gradual abolition of slavery by the declaring free of all children who should be born after a certain date. He embodied in his motion the statement that slavery is repugnant to the British constitution and the Christian religion. He was defeated, but he had sufficient support to win from the Government an undertaking that regulations would be drawn up to protect slaves. The avowed purpose was to ensure that slaves would be educated to enable them to be fitted for the responsibilities that emancipation would bring.

The campaign continued. The planters of the West Indies and other parts of the Empire remained recalcitrant and obdurate. It was still necessary to keep British people alive to the issue and primed with information about what was happening. Bull, as a returned missionary, still in touch with friends overseas, bore a share in this work. The task of quickening the unawakened conscience and of maintaining public interest was one from which he gained great satisfaction. The fight for the freedom of the slaves was a fight against vested interests, as are almost all movements for social betterment. The third phase of the fight was not a long one. Within a few years, the campaign, aided as it was by the blindness and stubbornness of some of the planters and the brutality and injustice of others, brought the issue to a successful conclusion. In 1833, slavery was abolished throughout the British Empire.

Apart from Bull's part in the campaign, it is of interest to us for two reasons. In the first place, during the campaign for limiting the hours of labour of factory children, the appeal was made to the same humanitarian instincts as those to which abolitionists had appealed and the support of those who led the campaign to end slavery was sought. Even more important is the fact that the method of influencing Parliament by this kind of outside pressure came to be the pattern for subsequent campaigns. Lectures, meetings, publications, well-organized rallies, the campaign culminating in mammoth petitions to Parliament and Parliamentary lobbying came to be the normal method of pressing upon the legislature the country's concern about some pressing social injustice. For some decades this was to be so, for the passing of the

Reform Bill did not achieve what its advocates had promised and what the unfranchised were led to hope for.

The emancipation campaign was gathering momentum when Bull went to Byerley in the winter of 1826/7, soon after Mary had given birth to their first child, Margaret. He had earned a reputation as a diligent pastor and a good teacher, but his reputation was enhanced by his vigorous speaking on the subjects that concerned many people, particularly this issue, so much to the fore, and temperance, becoming a subject of social importance and one with which he was concerned very early. At any rate, the reputation he had built up caused him to be invited to undertake work which gave him ample scope for his various gifts.

Byerley Chapel, now the parish church of Bierley, is situated some two or three miles from the mother church of the parish of Bradford. In 1826, it was the nearest chapelry to the parish church on the Wakefield side of Bradford. The curate, although assigned no district by law, was left free to minister to the township of Bowling. Even now, after some hundred and thirty years, it is possible to see that Bowling has grown up by the populating of a number of neighbourhoods some of which are still in a measure distinct from the others. When Bull went there, this process was but beginning. The factory owners were building shelters for their operatives. So far as they could be called "houses", they conformed to the view then current that houses were an extension of the factory, necessary to the factory system in order that workers may be accessible to the factory. They were not intended to provide more than shelter, and those who lived in the conditions of overcrowding, lacking even rudimentary sanitation, were not expected to want anything better. With the pastoral problems of the Curate of Byerley we are not here concerned, but it is relevant to the theme of this book to stress that the rapid growth of these pockets of industry created them. It was experience as a pastor that made Bull become the crusader for social betterment, especially for the improvement of the children's lot. As a rule, houses come to be regarded as slums as they decay and as the general standard of housing improves. The shelters built for factory people in Bull's day seemed to him to be slums as they were built. It is true that country conditions were bad, but they seemed to him to be preferable to conditions in the new buildings provided for factory workers. But the aspect of his pastoral life that caused him the more readily to join in the factory

PENTLOW PARISH CHURCH

movement was his concern that his people should be taught. The work of the National Society was beginning to develop, and he left ample lasting evidence of his enthusiasm for education in the schools he built. He found, however, that to build schools was not sufficient. It was important that children should be free to attend them and that they should be in a fit state to be taught when they did so. It was because he found that his children were too exhausted to learn that he plunged himself into a bitter controversy.

2

THE EMERGENCE OF RICHARD OASTLER

Bull had been at Byerley about four years when the West Riding was suddenly agitated by discussion about the need to limit the working hours of factory children. The rapid development of industrialism made it an important part of the whole social problem and the opposition to the factory reformers arose from the changing social outlook.

The eighteen-twenties had been years of depression and political agitation. After the French wars, the economic life of the nation had many ups and downs. The politicians and the educated classes did not understand what was happening. Lord Liverpool betrayed his own lack of grasp when he said that there was much over-production. The attempt to restore the pre-war monetary system had brought disaster, and indeed the banking system failed repeatedly in the financial sense and continuously in the social sense. The Government, "in the interests of sound finance", had followed a deflationary policy as thoroughly and persistently as it dared. Prices fell, but loans were not scaled down. Landlords could not afford to reduce rents and farmers could not afford to reduce the price of corn to the lower level of the deflationary period. Cobbett estimated that the agricultural labourer and his family consumed one-fifteenth of his total production. The hand-loom weavers suffered a decline in both money wages and real wages. In the newer industries, the workers were a little better off when they were working, but there was much unemployment. In 1826, the King asked the Archbishop of Canterbury to request the bishops to call for charity sermons in the churches of their dioceses that distress might be relieved and, no doubt, revolution averted. By 1830, the condition of the country was alarming. The ranks of the reformers were swelling. In the South, bands of labourers burned ricks, assaulted agents, threatened tithe-owners, and became increasingly daring in their violence.

Throughout that year, *The Times* was much occupied in reporting disturbances in the country. The low wages and high rents created hostility towards tithe owners. The gathering of tithes was unpopular. "The Clergy have the odium attached to their collection", said *The Times*. In the North, the condition of the unemployed was as bad and of the employed only a little better. In many homes, the paltry wages of the young children constituted the whole family income. Trade unions began to grow. In growing, they became more violent and seemed likely to become still more so. A Whig Government had succeeded Wellington's Tory Government. The Duke's assertion that the constitution was so near to the ideal that he would not take the responsibility of tampering with it had ended any hope that Tories would yield to pressure on the reform question. The Whig Government—or at any rate, Melbourne, the Home Secretary—repressed the risings in the South with uncharacteristic firmness and even severity. These risings were unco-ordinated, though frequent, but the fear of revolution returned because of them. Many people, including the King himself, urged Melbourne to take even more repressive measures. Other people thought him severe enough, and some of the judges supported him in a way that was reminiscent of the Bloody Assize. It is hard to apportion the blame for this blot on English administration, but much of it must be laid at the door of agitators who sought to further their own political purposes by using the grievances of the depressed classes to stir them to violence. The fear of revolution made it certain that any Government, particularly one that was pledged to reform, would repress the first signs of revolutionary violence.

To repress violence did not remove grievances or relieve distress, however. The North experienced less violence than the South and was spared the misery and horror arising from savage court sentences in consequence. There was plenty of unrest, and agitation for Parliamentary reform grew. Radical and Whig papers and pamphlets stimulated it. Men of the North no less than men of the South pinned their hopes on reform.

The campaign to secure factory legislation opened against this background some months before the troubles in the South became acute enough to call for Melbourne's repressive measures. It was not a part of the movement for Parliamentary reform. Indeed, the leaders were Tories, although Sadler and Oastler both suggested measures of Parliamentary reform that were more democratic than were most proposals. The real originator of the movement was John Wood. His father had built up a thriving business and left a large fortune. John Wood, Jr, had added to his fortune by launching out in the worsted trade. He was one of the best employers in Bradford, and his firm's mill was one of the most up-to-date. He had rented Horton Hall, a fine old house on the rising land to the south-west of Bradford and about a mile from the town.[1] With John Rand and Matthew Thompson, two like-minded employers, he had tried to persuade other manufacturers to limit the hours of child labour to ten. The discussions had broken down, and a minority of three could not hope to achieve reforms of this sort in the teeth of trade competitors. Wood was known to treat his workpeople as well as the prevailing conditions permitted, and he never ceased to long for the improvement of these conditions.

Some three years after his abortive attempt to secure a limitation of hours by the co-operation of the employers, he took advantage of the opportunity afforded him by a visit of Richard Oastler. They had in common their churchmanship and their political allegiance, and shared enthusiasm for the emancipation movement. Oastler, however, had no knowledge of factory conditions, although he lived within sight of the Huddersfield mills. He was more closely concerned with the affairs of the country estate which he managed and the activities arising from his position as agent for an absentee landlord. He had gained a local reputation as the result of taking the lead in a local dispute with Musgrave, the Vicar of Halifax, on a tithe question. He had not objected to the payment of tithes, but had resisted what he considered to be unjust demands. His leadership had won for him a place of standing in local circles quite apart from the status of his position at Fixby. Wood saw in him a man with the gifts that he himself lacked for the task he was anxious to see accomplished. He said on one occasion :

"I wonder you have never turned your attention to the factory system."

"Why should I?" asked Oastler. "I have nothing to do with factories."

"That may be so," replied Wood. "But you are very enthusiastic against slavery in the West Indies: and I assure you there are cruelties practised in our mills on little children which, if you knew, I am sure you would strive to prevent."[2]

---

[1] When the See of Bradford was created in 1919, Horton Hall was rented as a residence for the Bishop. The first two bishops lived there.

[2] "Alfred" (Samuel Kydd), *The History of the Factory Movement*, 1857, Vol. I, p. 96. *Home*, Vol. I, p. 53.

When Oastler expressed surprise, Wood told him of conditions in the Bradford mills, of the length of the working day of young children, of the scant opportunity allowed them to take their meals, and of the brutal treatment meted out to them by the overlookers. He made it clear that these conditions were fairly general, and that manufacturers who were given to works of philanthropy permitted these things to happen in their mills. He told Oastler of the hours of labour and the conditions in his own mill, where they were better than in most factories but where they were still bad—a fact which gave him sleepless nights and filled him with self-condemnation and a sense of impotence. Before Oastler left Horton Hall next morning, he was called to Wood's bedroom—it was not yet dawn—and persuaded to promise to use his influence and devote his powers to secure the removal of the cruelties from the factory system. It was the dawn of Michaelmas Day 1830, when Oastler rode off. There could be no better day than the Feast of Saint Michael and All Angels on which to embark on a campaign against evil in any of its manifestations, and neither Wood nor Oastler knew how fierce was the dispute they were starting, nor how long they would need to battle. The Church on this day is reminded that Michael and his angels fought against Satan and his angels, and the factory reformers believed themselves to be fighting the Lord's battle with the Lord's help. When they had occasion to rejoice because they thought they had achieved their object, their first thought was to give thanks to God.[1]

Whatever Wood's faults—and he could be difficult on occasion, although usually quiet and peaceable—to him belongs the real credit for launching the crusade. He it was who gave to the cause the sort of sanctions to appeal to people priding themselves upon diligence and generosity in humanitarian causes. Some months later, at his instigation, the aim of Oastler and his supporters was declared to be the reduction of the working hours of children to ten. Thereafter, they never entertained any suggestion of compromise. This too the movement owed to Wood. His gifts of money to the movement are said to have amounted to more than £40,000, and his influence on it was wisely exercised and greatly valued.

From the outset, the appeal was to the consciences of those who abhorred negro slavery for religious or humanitarian reasons. This is evident from Oastler's first move. He wrote a letter to *The Leeds*

[1] See Appendix B.

Mercury, which he headed "Yorkshire Slavery".[1] So anxious was he to appeal to abolitionists and to consciences they had awakened that he ante-dated his own awakening. He said that he had been stirred by a Leeds emancipation meeting of 22 September—"from none could more sincere and earnest thoughts arise to the throne of Heaven"—yet one shade obscured his pleasure. It was the failure to apply the same principle throughout the Empire. He wished that some of the able and pious champions of negro liberty had looked nearer home and directed the attention of the meeting to scenes of misery, acts of oppression and victims of slavery, even on the threshold of their own homes.

After amplifying this, he appealed to the Yorkshire Members to move for legislation and addressed himself to the children with sympathy. He pointed out to the abolitionists who were employers of child labour how inconsistent they were. Was it blindness or was it hypocrisy?

"The blacks," he said, "may fairly be compared to beasts of burden, kept for their masters' use; the whites to those which others keep and let for hire."

Bad as was the negro's lot, self-interest caused the owner to keep him alive and in good health, but he who hired the white slave recognized no such responsibility.

Baines, the Editor and proprietor of *The Leeds Mercury*, was so shocked that he withheld publication of the letter until he had verified Oastler's charges. Having done so, he prepared his readers for them and accompanied publication of Oastler's letter with another editorial regretting the warmth of Oastler's expressions. The whole story of the moves and counter-moves of those early days is told graphically and in detail by Professor Cecil Driver in *Tory-Radical*. At first, the discussions were carried on in the columns of the Leeds papers. Simeon Townend, a Thornton (near Bradford) manufacturer, accused Oastler of being unreasonable in comparing conditions in the worsted trade with negro slavery. Others besides Townend spoke of the benefits to the children of factory work—who acquired habits of early rising and punctuality, they said, as well as quickness and dexterity. Their arguments appear smug to us, but the doctrine of work for work's sake was being preached on many platforms and from some pulpits. One of Townend's anonymous supporters proved to be a prominent Dissenting minister.

[1] *The Leeds Mercury*, 16 October 1830.

It soon became clear that Oastler had not overstated the facts. Even the *Mercury*, although unwilling to support him, declared that in saying that children were employed from 6 a.m. to 7 p.m. he had referred to the best mills, and that in fact fourteen and fifteen hours a day were exacted from those children who worked in the worst factories in the towns, and that matters were even worse in country places.

A Bradford meeting of millowners held at the Talbot Inn, influenced by Wood and his two like-minded associates, Rand and Thompson, agreed to press for legislation to secure a sixty-three hour week for young people under fourteen years of age. Townend's opposition was unavailing at the meeting but was carried on with more success after it. He persuaded many who had pledged themselves to support the petition to be sent to Lord Morpeth, one of the York-shire Members, to support him in a counter-petition. Oastler wrote to the Press expressing his disappointment at the response of the mill-owners; he was particularly disappointed that no consideration had been given to the need for regulating the age at which young children should enter the industry.

Townend, and Ackroyd, his main supporter, gathered support. The Halifax manufacturers agreed with that section of Bradford manufac-turers which had condemned Oastler for his "inflammatory letters", and formulated fourteen resolutions stating their position. They said that it was no hardship for young children to work a twelve-hour day and that it was easier for them than for adolescents. They painted a grim picture of the economic consequences of the proposals before Parliament. They pointed to the taxes on corn, which hit labour, and to those on soap and oil, which hit industry. Their resolutions set out the implications of the doctrine of *laissez-faire*. It was in the nature of things that the poor and their children should work. Let matters take their course. Better still, they argued, remove existing restraints, and manufacturers and merchants would benefit. Legislation would do more harm than good, but if Parliament decided to enact legislation, it should provide for a twelve-hour day or a seventy-two hour week.

The proposals to which the Halifax manufacturers referred were embodied in a Bill sponsored by Sir John Cam Hobhouse, the Radical Member for Westminster. He proposed that no child under nine years of age should be allowed to work in a factory, that young people between the ages of nine and eighteen should work no more than sixty-six hours a week—eleven and a half hours a day and eight and a

half on Saturday—that there should be a half-hour break for breakfast
and an hour for dinner, and that no person under eighteen years of age
should work between the hours of 7 p.m. and 6 a.m.

As Professor Driver says, the discussions that followed were concerned with specific proposals and no longer with general principles
only. *The Leeds Mercury* took its cue from the manufacturers and
became the main exponent of the point of view expressed by the
Halifax resolutions. When the younger Baines, in the absence of his
father, "cut" Oastler's letter of reply to the Halifax manufacturers
and commented adversely on the rest, the breach between Oastler on
the one hand and the Baineses and the *Mercury* on the other was
widened if not yet complete. *The Leeds Intelligencer* published it in full
with some favourable comment. This was the beginning of the consistent support that paper gave to the movement and the healing of a
breach created by editorial criticism of Oastler during his difference
with the Vicar of Halifax.

Discussions by then were somewhat less local. London and Scottish
papers were aligning themselves on one side or the other. Discussions
about Reform took the first place, but by the middle of 1831 the
factory issue was beginning to interest a wider public. Some aspects of
the discussion puzzled people who were unfamiliar with factory conditions. The number of hours worked varied from mill to mill, but that
thirteen hours a day (with a short break for meals) was the normal
working day in the best of them was not denied. The conditions
inside the factories were unknown to people outside the textile trade,
however, and the fact that allegations made by some correspondents
to the Press were denied or minimized by others was a still greater
cause of confusion than differences about the length of the working
day. Many sympathizers had an uneasy feeling that the situation could
not be so bad as Oastler depicted. Even more was it felt that he was
guilty of exaggerating its seriousness when he likened working conditions in Yorkshire factories to slavery in West Indian plantations.
Bull, in spite of some little knowledge of the subject, could not at that
stage regard the issue as of the same urgency or seriousness as the freeing
of slaves. Later, when he had become one of the leading figures in the
campaign, he said that when Oastler wrote his first letter on the subject, he himself was actively engaged in the anti-slavery campaign. He
had taken serious note of what Oastler had written, but he could not
agree that here was "a slavery more horrid than colonial slavery". He

recollected that he had to go to Oastler's chapelry, and did so "in somewhat of a pugilistic humour, determined to dispute".[1] Oastler was not there, however. Bull added somewhat wryly that it was just as well, for when he made close inquiries of his Sunday scholars, themselves mainly factory children, he found that conditions were worse than he had imagined. He had for long been familiar with the sight and sound of children going to work early and returning home late, but he had uneasily accepted it as a necessary evil. He had no knowledge of what went on inside a factory. At any rate, his enquiries and observation led him to realize "the appalling mischief to health, social order, morality, and religion, which are inseparable from your ordinary system of nearly fourteen hours". It seems that there were three phases in Bull's awakening to the plight of the factory child. His meeting with Sadler made him aware of the problem, his stay at Hanging Heaton added to his disquiet, but his Byerley ministry and the shock that Richard Oastler gave him completed the awakening.

Some months were to elapse before he could publicly declare himself or take any action. Mill owners organized their steering committees to secure the rejection or modification of Hobhouse's Bill; the operatives and their friends with Oastler at their head, organized their committees to secure its improvement or at least its passing. The Bill, however, was modified and further modified so often that when it was passed it applied only to the cotton trade—in which some existing regulations were ignored—and much was emasculated. For the virtual abandonment of the Bill, the *Mercury* blamed Scottish and West Country manufacturers, but Oastler and his "short-time men" believed this to be but part of the truth. They blamed the West Riding manufacturers in equal measure. It was clear that much more intensive propaganda was needed, and when in the autumn of 1831 Sadler agreed to move a Ten Hours Bill, this propaganda became a feature of the life of all the manufacturing districts in the West Riding. Before the year ended, Bull was associated with it.

Hitherto, the argument had been carried on in the public Press, largely by people associated with the textile trade. Meetings had been mainly sectional, discussions by groups of people within the trade or amongst interested professional men. In the winter of 1831/2, however, the campaign followed the pattern of the anti-slavery movement.

[1] 19 February 1833. Reports in Leeds papers; also in *White Slavery*, Vol. VI. Oastler Collection, Goldsmith's Library, London University.

Public support was rallied by means of mass meetings in the main industrial centres. The second of these took place at Bradford on 27 December 1831. It was well attended. Some of the better employers, headed by Rand and Wood, supported the movement by their presence and commendations. The first speaker after Wood was J. C. Boddington, the Curate of Horton. Horton was, of course, the part of the parish in which Wood lived, and Boddington's name appears in the reports of the many Bradford meetings. He was one of the many Anglican clergymen who were active in the movement and he never ceased to support it, although his work was less spectacular than Bull's. Even at this early stage, a number of doctors were actively supporting Oastler. During the earlier phase of the campaign, Oastler had been able to quote from a book by Dr C. T. Thackrah, of Leeds, and more and more medical men were glad to support the movement. At this meeting, two doctors from Bradford Infirmary told of their experiences as they attended young factory workers and of the appalling effect upon child workers of the long hours of factory labour. Other doctors supported them. Oastler followed. He was developing a tremendous power of swaying an audience. Most of his speeches had been addressed to comparatively small meetings of his own supporters or of the committees. A public debate with the Baineses and the first of the great public meetings—at Huddersfield on the previous day—had given him some consciousness of his power. Indeed, in the days to come, there were to be occasions when he allowed himself to be carried away by his own powers of platform oratory and the heady wine of an audience's approval. On this occasion, however, he was superb.

His supporters heard him often and every speech was in some way memorable, but the Bradford meeting stands out in the history of the movement because it was the occasion on which Bull identified himself with it. The meeting was surprised and gratified by his speech.

I beg leave to support this resolution. As I entered this room, I heard a person say, "What have the parsons to do with it?" Sir, they have a good deal to do with it; and I conceive that a most fearful responsibility rests upon those Ministers of the Gospel to oppose all the influence they possess against any system which tends to prevent the moral improvement and religious advance of the people. I have not been invited to take part in the proceedings of the day, but I did not need an invitation.[1]

---

[1] Leeds papers of first days of January 1832. Also, *Oastler and the Factory Movement*, Oastler Collection.

He spoke of the many barriers to the moral and religious improvement of young people, of his five hundred Sunday scholars, "and," he added, "I feel my very heart smite me when I am scolding these poor children for coming late to school. It is not at all extraordinary that they should take an extra nap on Sunday morning." Others were to blame, not the children. Moreover, some of the most strenuous supporters of Sunday Schools were amongst those who employed the children. "What time was there for ABC?" he asked. In any case, such learning should be acquired on weekdays. On Sundays, the children should receive religious instruction.

Finally, he paid a tribute to Sadler, telling the meeting of his conversation with him seven years earlier. He could testify

> that this cause is dearest to his heart. We happened to talk upon Sunday Schools and he called my attention to the very system we are met to consider. I do declare without any reference to Parliamentary partialities but most conscientiously upon the word of a Christian that I believe the poor of this country have not a more firm and unflinching friend than Michael Thomas Sadler.

He pledged himself to work for the Ten Hours Bill. Oastler had a new ally, and Bull had added to his many interests a commitment which was to absorb much time, effort, and thought. It was one which he could not refuse as a Christian, particularly as he was a Christian minister working amongst people, especially children, who were victims of the factory system. During the years that followed, he often addressed himself to his colleagues, appealing for their co-operation on these grounds. If he earned for himself the title of "the Ten Hours Parson", he did so because he was driven by a strong pastoral sense.

3

ENLIGHTENING THE PUBLIC

THE TEN HOURS organization grew up in stages. Possibly Oastler had assumed that it was only necessary to draw attention to the facts for the public to demand the removal of the worst features of the factory system. Possibly he even hoped that a vigorous challenge to the humanitarian professions of the millowners would spur them to take action. It is unlikely that Wood cherished any such illusions. He knew from experience that the employers would not only refuse to take voluntary action but would make any restrictive legislation as innocuous as they could if they could not prevent its being passed.

No doubt he would be relieved at the measure of support given to him at the Talbot Inn meeting, but this reaction must have given way to a feeling of disappointment when so many of his supporters went over to the opposition. Their defection destroyed any hope of co-operation within the trade. The publication of the Halifax resolutions made it clear that a bitter campaign lay ahead.

It was certain that one or two public-spirited men could not cope with the powerful opposition that was being organized. Help came from many quarters. Men who were active in one or other of the many reform movements either offered help or commended the cause to their supporters. In some places, a group of textile operatives came together to supplement in their own locality the work that Oastler was doing and to influence local opinion as he was trying to influence opinion elsewhere. Sometimes, local committees were formed to further the cause. The Huddersfield Committee, which claimed to be the first of these, was almost entirely composed of Radicals, mainly tradesmen. At Leeds, where a committee was formed at about the same time, the membership was largely made up from the representatives of the mills. These two committees came into being spontaneously; others came into being as the idea caught on. Operatives and sympathizers formed committees in imitation of these two, while in other places they were formed as a result of the direct help and encouragement given by the leaders from Leeds, Huddersfield, and Bradford. Later, Oastler and Bull gave much encouragement to the formation of "Short Time Committees", as they were called.

They did valuable work at every stage of the campaign, although during lulls in it, following some partial success or some halting rebuff, some of them almost died. Each committee had on it varied types of people. Oastler's aim cut across party politics and brought together people who agreed on few other questions. Not all of them were dominated by Radicals so completely as that at Huddersfield.

Some of them came into existence in order to frame replies to the millowners. One of the most useful pieces of work done by any of them was the publication by the Leeds Committee of its reply to the Halifax resolutions. It was compiled to send to Hobhouse as a counterblast to the mill-owners' arguments. Reprinted, it became a handy *aide-memoire* to speakers. It was capably drawn up, well thought out, and an early indication that the millowners and their supporters would be matched in debating skill and reasoning powers.

Hobhouse's Bill was the occasion for the creation of many of these committees. It was generally accepted that his original proposals embodied the most that could be hoped for. They were not satisfactory, but it was agreed that it would be unwise, in view of the strength of the opposition, to press for better provisions. The committees, therefore, supported Hobhouse.

Methods varied. Some committees concentrated on pressing Members of Parliament to support the bill; some collected signatures for the petitions sent to Parliament, while others sought to enlist the support of the middle classes and of the clergy and ministers. They believed that if the facts were really known, the evil and injustice in the system would not be tolerated. All of them took every opportunity of proving true the allegations of cruelty in the mills and of the heartlessness of employers. The issue was not limited to a question of hours and children's ages; the hardness of millowners and the practised cruelties of some of their employees were important details adding strength to the reformers' case. The West Riding papers of this period contain many discussions between millowners on the one hand and the Short Time Committee men on the other. The committees had no concerted plan. Indeed, although they had come together to make the most of the opportunity Oastler's letters had given to them, they had no direct contact with him.

By the time Bull joined the movement, this had been remedied. Some six months earlier, the members of the Huddersfield Committee had approached Oastler with a request that he should assume the leadership of the movement. The dissolution of Parliament a month earlier had prevented the passing of Hobhouse's Bill, and it was necessary for him and his supporters to begin again. It seemed to the Huddersfield men that a well-organized and concerted campaign was essential and that all those concerned with factory reform must join forces. Oastler had written the fifth of his series of letters to the Yorkshire press, and he had for the first time declared his aim to be the passing of a Ten Hours Bill. Although Wood had tried to secure a ten-hour working day for children as far back as 1825, neither he nor Oastler had deemed it expedient to make the securing of this by law a first objective. By the end of April 1831, however, Oastler had become conscious that a policy of compromise and the setting of limited objectives was unlikely to win over any substantial part of the opposition. His all-out demand for a Ten Hours Bill provided a better rallying point than Hobhouse's Bill.

Oastler was less sure than the Huddersfield men about the wisdom of joining forces. He was reluctant to identify himself with them. He was a Tory: they were Radicals. He was a Churchman: they were Dissenters. He was anxious to do nothing to harm what had become his chief public interest, and he feared that he might alienate many who could help the cause if he made open alliance with men from whom he differed in both religion and politics. Churchmen and Dissenters were at variance on many matters, and sharp differences in politics made personal friendships hard to maintain. Oastler was justified in fearing that close personal contact with men so widely separated from him—socially, politically, and theologically—was unlikely to be easily maintained and might well be misunderstood by possible supporters and misrepresented by opponents. After some hours of discussion, their arguments and urgency bore him down. Oastler and his new friends agreed to keep party politics out of their discussions and to sink religious differences in the interests of the common cause.

"The Fixby Hall Compact" was adhered to, with the result that through the good offices and loyalty of his Huddersfield friends and his own devotion to the cause, Oastler was able to satisfy Radical doubters, and earlier suspicions were put to rest. *The Leeds Intelligencer* and *The Leeds Patriot* were strange allies, but in this campaign, allies they were. As Professor Driver says[1]:

> The Compact brought Oastler greatly increased power and soon made him the best informed man on factory conditions in the West Riding. The number of his working-class friends increased rapidly. They put him in touch with other short-time committees, and before long he was riding over to Leeds, Keighley, Bradford, and elsewhere, to attend their meetings as well. These and other well-wishers in the cause began to communicate with him directly. John Wood and his friends on the one hand, Hammond, Pitkeithley[2] on the other, were soon all keeping Oastler advised of their moves and intentions. Without any planning, Fixby Hall became the official central office of the whole campaign. By the end of the autumn, Oastler found himself the leader of a great movement.

Although a Ten Hours Bill was the avowed aim of the movement, Hobhouse's Bill was the only one likely to be presented in Parliament. To press for more would have divided the supporters of the Bill and lost the little it would achieve. The factory reformers campaigned in its support, therefore. When it was whittled away to next to nothing, and the little that was left not applicable to Yorkshire, attention was turned to the real aim of the movement. An organization grew that covered the textile areas of the West Riding. The Short Time Committee at Huddersfield invited the co-operation of friendly societies and trade unions. Most of them joined forces with the short-time men. They provided support in all the townships and villages of the Riding. Although the factory children were kept in the forefront by speakers and pamphleteers, both sides knew that a shortening of the working day of adult workers must follow any limitation of the hours of children's labour. Indeed, the Leeds Committee's reply to the Halifax resolutions included a definite statement to this effect. The Committee stated that its support for the proposals was due to this fact as much as was the manufacturers' opposition. Attempts to whitewash the opponents of factory legislation by saying that they did not oppose

[1] *Tory-Radical*, p. 89.
[2] John Hammond was the Secretary of the Leeds Committee; Pitkeithley was a member of the Huddersfield Committee.

legislation to protect *children* overlook these earlier statements.[1] The whole working-class movement was well aware of the implications of the reformers' proposals, and its leaders knew that in ranging themselves alongside the Ten Hours men they were helping forward their own cause. Some people, including Parson Bull, were drawn into the movement by their concern for the children—and Bull never ceased to regard them as his first concern—but the support of many working-class organizations sprang from recognition of the fact that not only children would benefit by factory legislation. No doubt the motives of many supporters were mixed—humanitarianism was often mingled with self-interest—but many knew that the movement embodied some of their own purposes.

Soon after Bull joined the movement, a parallel organization began to grow up in Lancashire. This was mainly due to the lead given by John Doherty, a trade union leader. He was trying to build a national federation of unions in a National Association for the Protection of Labour. His trade unions contributed much to the movement although the law had only tolerated them for seven years. The friendly societies, closely associated with the trade union movement, were much in evidence at the reformers' great rallies. The organization gathered strength as the smaller villages came to have their own committees or groups. Methods of propaganda previously used were adapted to the circumstances of the locality and intensified where work was already being done. Bull himself was soon drawn into this work. He was in demand in Bowling and Bradford and, very quickly, farther afield also. When it was decided to form a Central Committee, he became a member and was its secretary at a critical time.

The issue was bedevilled by the uncertainty in the political world. Another General Election seemed to be imminent and most people thought that the reform of Parliament was far more important than the reform of the factories. Moreover, the intense feeling and the sharp divisions in the political world made difficult the discussion of factory reform as a non-party issue, especially as the Liberal Press had by this time ranged itself against the reformers. Tory and Radical supporters of the movement were agreed on few, if any, other issues. But the movement was no longer confined to a few conscientious manufacturers, a few Christian men who had been shocked by what they had learned and a few groups of workers, with some Radical supporters.

[1] See G. M. Trevelyan, *History of England*.

It was more than a regional working-class movement headed by a small group of reformers. The range of interest had been widened, and people having no connection with the textile trade were being reached. It was far from being a national issue, however. In view of the furious campaign being waged to secure the passage of the Reform Bill it was not easy to reach a wider public. People not concerned in factory problems had to be made aware of their existence and of their serious-ness at a time when they were being pressed to decide about matters in which they had more direct interest. Factory reformers had to make a louder noise than Whigs and Liberals, who were concerned with problems of franchise and, in the main, opposed to factory reform. The fact that the columns of the Liberal papers were closed to the reformers, and that reports of meetings were either attenuated or distorted, was a further hindrance at that time.

When Bull first associated himself with Oastler and his cause, the campaign of public meetings was in its early stages. Earlier meetings had been organized for specific groups of people, but the series of the winter of 1831/2 were addressed to the public at large. The first of them was held at Huddersfield on 26 December, the day before the Bradford meeting. The Short Time committees had arranged one in each of the important centres of the West Riding. They were intended to rally support, to enlighten the general public, winning such support that Parliament—reformed or unreformed—must take notice. The anti-slavery campaign, then in its closing stages, had followed this pattern. The Reform agitation was being carried on by methods not dissimilar, except that speeches were more inflammatory in tone, more seditious in sentiment, and more violent in their immediate results. Public meetings, rallies, demonstrations, and petitions, had become the recognized means of rallying public opinion and exercising pressure upon Parliament. Professor G. M. Trevelyan, in his *History of England*, expresses the view that:

> The victory of the Anti-Corn Law League in 1846 had been a victory of new methods of political education and advertisement, which were another step along the road to democracy. . . . The sharp tussle between landlords and millowners, which had resulted in the Corn Law controversy had caused each party to champion the victims of its opponent. The miserable wages and housing of the rural labourer were proclaimed on League plat-forms: the wrongs of the factory hands were the most popular argument in reply. In this way, the unenfranchised had their wrongs advertised, and

in some cases remedied. The years of mutual recrimination between landlord and millowner saw the passage of Shaftesbury's Mines Act and the famous Ten Hours Bill for factories.[1]

This is not quite accurate. The emancipation movement inaugurated the "new methods of political education and advertisement". Subsequent movements adopted them. There seems to be little doubt that Oastler followed the methods adopted by Wilberforce, whom he admired. Nor was the ranging of forces as Professor Trevelyan saw it. If it can be said that either side replied to other, it was surely the Corn Law Leaguers who did the replying.[2] Opposing the factory reformers, they alleged that the Corn Laws made impossible the reduction of factory hours. Most historians ignore the first part of the factory reformers' campaign, yet it was during that part that the wrongs of the factory workers were "advertised". The public meetings and rallies were the means by which the whole country was made aware of the strength of feeling in the textile areas, for although the Liberal Press belittled the movement, the Tory and Radical newspapers gave ample space to it.

The Whig and Liberal Press, when compelled by events to take notice of the campaign, condemned Oastler as "an incendiary" and Bull as "a rabble-rouser". This was unjust and hypocritical. They were trying to do for their cause what was done for others by the same methods. It is true that abolitionists did not address slaves and that audiences could take a more impersonal view than could an audience which included a considerable body of factory workers when it was addressed by leaders of the movement. The same could not be said of the Reform agitation. Speakers led their audiences to believe that the wrongs suffered by the underprivileged would be swept away by the passing of the Reform Bill. They led hungry, workless, and dispossessed people to believe that the reform of Parliament would settle almost every social problem. They made it appear that opponents to reform proposals were opposed to schemes for the betterment of the poor and of the industrious classes. They were the men who decried the factory reformers. Baines, who vilified Oastler and Bull, could call upon a Leeds crowd to give "three groans for the Bishops, three

[1] Trevelyan, op. cit., pp. 646–7.
[2] See also *The History of the Anti-Corn Law League,* N. McCord, Allen & Unwin (1958).

groans for the Queen" at a Reform rally at which the Crown was ridiculed and revolutionary emblems were much in evidence.[1]

It is true that Oastler grew more aggressive as he became more exasperated by the tactics of his opponents. From the first, John Wood had wished that he had written in a more restrained manner and more than once regretted Oastler's vigour of speech. Yet the movement was never a threat to the constitution. The Radicals honoured their agreement with Oastler and kept party politics out of it. When the organization became less active for the time being, some of them joined some other of a more militant kind, but they did not hinder the cause of factory reform by making seditious speeches. The movement led by Oastler had too many Tories associated with it to permit it to become unconstitutional. Bull was one of them. He would associate with no movement that threatened to overturn the Constitution or which advocated violence.

The meetings would have been of little value had they not been stirring. Besides informing people in the factory areas—for it is possible to live there and to know little of factory conditions—and winning their support, publicity was important. The whole country needed to be made aware of the need for legislation. One of the most effective of the whole series was the Leeds rally, held ten days after the Bradford meeting. Workers from Leeds and the surrounding districts assembled in large numbers. The numbers were so great that it was held in the yard of the Mixed Cloth Hall instead of indoors. The Leeds Short Time Committee left nothing to chance in organizing it. The variety of banners demonstrated the variety of political creeds represented there. The speeches were forthright and made clear the unity of the gathering—apart from a few Liberals whose support for the opposition speaker provided a discordant note. Dr Thackrah, the Vicar of Leeds (Dr Richard Fawcett), Oastler himself, and William Hey, the Mayor, were amongst the speakers. Marshall, one of the leaders of the opposition was given the opportunity of putting his case. Contemporary reports say that there were 12,000 people present, and it is certain that more than 18,000 people signed the petition that was sent to Parliament as a result of it.

Parson Bull was soon pressed into service. His Bradford speech and his reputation as a speaker would help Oastler to see in him an acquisition to the movement. At any rate, he was one of the speakers at the

[1] *Leeds Mercury Extraordinary*, 15 May 1832.

Keighley meeting on 30 January (1832).[1] As it was his first as a Ten Hours campaigner, it affords some evidence of his approach to that work. He half-apologized for being there at all, being "nearly a stranger to the town", but he had the authority of Dr Dury, the Rector, who was prevented from being present by a prior engagement in Halifax. He read a letter from a Wesleyan minister named Marsden, recently returned from the West Indies and prevented by illness from attending the meeting. Mr Marsden said in the course of his letter:

> In those parts of the West Indies where my lot was cast, I saw nothing so oppressive as fourteen hours labour in a confined place, nor is there, I am persuaded, anything similar to it in the negro colonies of the British Empire.

Bull went on that he could say that he came as the representative of two ministers of the Gospel as well as on his own behalf, "but", he added,

> If I represented nobody else I would try to represent the poor oppressed children. They do not need representatives: we are all their representatives and we all feel that much must be done for them to place them in their proper scale of rational and intellectual creatures. At present, they are deprived of these advantages which in justice and humanity they ought to possess.

He denied that the movement was politically inspired or that he and his friends desired to irritate master manufacturers. He pointed to the array of speakers drawn from different political creeds but hoped that they were all agreed on the creed of humanity. After mentioning the comparisons that had been made between what Oastler had called "Yorkshire Slavery" and "West Indian Slavery", he said,

> Now undoubtedly there are some features of the factory system which are as odious and bad as some features in the West Indian Slave System, but we are quite sure we cannot be just in drawing comparison between the two; because we are not bought and sold nor can husband and wife be separated nor can we be laid down to receive thirty-nine lashes.

He went on to say that people who were doubtful about the movement because it seemed to lack influential support, who asked, "Who are the supporters of this cause?" and "Do you carry with you the

---

[1] Reprints of the reports of these meetings, which were reported in the Leeds papers, are in the Oastler Collection.

respectable and influential weight of Society?" were not asking a fair question.

The question ought to be:—

Is it a good cause? The supporters of the cause are not the point at all: and if the more influential portion of society will not support a good cause, it is time the less influential did. We cannot help that we are to be twitted with the absence of the more respectable portion of society. If they should come, we would be glad to see them; there is none but would be welcome to plead the cause of the factory children; and if anyone can prove to us that factory children are treated as Christian children ought to be, we will sit down and put our hands on our mouths.

He dealt with the physical effects of factory work, quoting the evidence of Leeds and Bradford doctors. He said that if anyone could prove their statements untrue, "we have them on another tack—on the score of morality". He referred the meeting to Mr Sharp, an overseer of the poor, who was on the platform, for confirmation of this. The condition of factory life led to all kinds of immoralities amongst young people. This he considered to be one of the strongest arguments in any appeal to a Christian audience. More than one leading ecclesiastic gave support to the Bill because of the moral dangers and temptations where young people of both sexes were gathered together in factory conditions. Referring to the anti-slavery movement, he said,

I have travelled many, many miles for that cause, for I hate slavery in every shape and form whatever, and indeed we want nothing better to fight with than the arguments that are made use of against West Indian slavery. These arguments will exactly suit us; they are ready made to our hands and we have only to use them properly to ensure our victory.

From the beginning of his campaigning to the end of it, he could not forbear to stress the impossibility of giving education to young people in the prevailing conditions:

I am a Sunday School teacher and I know that the children have not the means of improvement they ought to have. Some people say that pastors have no business to meddle in matters of this sort and that they ought to confine their exertions solely to the spiritual edification of their flock. I do so, and I feel obliged to lift up my voice against this system. I do not dictate to any other minister what his duty should be but I say these poor children should have less work and more time for improvement than they have now, and while I have tongue to speak and pen to wield, I pledge myself to advocate their cause until I see them in far better circumstances.

During the course of the meeting, a point was raised about West Indian conditions, and Bull was able to refer to newly issued Orders in Council. It is clear that he was well-informed on these matters and that he continued to support the abolitionist cause. He became less and less active in that cause as his colleagues in it attacked him for his activity on behalf of the factory children.

The half-apologetic note in this, his first speech of the campaign, was less in evidence as time went on. In particular, his tolerance of ministers who would take no part in the campaign wore thin. In those first days, however, he had only begun to know the opposition that increased in its intensity, and he was clearly anxious not to alienate potential supporters or to create needless opposition.

Replying to the vote of thanks accorded to him, he said that he was exceedingly thankful and grateful for it but ventured to think "that we shall be much better employed in encouraging one another than in thanking one another". He expressed delight that there was a spirit in Keighley to support the Ten Hours Bill and added that "we shall never desist till the whole country has said 'Amen' to it". There were to be many occasions on which he was to call assemblies to recollect the religious sanctions for the campaign. He came to be called "Chaplain to the Ten Hours Bill"—affectionately by his friends, scornfully by his enemies. On this first appearance on a Ten Hours platform, he expressed his thankfulness for the Christian spirit of the meeting and suggested that the Doxology should be sung. It was sung, says the newspaper report, with reverence and decorum. Meetings often seem to have been almost like revival meetings. Most of the leaders were religious men and it seemed to them to be in no way incongruous to end a meeting with an act of praise.

Of all the meetings in this series, the most difficult was the last of them at Halifax. At Huddersfield, Bradford, and Dewsbury, some of the influential manufacturers were taking part in the campaign and others were in sympathy with it. Even at Leeds, where there was a strong opposition, there was a strong body of middle-class support and even some of the manufacturers gave active help to the campaigners. The toughest opposition came from Halifax, where the manufacturers adhered to their resolutions and the middle class gave scant support. That section of the Whig Party most influenced by the Liberalism of the political economists and those who could already be called "Liberals" in the party sense were becoming more bitter in their opposition. The breach between Baines, their chief spokesman in Yorkshire, and Oastler had widened. The Radical Press and much of the national Press supported the reformers. The national Press was being compelled to take notice of the campaign. The first interchange of letters, the local discussions, and the first meetings, although creating considerable interest in the textile areas, were of limited interest in other areas. But the series of mass meetings had widened the interest considerably. Oastler, who had increased in power as he gained in confidence, was like the conductor of an orchestra working his players up to a crescendo.

From the first, he had been the object of attack for many reasons. He was a Tory, and his campaign was said to be part of a political campaign to divert attention from the Reform agitation. He was not a manufacturer and knew nothing of the problem. He was guilty of exaggeration, it was said. As the correspondence had proceeded, the bitter hatred of some of the manufacturers became more marked. It was fitting, therefore, that the concluding meeting should be where that bitterness was greatest. Oastler made clear his determination that the aim of the movement must be the passing of a Ten Hours Bill. Even this he had come to regard as a compromise, for he thought that eight hours of factory labour was quite enough. Moreover, conditions of work and the cruelties perpetrated on the children had come to be hardly less important issues than the question of hours. Some of the worst of these cruelties were perpetrated in the Akroyd mill, whose owner was one of Oastler's bitterest critics. References to specific instances of cruelty and harsh treatment were not lost upon the audience. Each scandalous case that Oastler mentioned was recognized, and roused the audience to greater indignation. The meeting was not concerned with argument: every person in the room knew all the arguments. It was concerned with the urgency of the matter, with the contrast of wealth and poverty as exemplified by the stately mansions of the manufacturers and the crowded hovels of the workers. It was concerned with the certainty of social disaster unless the worst abuses of the factory system were removed. The fight was on. For the next eighteen months an intensive campaign was waged by both sides. The reformers were concerned that considerations of humanity should prevail and that justice should be done. They were opposed by vested interests which could invoke convenient current philosophies to justify their attitude.

4

PARSON BULL STATES HIS CASE

THE BITTERNESS shown towards Oastler by Baines and the millowners was naturally extended in some measure towards all those who took leading parts in the campaign. Bull was quickly in trouble. At first, his worst trouble came as a result of a whispering campaign in his own district. It is one of the hardships of a clergyman that he is liable to be misunderstood or misrepresented whatever course of action he follows. If he is cautious because he fears that his pastoral work might suffer as a result of his incursion into public affairs, he is accused of indifference or cowardice. If he concerns himself about public affairs he is accused of going outside his proper sphere by those who do not agree with his opinions. He is liable to misunderstanding in what he says and hardly less in what he does not say. The people whom he seeks to benefit are often amongst the first to misunderstand him.

In those days, the Church was not in good odour. The bishops in the House of Lords and the clergymen in the parishes were regarded as the main opponents of Parliamentary reform. Most of them were Tories, although that label carried a different meaning from that which we attach to it. Bull was a Tory. For other reasons, notably his forthright speaking about the intemperate habits of many working-class people, he had made enemies. His work for the Ten Hours movement increased the number of his enemies although it added to the number of his friends.

There were two reasons for this.

The millowners made it seem that factory reform would reduce the workers' income. Some parents earned little themselves and relied on their children's earnings. Sometimes this was due to shiftlessness; often, it was due to the state of the labour market. In any case, the reduction of the working hours of children could only result (it seemed) in the reduction of the working hours of adults. The factory reformers argued that this would enable the work to be shared amongst more people—the term 'full employment" could not be used, for there was much uncertainty of employment. The reformers argued that there need be no reduction of income because trade was expanding. But in view of the resources for propaganda possessed by the millowners, it is not surprising that some of the poor—particularly the less thoughtful amongst them—should conceive a suspicion of the leaders of the movement. When it is remembered that not only Bull but also Sadler and Oastler were Tories, the grounds of suspicion and hostility are obvious.

The second reason for local criticism of Bull lay in one of his reasons for criticizing the factory system. While he always paid tribute to those remarkable women who triumphed over the shocking conditions in which they had to live, he deplored the inability of many other women to do the same. It was due, in his opinion, to the sheer impossibility of training girls to care for a home and a family. To master the arts of housekeeping is more important when the difficulties are many than when they are few. Bull said that the difficulty of training the future housewives was mainly due to the factory system. It was this part of his argument that gave great offence. Some of the people of Bowling and Bradford regarded what he said as a slight upon them. Some of them, who did not know his mind, as well as those who did not like his views, chose to regard what he said as a reflection upon factory workers. The working classes had many detractors who argued from the particular to the general, lumping them together in much the same way as people from slum clearance areas have been said to use their bath for storing coals. To people accustomed to this kind of generalization, Bull would seem to be criticizing a class of people. His enemies and opponents made it appear so.

Soon after he joined the movement, he wrote a pamphlet setting the case for factory reform. Cheap pamphlets were invaluable at a time when a few coppers constituted the price of a meal for a poor family. They could be passed from hand to hand and groups of people could make use of them. This particular pamphlet was the first of many written by him, and was in circulation less than three weeks after he had joined the movement. He not only set out his own reasons for supporting Oastler; he showed that the traditional Christian view of society was still held by ordinary parish clergymen. There were no

4

leaders of any school of Christian social thought within the Church, and social and political thinkers were propounding the teaching with which the factory reformers had to contend. The difficulty of keeping alive traditional Christian social teaching was increased by the fact that the Convocations were silenced, for between 1717 and 1852 they were only allowed to do formal business—a point overlooked by critics of the Church's social record of that period. There was no official Church body which could discuss current social problems or even, for that matter, ecclesiastical problems. But the social witness of the Church has been expressed more often in the pastoral work of parish clergymen and in the prophetic witness of a minority of Churchmen than in the pronouncements of her official bodies. In the early nine-teenth century, there were still many who retained some hold on tradi-tional Christian social teaching, inherited from the Middle Ages and related to later conditions by Hooker and other thinkers. Some of Bull's writings show that he took for granted much of this. The Liberals sought to impart a new body of social thought and to lead the nation to a different way of life. Oastler, Bull, and their friends, sought to adhere to the traditional way of life and thought, not by "impeding progress", as their modern critics would say, but by dealing with the new situation consistently with the social teaching traditional to Christ-endom. This is why Tories and Churchmen were allies for so long. There was something natural about the alliance. Bull was not an origi-nal thinker. He fashioned no body of original thought. It seemed to him that certain things ought to be done in common justice and that a Christian country could not tolerate the evils and the injustices which so much concerned him.

His first approach to the factory problem was on a practical level. In this first pamphlet, he showed this. After the courtesies of his opening remarks and an apology that his duties did not allow him to set out his appeal as he could have wished, he dealt with the meeting of the pre-vious month. He discussed the different views about the kind of legislation required. Should the bill provide for a ten-hour or eleven-hour working day? He reminded his readers that there was strong opposition to any legislation on the ground that it would be vexatious. Having discussed these positions, he went on to expound his own conclusions, born of experience in factory districts.

He said that the moral evils were of tremendous magnitude and that the education of the factory child was neglected.

THE OLD RECTORY, PENTLOW, THE HOME OF G. S. BULL'S CHILDHOOD

What knowledge having a religious or moral tendency can the factory child acquire? Suppose children have learned in infant schools or national schools to read the New Testament tolerably well before they become Factory Children, which is commonly the case at 8 or 9 years of age, what chance have they of improving on or even maintaining what they have learned? At 5 a.m. (or even at 4 a.m.) they leave their beds; they return at 7, 8 or 9 p.m. The factory system annihilates, as nearly as possible, the offices of parents or religious instructors to all moral intents and purposes.

Those children, "tied to the bell", who attended Evening School usually fell asleep from absolute exhaustion and could not profit by going to school.

To those who objected that to educate "the lower orders" was "to lift them out of their station and make them aspiring and discontented" and who made comparison between town and country "where the bliss of ignorance prevails", he had much to say.

This (he said) looks plausible, but the illiterate become dupes of the better informed—a fact which accounted for much of the incendiarism lately experienced in the Southern Counties. There is more servility in the agricultural areas; there is more of sincerity in the manufacturing areas.

(Again) I can testify, that in my humble exertions for the spiritual and temporal welfare of these people, though I have seen no little ingratitude, I have also witnessed much sincere and grateful affection—from the children especially. There is a rude and vulgar sternness among the working classes, but I believe it will wear off by better acquaintance. Respect begets respect. If the better conditioned classes shew little or no respect for the humbler classes, treat them with indifference and accustom themselves to speak of them with disrespect, they can hardly be surprised if they meet contempt in return. I have no wish to excuse or palliate want of proper respect in lower ranks of life, I am not afraid to rebuke openly.

In any case, he argued, critics who doubted the benefits of education could hardly say that it had been tried and had failed. There had not been schools commensurate with the population. He challenged every such critic to demonstrate that the factory children of the previous seven years, who had grown up "as complete dunces as heart could wish", had become the "most respectful, orderly and provident, portion of society". His insistence on the duty and the wisdom of educating the poor led him to regret the lack of opportunity left to do it. He had discontinued teaching to write at Sunday School. It had caused backward children to leave. In any case, to neglect teaching the Bible and religion at Sunday School was "a guilty indifference to the Royal Law". The whole problem was created "from cursed lust of gold". He went on to intreat

those who are active in promoting Sabbath institutes by their money and personal labours but who at the same time exact in the week day such a portion of labour from our tender youth as incapacitates them from profiting thereby not to deceive themselves any longer. Gain is not godliness and Mammon's logic will not be heard in Heaven's righteous Court.

Another moral evil of the system, he went on, was the tendency to obstruct and impair filial affection and parental authority. Not only did parents and children see too little of each other, but the labour the parents were forced to exact of them was "such as to blunt all the best of the affections of the heart in both parties". The duty to parents taught at Sunday School must seem unreal to children:

When their masters were Pharaohs and their parents Labans, their instructors must seem to be convenient apostles of both.

From this must follow the absence of parental authority or the gross abuse of it and the total want of affection and respect in children. Children, he pointed out, were with their parents less than one-twentieth of the time.

Do not parental authority and filial submission lie at the basis of the social edifice?

Are those who drag weary limbs to Sunday School and to the sanctuary of God likely to reverence religion in mature years? Or to prove impervious to the keen shafts of infidelity which would suggest Christianity to be a mere convention for those who would subdue the many to enrich the few?

Bull urged that the heartless factory system made children unfilial and anti-social. There was harm in the conditions in the factories, the indecent familiarities at an early age leading to revolting and obscene habits.[1] It was all taken as a matter of course, he said, but everything

---

[1] "I know the moral conditions of our factories well, but they are too scandalous and infamous to be told, even to a searcher after truth like you. They can only be alluded to. You may, however, form a vague idea of the evil consequences when you are told that girls are willingly debauched at 12 years of age; that girls and boys have less regard to decency than cattle; that overseers and others in office are debased below any other description of persons, and permit, if they do not promote, such atrocities as none without the most positive and credible evidence can believe is possible.

should be done to reduce the evils and to remove the dangers. The sexes should be separated and there should be female overlookers. The Factory System gave the death blow to education, moral improvement and religious instruction.

He called upon his readers to:

> View it in the sight of that tribunal where a man shall not only be called to answer for his own direct violations of the law of his Maker, but where he shall be equally responsible for the indirect influence of his conduct and pursuits upon his neighbour. The eager pursuit of wealth, busy commercial occupation, is always an opportunity of developing the selfish side of our fallen nature.

He told of instances of exploitation of young people known to him and went on to say:

> Power without due responsibility or control is too great for fallen human nature to resist and power is often in the worst hands.

After quoting relevant Biblical passages, he re-asserted, "Verily, there is a God that judgeth the earth." There was much of the Old Testament prophet in his make-up, and his approach was strongly reminiscent of Amos. Throughout the campaign, he continually adopted this Biblical and prophetic tone.

It was a main part of the argument against legislation controlling factory conditions and hours of labour that trade would be harmed by any such "interference". Indeed, the manufacturers were pressing for the removal of taxes that interfered with the freedom of trade. To the kind of argument advanced by the reformers, they replied that religion had nothing to do with trade and that no reason advanced on religious or moral grounds was valid. Bull showed the inconsistency of some of the manufacturers who advanced this argument.

> A man may be held up as a pillar of a religious society while he gives an eight year old worker a shilling a week. He swallows a camel on Saturday

---

"From enquiries I made some time ago, I was informed by two spinners of Stockport that there were 31 persons who were known to them each of whom was a grandfather; and yet not one of them exceeded 37 years of age.

"Girls become unchaste at a very early age as a matter of course; the whole family lived in one room, and hearing what they hear and seeing what they see, they never arrive at any notions of self-respect."

Letter from Francis Place to Harriet Martineau. Quoted by Vaughan Wilkins in *Endless Prelude*, pp. 10–11.

night and strains out a gnat on Sunday morning. Politicians may welcome such reforms but I want nothing to do with them as a Christian.

He enlarged on the difficulty of teaching a woman to be a good housewife, dealing with the ill effects of the factory system upon the cottage home. It was this part of the pamphlet, together with his criticisms of the moral conditions in the factories, that gave so much offence to some of his people. No doubt he had said something about this before he became active in the movement. Indeed, it is probably one of the aspects of social life which had driven him to Oastler's meeting. Here, he said:

The best housewife in England cannot save the home of a drunkard. The same misery comes from a wasteful wife.

He maintained that the girl who had to work long hours in a factory could not be prepared for her duty as a housewife in a cottage economy. Legislators did not know the system and its harmful effects on home life and education.

Wood's appeal to Oastler had been on the ground of their common interest in the emancipation movement. Oastler's first letter to *The Leeds Mercury* had argued that Yorkshire conditions were akin to West Indian slavery. From the outset, the appeal had been to people who were determined, on religious and humanitarian grounds, to free the slaves. Bull himself was active in the campaign to bring about their emancipation. In his pamphlet, he urged that slavery emancipation should be linked with the improving of conditions in England. The emancipation movement should go hand in hand with the campaign to end injustice in England. Otherwise, it was "foreign philanthropy", "one-handed, and of a left-handed character". He did not, at this stage, belittle the importance of the abolitionist campaign. He was anxious to make clear his belief that slavery, oppression, and injustice, should be resisted and their outcome removed whoever their victims might be. It was a constant source of disappointment to the leaders of the Ten Hours movement that so many of the leaders of the emancipation movement should be indifferent to the factory problem and, in many cases, fiercely opposed to factory legislation. In the early days of 1832, Bull still hoped to combine his work with the abolitionists with his work for the factory children.

Even so early in the campaign, he found it necessary to reply to critics who resented his own incursion into the discussions. Advocates for the cause of the factory children who were not engaged in the trade were called, "Busy-bodies in other men's affairs", he said, and were accused of being "inciters to Communism"—even in 1832! It was bad enough when an outsider like Oastler intervened. He was not engaged in the textile trade. For a parson to join him was regarded as monstrous. It was said that clergymen had better leave such matters "and be scarce at all meetings where politics and commerce are involved; let them attend Bible and Missionary Society Meetings; let them visit the sick, and not injure their usefulness". This, of course, is the line usually taken by those whose interests are being attacked when any clergyman takes part in a public discussion of this kind. It was not always the case, but the social witness of the Church had been weakened by the Revolution of 1688, the silencing of Convocation, and the Erastianism of the eighteenth century. The Dissenters, for the most part, preached the duty of the poor to submit to lawful authority and to accept the contrast between extreme wealth and abject poverty as divinely ordained. Evangelical Churchmen, as well as Dissenters, could call upon the poor to be thankful that they had not the rich man's hindrances to the gaining of eternal life. The growing concern of the clergymen of the industrial areas and the militancy of parsons like Bull were a new manifestation of the Church's social witness. But the Industrial Revolution had created a new situation and called for a counter-revolution. Bull had learned how great were the difficulties of pastoral work in the new social conditions. He answered those critics who called on the clergy "not to injure their usefulness" : "To whom? I take both sides, for the same arguments apply." "Is not our province invaded?" he asked his fellow ministers.

He was quite right, of course. Even apart from abstract principles of justice and humanity, hindrances in the way of the preaching of the Gospel and conditions that make it seem irrelevant and hinder its acceptance constitute a challenge to those who discern them. The setting of men's lives and the assumptions of the community in which they are lived have a powerful effect upon men. Assumptions unconsciously held affect a person far more than his consciously held beliefs and might well be the main hindrance to his accepting a right way of life based upon what he thinks he believes. Bull sought to resist the acceptance of avarice as a national virtue and commercialism as a way of life. These idolatries were being propagated by men who claimed to be Christians and combined the worship of God with the worship of Mammon. They could justify by sound economic teaching the double life they lived.

The severely practical issue that concerned Bull first was that of securing for factory children sufficient time to be educated and particularly to be taught the elements of their religion. In both these respects, he contended that his province was being invaded by the demands of the factory system. He ended his pamphlet by commending his case to "the candour of his readers" and to the blessing of God.

He earned some local unpopularity by the publication of this pamphlet. Indeed, it seems to have created some bitterness in Bowling. The second edition carried a footnote. In it, he referred to the very loud complaints of the manner in which he had treated the evils of the factory system. The complaints had come, in the main—"I am happy to find," he added—from the drunkards, disorderly persons and gossips. He stressed that he had allowed for the exceptions when he had dealt with the homes of the factory workers, but that he had stated what he knew to be the conditions generally obtaining. He had no wish to hurt them, nor did he treat inability as a fault. Their inability to make the best of bad conditions was due largely to the factory system which he was attacking. Indeed, he had referred to their lack of ability in that connection. He was anxious that girls should have a chance to acquire abilities they so often lacked through no fault of their own. He told of one father who had warmly approved of what he had said and had written on this aspect of the subject, supplying him with another instance supporting his contention. This man had watched his daughter darning and nodding in sheer exhaustion after her long day in the factory. Parents who were concerned about their children agreed with him in general, although opponents' propaganda created bitterness against him.

He reconciled himself to the prospect of misrepresentation and hostility by recalling the hostility encountered by our Lord and the martyrdom of the first Christian leaders, especially of Saint Paul, Saint Peter, Saint James, and Saint Stephen. He knew that he would be called upon to endure much less than they endured, but he felt himself to be in good company.

Although Bull developed his arguments as time went on, the reasons he outlined in this first pamphlet remained broadly the case he made for his own support of the cause. The difficulty of fulfilling his duty as a pastor, especially as a teacher of religious truth, the ill-effects of the factory conditions on the health and the morals of young people, the wicked injustice of treating people made in the image of God as mere instruments in the accumulation of money, and the idolatry which justified these evils, were the themes upon which his writing and speaking were variations. But he never ceased to be convincing. As his knowledge increased, his convictions were strengthened.

5

CHALLENGING VESTED INTERESTS

THE FACTORY reformers were faced with a stupendous task. They had to persuade the whole country that factory laws were necessary. If possible, they had to win over the opposition. In any case, they had to withstand the arguments and counter the propaganda of the vested interests. There were still many people in the textile areas who had not made up their mind, and, of course, large numbers of people in other parts of the country who had given no thought to the matter. A doubt in friendly quarters caused the wisdom of an all-out demand for a *Ten* Hours Bill to be questioned. Hobhouse in Parliament and Matthew Thompson in Bradford were doubtful. Hobhouse doubted the practicability of a ten-hour day, and Thompson was inclined to think the demand bad tactics. Throughout the campaign, this wavering had to be contended with. During the early days, it was a danger to the unity of the movement; later, it divided it and caused crippling dissension. When Hobhouse had failed to secure Parliamentary approval for the wider application of his own bill, Oastler had written to him to find out by whose influence he had been virtually defeated. In the course of the correspondence, Hobhouse had expressed the view that if Sadler attempted to secure the passage of a Ten Hours Bill—as he had heard that he intended —he would not be allowed by Parliament to proceed a single stage. The opposition of the manufacturers and the political economists was so great that well-meaning people like Lord Morpeth were shaken. When he expressed the hope that, if a further appeal were made, the movement should have the advice of men with practical experience, he did so because the strength of the opposition had surprised him. Wood, his partner Walker, and Rand, as well as other manufacturers, were known locally as supporters, but the leading speakers for the movement were not manufacturers. That Sadler was not a manufac-

turer was made much of in Parliamentary circles, and the fact that the
best-known campaigners were not made it easy for the opposition to
represent them as either dreamers or agitators.

The opposition had lobbied as assiduously as had the reformers.
They had met secretly and had supported the manufacturers from
Scotland and the West of England, who were not faced with an organization so strong as that built up in Yorkshire or even in Lancashire.
The millowners' refutation of the reformers' evidence of cruelty in
the factories was given prominence in the Liberal newspapers, which
had supported them in their editorials. As the campaign developed,
The Leeds Mercury in Yorkshire, *The Manchester Guardian* in Lancashire
and *The Morning Chronicle* in London, gave constant support to the
millowners. *The Edinburgh Review*, founded by Henry Brougham and
his Liberal friends, regaled the Whig and Liberal intelligentsia with
essays on the foolishness of trying to interfere with the natural order of
things. For the advocates of *laissez-faire* contended that factory legislation would do so. The millowners were able to quote in support of
their case the most up-to-date economic theories, which was very nice
for them. It was to their great advantage that they were supported
by the writings of men who were shaping the nation's thinking and
revolutionizing her way of life. The first important issue to be decided
arose from this contention that "economic laws" have the force of the
laws of Nature. If it is right, the contention that the state ought not
to interfere between two sets of free agents—employers and workers—
logically follows. The factory reformers denied the truth of the Liberal
premise.

There was, however, a second point.

Could it be said that the industrious classes were free agents?
Oastler and Bull constantly stressed how little freedom they had. If
there is competition for work, the person with power of appointment
and dismissal may be a free agent, but the person who goes hungry if
he does not get work certainly is not free. Hunger or the fear of hunger
is as potent an instrument in the hands of men with a slave-driving
mentality as is the overseer's whip. Even to-day, there are those who
advocate a "pool" of unemployed workers to ensure the competition
for jobs that would curb the demands of the workers. Any intelligent
observer of the industrial scene must know that fear of unemployment
is a frequent cause of trade dispute. Those who have less respect for
"economic laws" than advocates of a labour "pool" have said that the

fiercely competitive nature of trade arises from the fact that successful trading exports the unemployment problem. If the force of events and the strength acquired by the working-class movement have combined to expose some of the fallacies of the *laissez-faire* school, this exposure was in the future in 1832. That people with nothing but their labour to sell are not free agents is a fact that was not then established. The reformers found it difficult to persuade Parliament that young children were even more certainly not free agents. As we shall see, a Select Committee and a Royal Commission were necessary before this was established. The millowners had the support of most of the intellectuals. Men like Coleridge and Southey did something to stem the tide, and the nation's way of thinking had not yet been completely dominated by the new social philosophy. But the fact that political power was passing to the class of people to whom the new teaching was highly beneficial enabled it to be propagated the more easily.

The campaign to secure the passing of the Ten Hours Bill was one aspect of the attempt to retain the old standard of values and ways of thought. The humanitarianism which prompted the leaders and many of their supporters was not sloppy sentimentality. It was rooted in their conception of man's nature and needs, his rights and worth. It is true that their revolt against the working conditions in the textile areas arose from instinctive reactions rather from any worked out social philosophy, but this does not alter the fact that the movement owed its strength to their grounding in the Christian Faith. Later, they found themselves more or less compelled to think out their position. Partly to answer their critics' arguments and partly to give intellectual reasons justifying the stand they had taken, they worked out in a modest way a political creed in which the influence of Christian thought is plainly discernible. Professor Driver deals with Oastler's attempt to work out a Tory-Radical philosophy, for his experience of Tory-Radical co-operation made him believe this to be possible, and it seems that this might have been done at a higher level had not the Tories accepted much of Liberal social and economic doctrine. Mrs Frances Hawes, in her life of Brougham, says that "Peel's extraordinary delusion that he was a Tory persisted all his life and eventually transformed not himself but the Tories".[1] That transformation had not yet begun, however, and it was still possible for the factory reformers to

---

[1] Frances Hawes, *Henry Brougham*, p. 200.

appeal to Tory tradition. The tentative suggestions for Parliamentary reform made by Sadler and Oastler, if put into effect, would have made Parliament more representative of "The Two Nations" of which Disraeli was to write a decade later. Oastler's slogan, "The Altar, The Throne, and The Cottage", coined by him during the election campaign of 1832 and later used as a caption for *The Fleet Papers*, indicates the way his mind was working. Bull thought along similar lines, and their co-operation in the factory movement was but one aspect of their common religious beliefs.

This religious basis of their political creed is to be discerned in their reply to the defenders of the factory system that it would not work because it was wrong. They refused to believe that a system which offended against even human standards of justice could possibly be of God. Chaos and disruption must result. They believed that the system carried within it contradictions which made it unworkable. Long hours of work were physically harmful and an unjust imposition upon factory children. The large numbers of unemployed workers not only provided further evidence of the injustice of the system but also pointed to its irrational nature. The share-the-work-plea figured in much of the literature of the movement and in one or other of the speeches at most of the meetings.

Sadler moved his Bill in March 1832.

The organization which had grown up to support Hobhouse was strengthened so that Sadler would have support from a wider public in the textile areas. A Short Time committee was formed in almost every village in the West Riding; where this was not possible, a sub-committee of the nearest committee was formed. They saw to the distribution of the growing spate of literature. The Central Short Time Committee at Leeds co-ordinated all the work. The movement in Lancashire developed along similar lines, especially after a series of meetings in the March of 1832. After this, the arguments in the public Press were intensified. George Condy, of *The Manchester and Salford Advertiser*, contended with Vernon Royle, an apologist for the mill-owners, and with Holland Hoole, a vigorous and not over-scrupulous campaigner against factory legislation in general and Sadler's Bill in particular.

Although the meetings reached a wider public, it was important that sympathy should be turned into active aid. It was particularly important to win the support of the middle classes. To achieve this, two committees were formed. A Leeds Committee, called a "General Committee" to distinguish it from the Central Short Time Committee, was composed of members of the middle class and clergymen of Leeds and district, and was actively presided over by Dr Richard Fawcett, the Vicar of Leeds. Shortly after Sadler moved the Second Reading of his Bill, a society was formed in London with similar objects. The Duke of Sussex was its President, but his undoubted interest was never translated into active help. Although its members were mainly influential people, it achieved little when its work is compared with its active counterpart at Leeds. Perhaps its main value lay in its bringing the issue before some of the socially and politically influential people in London. The propaganda carried on by the Leeds Committee was of greater immediate importance, however. The existence of these two committees did something to meet the criticism of the movement with which Bull had dealt at Keighley. They harnessed the support of "respectable people".

Bull was mainly engaged in work in his own locality. He wrote a good deal, and his writings must have occupied more of his time than the meetings that he addressed. He spoke at a number of local meetings besides the Keighley and Dewsbury mass meetings, for it was important to strengthen support in Bradford and Bowling. In addition to his pastoral work, he spent much time preaching for missions, addressing meetings on temperance, the Bible and education problems. He was still playing some part in the emancipation campaign.

During the same March, an event took place which had repercussions later. At that time the Whig Government was concerned about Irish Education. How were the Irish to be provided with educational facilities with due regard to the susceptibilities of the Roman Catholic population? When Edward Stanley, the Chief Secretary for Ireland, withheld a grant from the Kildare Place Society, which had been doing educational work in Ireland, the supporters of the principle of "reading the Bible without comment"—which it had followed—organized protest meetings. Bull was the main speaker at one of them at Liversedge, not far from Bradford and on the road to Dewsbury. By this time, Dissenters were identifying themselves with the politics of the Whig Government and the social views of the Liberals. The protests seemed to them to be politically inspired, and they attended the meeting in militant mood. The meeting itself is not important to us here except that the accounts of it in *The Leeds Mercury* marked a decline in the relations between that journal and Bull. In spite of his activity in espousing the cause of the Church and withstanding Dissenters' attacks upon her, his activity in causes supported by the *Mercury* had won him some favourable comment. The references to him in the report of the Liversedge meeting, however, show that he was an object of bitter attack second only to Oastler.[1] At any rate, as a result of this affair, he won Baines's lasting enmity. The *Mercury* was growing in influence. Cobbett had named Baines "the Great Liar of the North" on account of the misrepresentations and distortions in it. If this was deserved, it did not lessen the circle of his readers. Even today large numbers of people read papers published by men they do not trust, and they are usually more influenced by what they read than they admit. Certainly, the influence wielded by the Baineses—father and son—was not confined to Whig and Liberal circles.

The meetings at Liversedge and Dewsbury in connection with the Irish Education question serve to show how the differences between the Church and Dissent were being reflected in the political field. This is important to us in considering the alignments on the factory issue. On that issue, Dissenters were divided, but on most others they supported the Whigs and the Liberals. On the Irish Education issue, it must be admitted that Bull and his friends were not on very good ground, but their opponents made no attempt to argue the question on its merits. They were content to leave the matter to the Government on account of its colour. The gulf separating Churchmen from Dissenters on religious matters was to be further widened by their political alignments and by the difference in their approach to social problems. Even on the factory question, the same tendency developed, although other factors more obviously came into consideration.

The drive to win support for Sadler went on throughout 1832, although it became involved in the campaigning prior to the imminent election. The Spring provided occasion for a spectacular rally which could not fail to attract attention. All the resources of the movement in Yorkshire were behind it, and it was the climax of this phase of the agitation. It took place on Easter Monday, a little more than a month after the Second Reading of the Bill. York was decided upon as the meeting place because of its associations. York and its Minster are dear to Yorkshiremen. The Castle Yard, where the rally was held, had a tradition for county meetings organized to focus attention on

[1] *The Leeds Mercury*, 10 March 1832.

important social or political issues or to rouse the nation to deal with them. A notable one, in 1779, had had nation-wide repercussions, for Christopher Wyvill, a parson who lived on his Yorkshire estate (instead of in his parish), had organized a meeting of nobles, gentry, and freeholders, which had petitioned Parliament "in favour of economical reform"—a petition directed against the corruption of George III's Parliament. It was signed by nine thousand freeholders. Ramsay Muir says that "It was the beginning of the use of public meetings for political ends".[1] Nearer in time were the meetings that had sent Wilberforce to Parliament. Some of the prominent leaders of the factory reform movement would be present at the 1807 meeting. Those meetings, it is true, were gatherings of people with political influence, voters and freeholders. The proposed meeting would include a minority of such with a preponderance of artisans and workless people. Yet to organize in York Castle Yard a rally of people from the West Riding was to draw the attention of the whole nation to the importance attached by textile workers to Sadler's Bill. It was an imaginative move to make the passing of that Bill a national issue and to ensure that the discussions should be nation-wide.

It was a tremendous undertaking and only possible because the Yorkshire organization was so good. The rally was looked upon as a pilgrimage besides being a demonstration. There is in Birmingham Reference Library a pamphlet dealing with it. It is a copy of an edition published twenty-five years later and carries a foreword by Bull and a dedicatory note addressed to the Earl of Faversham, previously the Honourable William Duncombe. He was one of the Yorkshire Members and a loyal supporter of Oastler. He was present at the York Rally. The pamphlet is entitled *The Pilgrimage of Mercy*, and adds to the information gleaned from newspaper reports and contemporary accounts.

Whether or not the majority of the pilgrims had heard of the Pilgrimage of Grace, it is certain that the leaders had, and they imparted to their followers something of the pilgrim spirit. The spectacle of thousands of them trudging along the road from the West Riding to the ancient city was bound to be impressive. The company grew as the journey to Leeds proceeded. Village companies, many of them led by a band, set out for the nearest centre. There they joined a larger company which was led by one of the leaders of the movement.

[1] *A History of the British Commonwealth*, Vol. II, p. 103.

Oastler, with the men of the Fixby Hall Compact, led the Huddersfield contingent. Some of the men from the villages beyond Huddersfield, who helped to swell the Huddersfield contingent, had left home in the small hours of the morning. The return journey was to take them three days. Parson Bull led the Bradford column, and others went from the other industrial centres of the West Riding. These columns converged on Leeds, where they were greeted by friends and foes who lined the streets. The bells of Leeds Parish Church welcomed them. The Vicar of Leeds was making the Ten Hours movement one of his main concerns at this time.[1]

As the contingents poured into Leeds on Easter Monday, they presented an odd spectacle—a mixture of grim purposefulness, of poverty and want—whose drabness was relieved by the banners bearing the movement's slogans. Most of the men wore clogs; some of them had borrowed boots or shoes. Few had overcoats, and many marched wearing a piece of woollen cloth to serve as a cape. They assembled in orderly and disciplined fashion. When they had assembled a storm broke, and several hours of rain delayed their departure. When the rain showed no sign of abating, the procession set off on the twenty-two-mile walk to York. Contemporary accounts give no hint of any dampening of their ardour. The long, winding procession went on its way through the wet night. The men sang hymns and local, traditional songs. They lighted their way with torches, roughly contrived. As they crested each hill and dropped down into the next dip into the road, "they left a long loud cheer behind," as one observer tells.[2] On reaching Knavesmire, the race course, where beer and bread and cheese were due to be served, there was another disappointment. The beer was there, but the bread and cheese had not been delivered. The situation could easily have got out of hand, but Oastler saved it. The *Mercury* had lately gibed at him, saying that he was getting above himself and imagined himself to be a king. The men had seized on this gibe and turned it to a compliment, dubbing him King Richard. On this occasion, at any rate, the title was deserved, for they responded to his appeal for patience and good order. They behaved as good subjects. The rumblings were stilled.

On the next day, the vast crowd stood in the Castle Yard and listened to speech after speech. The capacity of the people of those days for

[1] C. J. Stranks, *Dean Hook*.
[2] W. R. Croft, *Oastler and the Factory Movement*, pp. 59 ff.

listening to speeches seems to have been unlimited. These twelve thousand people listened to speeches from Sadler, Wood, Oastler, and Bull, who were their leaders. They listened to speeches by men whose influence was exercised on their behalf in other circles—Duncombe, who served the cause well in both Houses of Parliament, Dr Smith, of Leeds, and others. The leaders renewed their pledges and the rank and file cheered them. Emotions were stirred and wills were strengthened. If the mass meetings worked up the movement in a crescendo, here was the fortissimo.

There had been fears that so vast a body of men with so many grounds for discontent might get out of hand, but those fears proved to be unfounded. Oastler's confidence that there would be no trouble was justified. The High Sheriff of York, to whom he had given a guarantee, spoke to the crowd and congratulated them on their seemly behaviour and orderliness.

The return journey began badly. It rained heavily, and many of the pilgrims fell by the wayside. It should be remembered that a whole company of them were unemployed and that even those who were employed received very low pay. Great numbers of them were undernourished, and the privations of the outward journey, caused by the unusually bad weather, must have taken toll of them. Bull, however, with some of his fellow committee-men, scoured the city and hired covered vehicles, which were paid for by John Wood. Bull and his friends followed in the wake of the procession, picking up those who had dropped out and giving them refreshment. After a few hours rest at Tadcaster, the last dozen miles to Leeds were covered the next morning. The weather had improved and the morning was brighter. The men's spirit revived. It is recorded that someone began singing "Praise God from whom all blessings flow", and that this was taken up by others and passed to the rear. Nothing could better illustrate the spirit of the occasion—indeed, of the whole movement—than this picture of some twelve thousand men, most of them pinched and shabby looking, mudstained after two marches in the rain, singing of God's blessings many of which were denied them through the blindness of some men and the selfishness of others. They were not rebels planning violence or insurrection. They were decent men, most of them holding on to their religion, glad to follow the lead of Christian men who were trying to win for them and for their children some of those blessings, which flow from God. When Baines, in *The Leeds Mercury*, represented the whole affair as disorderly or worse, he maligned them and earned the demonstration against him which followed. There have been few occasions, if any, when so large a number of men with no political power rallied to impress those having political power without there being any breach of the peace. Their exemplary conduct was a testimony to the influence of the leaders of the movement and clearly demonstrated their regard for law and order. Yet the party in power and the Liberals, who aspired to power, pledged to reform and paying lip-service to democratic ideals, represented those leaders as incendiaries and public enemies.

6

SADLER'S TEN HOURS BILL

IN ADDITION to the strengthening of the Yorkshire organization, the early part of 1832 saw the campaign develop in Lancashire. In Manchester, medical opinion expressed itself strongly in favour of factory reform. Dr Bardsley, at a meeting at the Manchester Exchange on 8 March, said that he had suggested in 1796 that the system be ended. He found that night workers were susceptible to typhus during epidemics. He was concerned with the health, the morals and the comfort, of the working classes. He spoke of the moral dangers of night work, particularly to females. Like Bull, he deplored the lack of family intercourse caused by the factory system as well as the inability of young women to acquire the knowledge and experience to fit them to be housewives in a cottage economy. Another doctor, deploring the frequenting of dram shops by factory workers—even women and children—asked, "and to what but the diseased and relaxed state of their bodies could be attributed the participation and necessity of such stimulants?" The literature of the movement contains reprints of much medical testimony in condemnation of the system and the need for its reform, and the Manchester doctors contributed much of it.

Dr James Kay, of Manchester, surveyed the conditions of life and reported on them. He painted a grim picture of life (and death) in Manchester, of the short average span of life and of the low moral standards. He was, however, one of the very small minority of medical men who refused to allow that factory conditions were a cause. He said:

> The evils here unreservedly exposed, so far from being the necessary consequence of the manufacturing system, have a remote or accidental origin and might by *judicious management* be entirely removed. Nor do they flow from any single source, and especially in the present state of trade, the hours of labour cannot be materially diminished without occasioning the most serious commercial embarrassment. We exhibit a frightful picture of

the consequences of injudicious legislation. The evils of a restricted commerce affect not the capitalists alone; for the working classes are reserved the bitterest dregs of the poisoned chalice.[1]

There speaks an adherent of "The Manchester School" whose judgement was blinded by his adherence to economic theories. He was at variance with most of his medical colleagues, who decried the factory system, and particularly the long hours of children's labour, in no half-hearted fashion. Indeed, the consensus of medical opinion being on the reformers' side was one factor in winning the support of many people who could only judge the issue in the light of the evidence.

In addition to the meetings addressed to the general public, many were held to win the support of the clergy, ministers, and the gentry. They were often addressed by Bull or one of the other clerical supporters and one of the doctors anxious for Sadler's Bill to become law. These meetings were important because they were attended by people who influenced public opinion and who themselves wielded political influence. The appeal was to the evidence of clergymen and doctors, who between them knew more about the lives of the people than any other publicists. For the most part, the clergy in the textile areas supported the reformers, and some of them were very actively engaged in support of the Bill. Generally, the professional and middle classes were influenced by the kind of experience that doctors and clergymen could draw upon. The movement canalized and co-ordinated the efforts which many of the doctors were glad to make.

Shortly before Sadler presented his Bill, the Archbishop of Canterbury presented in the House of Lords a petition from some of the people of Rochdale. He said:

> Up to the age of 14 or 15 the time was that of innocent pleasure and enjoyment, whereas under this system they were confined for an unreasonable number of hours each day at their labours without time for relaxation, or even for proper refreshment, and that too with very few holidays in the year. The effect of this was most pernicious to their health and it ought to be recollected that it was attended with most serious injury to their morals. It was a disgrace to a Christian and civilized country to allow such a system to continue, merely for the sake of putting money in the pockets of the master manufacturers.[2]

---

[1] *The Moral and Physical Condition of the Working Classes*, 1832.

[2] House of Lords, 1 March 1832. *The Times*, 2 March 1832. *The Leeds Intelligencer*, 8 March 1832, refers to the *Rochester* petition. Evidently a printer's error.

Sadler moved the Second Reading as the volume of support grew. The improved organization had given a fillip to the movement. The growing support of clergymen and members of the middle class in parts of the country unaffected by the problem indicated that the issue was ceasing to be of local interest only. National newspapers were giving more space to reports of meetings and their own comments on the discussions. *The Times*, as well as some of the other London newspapers were giving support. Even the opposition of *The Morning Chronicle* had value, for however infuriating that paper's *laissez-faire* attitude might be, it drew attention to the question which Parliament was to debate.

Hobhouse, in forecasting that Sadler would not be allowed to proceed with his Bill, was nearly right. For Sadler was only permitted to move the Second Reading on his agreeing to the appointment of a Select Committee to investigate factory conditions. He protested that the facts were well known and that the proposal to appoint a Committee was a delaying device. But the Government included too many opponents of factory legislation and Sadler had no alternative—except to drop the Bill. His speech was moving and dignified. He spoke of the long hours, the atmosphere, and the working conditions. He stressed the lack of opportunity afforded to the children for taking refreshment, especially during times when the pressure of work was very great, and the very limited opportunity when work was normal. He produced whips and other implements used by overseers and overlookers to chastise children and gave the House a horrifying but true account of the lot of factory children. He answered the objection that legislation would limit the freedom of millowners by saying that all legislation limited the freedom of those it affected. The Christian Fathers who taught that the State and its laws are made necessary by man's fallen condition would have supported his argument that the law was necessary to protect those who could not protect themselves. He repeated the reformers' arguments that men with no property to support them, relying on the wages they could earn, could not match the power of the employers.

Some time was to elapse before trade unions gained anything like sufficient power to bargain with employers, and legislation was necessary to redress the balance. The holding of most of the nation's wealth by a comparatively small number of people made nonsense of the argument that operatives were free agents. This point needed

MICHAEL THOMAS SADLER

constantly emphasizing at a time when the political economists were gaining in influence. Professor Trevelyan's scorn of the idea that this was a period "obsessed with *laissez-faire*"[1] looks sadly out of place when the speeches made during this debate are read. The doctrine of *laissez-faire* dominated the debate. Because so many members of the Government and of the House were believers in it, Sadler's opponents based their arguments on it. He had to devote much of his speech to refuting it. Only those obsessed by it could have been proof against his argument that men who starve if they or their children do not get work are free agents. In any case, as he pointed out, it is surely undeniable that young children—some as young as six years of age—could not by any stretch of imagination be regarded as free agents. He made good use of medical testimony that prolonged factory labour was harmful, quoting documents by Thackrah and Smith. On the general principle behind the movement and to discount the disadvantage that he was not a manufacturer, he quoted a document that Wood had prepared. He pointed out that the Orders in Council, to which Bull had referred at Keighley, prescribed for West Indian slaves a maximum working day of the same length that he was asking for British young people between the ages of nine and eighteen years. The Government was accepting as valid arguments advanced by the millowners identical with those they rejected when advanced by the slave-owners. In spite of every attempt to argue the case on its merits and without reference to the kindred problem of slavery, the inconsistency of some opponents and the hypocrisy of others made the comparison inevitable.

Sadler's Bill provided that no child under the age of nine should be employed in a factory and that none between that age and eighteen years should work more than ten hours a day. This, with the breaks to be prescribed for meal-times, really meant that the Bill could properly have been called a Twelve Hour Bill. *The Times* pointed this out,[2] and Bull more than once stressed it. It seems that he regretted that it had not been given that title, being more accurate and therefore less misleading. Moreover, the propaganda value of that title would have been great, meeting some of the arguments of opponents, and saving much explanation to people who knew nothing of factory conditions.

---

[1] G. M. Trevelyan, *English Social History*, p. 544.

[2] 2 February 1832: "Mr Sadler's Bill is erroneously called a Ten Hours Bill. It prescribes ten hours of actual labour, which with the interval for meals, will keep these poor children for twelve hours a day in attendance on the factory."

The Bill really provided for a twelve-hour day—with eight hours on Saturdays—but that two hours of the twelve were to be allowed for meals. It also provided that no night work was to be done by young people under twenty-one years of age. These provisions do not seem to us to make over-generous concessions to young people, but they were revolutionary when proposed. In the woollen, worsted, and flax trades, there was no regulation. The length of the working day varied from twelve and a half hours a day to fifteen and even more during rush periods. In the cotton trade, the Hobhouse Bill provided for a restriction of the working week to sixty-nine hours, but it was well-known that its provisions were evaded.

The debate showed that Members were not convinced that this was a proper matter for legislation. Just as discussions on economic problems have often been carried on in terms suggestive of belief in a malignant Fate rather than a beneficent Providence, so during this debate there were those who argued that to act on considerations of humanity would be fatal to the country's interests. It was a repeat of the various debates in the columns of the newspapers, between the pamphleteers, and on the platforms. The argument that shorter hours would lead to increased prices, with consequent loss of trade and unemployment, was countered by the argument that employment should be shared more and that a wider distribution of wealth was just and would be to the common good. Some said that children must work or starve because it seemed to them that "economic laws" decreed this. Their speeches read badly now, but they honestly believed that legislation would hinder trade. It is easy even to-day to speak of "increasing the national income" in a way that suggests the enrichment of everyone, but we are well aware that any such increase does not automatically benefit sections of the community lacking economic power or political influence. In those days, when the new theories were only beginning to be applied, it was too early for this lesson to have been learned. The increase in the national income was there to be won by competition, and the successful deserved the spoil. "Enlightened self-interest" was not very enlightened.

There were many Members who could not make up their mind. They were honestly puzzled. Eighteen months of propaganda had made them uneasy about the lot of the factory children and the state of the factory areas, but they did not know how to deal with the problem. The reformers made no attempt to deal with the arguments of the political economists. They denied their basic assumptions and argued on quite other lines. The waverers, therefore, had to decide not only whether they ought to ease the lot of the factory children but also whether the opponents of factory legislation were right that legislation would create worse problems. It was not easy for them. It only seems to us, wiser after the event, that they ought to have found it easier. Their difficulty serves to stress how great a hold on the minds of responsible leaders the new theories had already taken. The reformers were challenging a way of life and a mode of thought as much as one of the results of their acceptance. They would not accept the new mode of thought as worthy of respect even as economic doctrine. Certainly, it would not do for them as the basis of the nation's economic life. They were in much the same situation as their spiritual descendants, monetary reformers, are at present. The latter, it is true, challenge assumptions which have become part of the make-up of everyday thought, while the factory reformers could appeal to a tradition which was not quite forgotten. If it is admitted that the waverers were in a position of some difficulty, it must also be recognized that much credit is due to these men who saw more clearly what was right and just. The waverers, voicing their uneasiness, were clearly glad of the delay that the appointment of a Select Committee would bring. Many of them genuinely hoped that it would enlighten them, enabling them to come to a decision.

The most ominous speech was made by Lord Althorp, the Leader of the House and therefore spokesman for the Government. He spoke of the danger of exaggeration by Sadler and showed himself to be influenced by the new dogmas. He went so far as to say that he would not pledge himself to support the Bill even if the Select Committee reported in its favour.[1] It is easy to gain a wrong impression of Althorp from the part he played in this controversy, especially when the reformers' account of it is the basis of judgement on him. Lord David Cecil sketches his character and the extent of his influence in a paragraph:

He was a curious and lovable character of a peculiarly English type. With his heavy figure and plain weather-beaten face, he looked like a farmer; and in fact there was a lot of the farmer about him. . . . Yet beneath this John Bull exterior lurked a quixotic strain of enthusiastic idealism which led

[1] *The Times*, 17 March 1832.

him far from the path Nature would seem to have marked out for him. . . .
He also threw himself into the cause of Reform against all his natural instincts as a landowner, simply because he thought Reform was the cause of
justice. The same motive kept him still in office afterwards, though he had
no ambition and was as miserable in London as a sporting dog. . . . Althorp's
influence with his colleagues was considerable. With the House of Commons
it was more. Who could resist so endearing a mixture of honesty and
modesty and homeliness? That fact that he was a poor, halting speaker
somehow only made members like him more. He could do anything he
liked with them. Once when an opponent had raised a point against the
Government, Althorp replied that he had some facts with which he was sure
he could answer it, but for the moment he had mislaid them. Both sides of
the House at once accepted his answer as perfectly satisfactory. Indeed, so
far as the management of Parliament was concerned, Althorp was the most
important member of the Government.[1]

Nothing could better illustrate the dilemma of the waverers than
this sketch of Althorp, whose concern for Reform drove him to occupy
an office he did not want, but whose idealism was not proof against
the cold logic of the economists. At any rate, the reform for which he
had zeal did not include factory reform.

In the face of such opposition, Sadler's plea that a Committee was
unnecessary and that the Government had legislated on other matters
without following that procedure was unavailing. Many of the
newspapers were critical. *The Times* said:

> Why a Select Committee should be required to ascertain whether it be
> right and proper to confine infants of seven, eight, nine or ten years of age
> more than twelve hours a day as unremitting labour in the atmosphere of a
> factory is beyond our imagination.[2]

Some of them saw it as a device to give an air of authority to the millowners' contentions, others as a delaying tactic. Only those opposed
to factory reform could see any useful purpose in such a Committee.
What could a Committee say to alter the admitted fact that children
of six years of age were compelled to work twelve or more hours a
day? A leading article, typical of many in newspapers published in
districts themselves unaffected by the problem, was one in *The Derbyshire Courier*:

> It is said that the measure is unnecessary, for the enormities of the factory
> system are exaggerated, that its enactments would injure the children and

---

[1] Lord David Cecil, *Melbourne*, pp. 200–1.   [2] *The Times*, 17 March 1832.

their parents by compelling the masters to reduce wages; and that it is an unjustifiable interference with the rights of property.

The writer went on to refute the first part of the argument by quoting some of the medical testimony dealing with the effects on the children of their work in the factory. He went on to say:

> Secondly, any fall in wages would be momentary, and thirdly nearly every bill affects property.
>
> And who shall presume to stand forth as the Champion of Property with a tacit affirmation that Humanity has no claim to consideration? Wealth, commerce, luxury, do not constitute a nation's strength. We make laws to provide protection for the Negro, let us not be less than just to the children of England.[1]

The composition of the Committee caused some of the newspapers to express the fear that it would prejudge the issue. Sadler was its Chairman, and he was supported by some sympathizers, but the number of avowed opponents appointed to it justified their fear. The appointment of Poulett Thomson, Vice-President of the Board of Trade, seemed to many to be ominous. These fears were shared by the operatives and the leading reformers.

Oastler and Bull pointed out that the cost of the journey would make difficult the attendance of operatives. They said that those who did make the journey would be overawed by the occasion when appearing before such an august body. They organized the building up of funds in order to pay for witnesses sent. Collectors received subscriptions from well-wishers as well as from members of the Ten Hours organization, and successful appeals were made to groups and church congregations. This was the first and obvious task of the Central Committee.

The second was the briefing of witnesses. It was important that they should be able to give evidence convincingly and stand up to close examination and to rigorous cross-examination. Witnesses must tell only of what they knew. Hearsay evidence would harm their case and impair the value of their genuine evidence. Every care, therefore, was taken to test the veracity of every witness. A document, largely the work of Oastler, was issued by the Central Committee and stressed all this. It posed twenty-two questions covering the ground that the

[1] *The Derbyshire Courier*, 17 April 1832.

Select Committee was likely to cover. The opening memorandum shows how great was the importance attached to the accuracy of the evidence and the trustworthiness of the witnesses.[1] In view of the later charges of exaggeration, it is important to notice that this care was taken.

The massive Report embodies the evidence of witnesses of all kinds. Not only was evidence given by people with a life-time's factory experience; social workers and other observers gave evidence of what seemed to them to be the effects of the system. William Osburn, a member of the Leeds Committee, a trustee of the local workhouse and a former town overseer, was one of them. Of the eighty-nine witnesses, sixty were factory workers. Their evidence was very telling. They told of the conditions of work, of the cruelties practised, and of the plight of the children. There is small wonder that the millowners tried to belittle its worth by saying that it was exaggerated. Many of these men lost their work for giving evidence. Sadler stopped calling factory workers for this reason, although it is doubtful if they could have added to the value of the evidence already given.

Twenty-one doctors gave evidence. Those who had long been known as supporters of the movement were reinforced by others. Bull himself was examined on two separate occasions. He was first examined about his criticism of the factory system. He was extremely careful to tell only of what he knew. For example, he was asked about the practice of hiding sickly-looking children from view when visitors were being shown round. He said that he knew on good authority of one factory where this had been done; he had heard of others and did not doubt that it might well be so, but he could not say with certainty that in those cases it was so. When pressed to divulge the source of his

[1] Memorandum: "The local committees and others to whom a copy of these notes is entrusted, will take especial care that they are not shewn to any but well-known friends. These notes apply solely to that branch of the evidence that must be got up by the Operatives themselves. A short minute of the general evidence has been previously communicated. The Committee will be pleased to consider it as absolutely necessary to attend to every particular head of evidence herein stated; to be very careful to ascertain as many facts under each head as they possibly can; and communicate them, with names and persons and places, to the Central Committee, at Leeds. It is essentially necessary and must always be borne in mind that any pretended or assumed statements which cannot be fully and clearly substantiated, would materially mar the cause."

The document, with its twenty-two instructions, is to be found in the Oastler Collection and is reprinted in *Tory-Radical*.

information, he said that he was concerned with the system and not with individuals.

As he was accustomed to do, he based his criticism of the system on his parish experience, particularly as a teacher. He described his work in Bowling, a township of between 6,000 and 7,000 people. There were, he said, seven Sunday schools, of which three were his Church Sunday Schools. There were also three Wesleyan Methodist and Primitive Methodist Sunday Schools. He was on friendly terms with their responsible officers and had collected statistics from them. There were some 1,135 scholars, of which 516 were in his own schools. He said that the Sunday School teachers were at one in their belief that the children could not be expected to gain much benefit from attending in their overworked state. He said, as he had said on many occasions, that he felt bound to excuse late attendance in view of the children's week's work. Instead of going to Sunday School at 8 a.m., many of them went nearer 9 o'clock.

He deplored the effect of the factory system upon home life. The children were sent to work at a very early age and were denied the opportunity of learning good domestic habits.

They go very early in the morning; many of my little children (I call them mine) set off regularly at 5 o clock and do not return until 8 o clock almost all the year round; perhaps in the course of the winter some weeks of shorter employment take place. They see, therefore, very little of their parents and when they go to the mill, their first impressions (and first impressions are generally the deepest) are of a very injurious kind.

Answering questions, he said that although some children went to work as early as six years of age, the most usual age at which children began to work was eight or nine. Parents were often driven to send their children to work by the family need, and many of them regretted it. Of course, there were degraded parents who cared little. He added that they were, in the main, themselves products of the factory system. Asked whether factory workers considered themselves in a state they ought to be in, he said:

No: they call themselves slaves. Of course it is my continual desire and object as a minister of Christ, and as a friend of the social order to soften all such impressions as these, and to endeavour to encourage kindly feelings and feelings of contentment; but I am sure I find it very difficult under present circumstances to make that impression upon their minds in this respect which I could wish, for they immediately refer me to the increasing duration of their labour and its decreasing remuneration; the only salve that I can apply to such a wound is to hope that their condition will be ameliorated.

He stressed that the movement's demand for a Ten Hour Bill was in the nature of a compromise and agreed that there would still be many unable to attend evening school even if that Bill became law. He added:

But we are obliged by the opponents of the measure (for I do not hesitate to confess myself in favour of the measure) to be as moderate as possible in our request.

He would prefer an even shorter working day, but in the existing circumstances he thought that a reduction to ten hours "would be far better for the improvement of the children than the twelve and a half hours" they normally worked. He spoke of the stunted and deformed children and said that strangers to manufacturing districts were deceived by appearances. The most unhealthy looking children are often the strongest, having become acclimatized to the atmosphere and conditions of the factory. He added:

I am in the habit of attending the sick in their homes every month in the year more or less; there are several factory children in my schools whom I do not expect to live the year out; and some one or two whom I left very poorly when I came from home, whom I never expect to see again.

In Church circles, the effects of the system on moral standards were amongst the most telling reasons for supporting the reformers. Bull had much to say about them. There was no time for adequate instruction. Children should be able to return to their homes earlier so that it could be given to them. It was bad to bring together young people promiscuously, and regulation was needed to mitigate these evils. He told of assignments made at the factories with girls and said that over-lookers and masters seduced the girls. He was examined at some length about the relative moral standards of country and industrial communities, for opponents of factory reform were fond of comparing the manners and morals of town and country people. Bull was asked about the comparative number of illegitimate births in them. He said that he did not know the figures, but in any case they meant nothing. Many factory girls became prostitutes, he said, and added, "I have never yet observed that prostitutes become mothers." He told of the "hints and remarks" made to him about practices of abortion and the conversation amongst factory young people about these things, and said:

> I confess that my own disgust has been such as to prevent me from pursuing the conversation and I have turned it into another direction.

He had walked from Bradford with a group of young millworkers and had been shocked by what he had seen and heard. Having known sea-ports, he was not easily shocked, but the language of even young children had appalled him.

He did not take kindly to a suggestion that children might work in six-hour relays because this "would tend to increase rather than diminish adult labour". He had seen a deterioration in the lot of the poor. He was not in a position to quote percentages, but from his own observation he had come to that conclusion. He did not agree that factory children were better off than children had been under the domestic system. They were driven by the pace demanded by the steam engine instead of the pace and amount of work being related to their strength. Moreover, conditions had been less inhuman than they were under the factory system. Factory children were often punished if they so much as spoke while tending their machine.

As it had emerged during the course of his evidence that he had served a country curacy, the Committee was anxious to have such help as his knowledge of both town and country enabled him to give. He was recalled a week later—his thirty-third birthday—and questioned to this end. He gave evidence which showed that he had knowledge of country conditions, recently brought more up-to-date by visits to his old home. In spite of changes for the worse in the country, he thought that the lot of the agricultural labourer was still preferable to that of his opposite number in the factory areas.

When questioned about the town labourer's conditions, he said that men, on an average, earned about 10s. a week, girls from 4s. 6d. to 5s. In the worsted mills, a fifteen-year-old girl would earn 6s. 6d. to 7s. a week, but a twelve-year-old girl in the spinning room would earn 3s. 6d. to 4s. He did not see how any of the benefits enjoyed by the countryman could be accorded to the townsman. There was no land available for gardens in the industrial areas. In any case, the hours of labour were too long to enable the factory worker to cultivate a

garden. He pointed to the wastefulness of a divided family meal and
other expenses incurred in factory labour—more washing and repairing
of clothes—which he estimated at two shillings a week. He told of overlookers who had tubs into which they threw the workers' food when
it had been rendered uneatable by the atmosphere or by delay in
eating it. They kept pigs on such leavings. He told of the housing
conditions:

> I have frequently visited by night the cottages of the operatives for the
> purpose of baptizing a child that was expected to die, and have sometimes
> found five persons in one bed, three children lying at the feet, and their
> parents at the other end with a little baby between them.

There were clean and trim houses, he said, but they were usually the
homes of country-bred housewives. His evidence throws a side-light
on the pastoral work of the Church at that time, but its main value
here lies in his experience of the factory workers and the conditions
under which they lived and worked. He spoke of the things he knew.
When pressed for an answer that could not be authoritative, he made
clear that his answer must be qualified. He was not opposed to the
factory system; he was opposed to the existing factory system. "Under
proper regulations the factory system might be advantageous to the
poor", he said. Early habits of industry were important. He was sure
that no child under nine years of age should go to the factory and that
young people under eighteen years of age needed protection. He had
given no thought to the proposal to restrict moving power. He
stressed that most operatives were anxious for working hours to be
limited to ten even if a reduction in wages followed. He made no
secret of the fact that they regarded the formation of a Select Committee as a delaying tactic or that they expected the next Parliament
to be even less friendly towards the Bill. When asked why, he said that
it would contain many more of the manufacturers and their friends.
He forecast that if a new Parliament turned the Bill down, there would
be a clamour for universal suffrage and a vote by ballot. His assertion
that the demand for a limitation to ten hours was in the nature of a
compromise led to repeated attempts to persuade him to say what he
thought should be the length of the working day. He refused to be
drawn. For the time being, the Ten Hours Bill would do for him.

7

THE MACAULAY AFFAIR

BEFORE THE Committee issued its Report, Parliament was dissolved. The election that followed was one of the most important in history for many reasons.

It was the first after the passing of the Reform Bill. Men who had never previously voted in a Parliamentary Election were empowered to do so. Most of them desired changes in many aspects of the national life. To those who feared those changes, the election was important because they were defending a position undermined by the years of Radical propaganda. Those who desired them hoped to get a mandate for making them.

Even within the Government which had sponsored the Reform Bill, there were various degrees of enthusiasm for it. Stanley, Melbourne, and others like them, supported it because the state of the country made some such bill inevitable; the feeling outside the House determined the action of those inside it. Melbourne feared that upheaval would follow the disappointment that would follow when it failed to fulfil the hopes and promises of the advocates of reform. "However," says his biographer, "it was one of his fundamental principles not to stand out against a widespread popular movement."[1] On the other wing of the Whig Government, were Grey himself with Durham and Charles Wood. The latter was consistently an opponent of factory legislation, and his enthusiasm for Parliamentary reform is further evidence of the mistake of assuming that Parliamentary reform and factory reform went together. Mr A. C. Johnson, in his life of the present Lord Halifax, the third of the line, tells of Wood, at that time Member for Wareham, having had

> considerable acumen—or inside information—about the Bill's hazardous journey through Parliament, for he is reported to have given the correct

[1] *Melbourne*, p. 173.

forecast of the majority of nine which it duly received after a dramatic debate in the House of Lords. He sprang from his seat, shouting, "We have won"—exuberance which provoked Lord Stanley into retorting angrily, "I could kill you". Lady Mary Meynell recalls in her *Memoirs* that when the Bill became law Charles Wood and John Grey "ran hatless and hallooing into the streets in the early hours of a June morning."[1]

Although some Tories agreed that a measure of reform was necessary, after the death of Canning and Huskisson they lacked influence within the Party. It was dominated by Wellington and those who thought like him. The Tories feared the growth of the political power of the manufacturing and trading classes, with their jealousy of the aristocracy and squirearchy. Churchmen feared disestablishment. The bishops' opposition to the Reform Bill was due not so much to anti-democratic principles as to fear for the Church's interests. The Bill, after all, did not give political power to all citizens. It did not even give them voting power. The alignments might have been different had it done so, although it must be admitted that opposition was not due to democratic principles. It was due to fear of people to whom it was proposed to give voting power rather than to sympathy with those to whom it would not be given. Most reformers demanded reform as a means to an end, and opposition to the Bill arose from fear of those ends being pursued. Tories and Churchmen had cause to fear. Their interests were threatened. If the election should result in Parliament being flooded with representatives of the newly enfranchised, they could be expected to carry out reforms to the liking of neither Tories nor Churchmen.

The Election was important to the factory reformers because the newly enfranchised were their most bitter opponents. Bull's testimony before the Sadler Committee that the operatives knew that the Reform Parliament would be ill-disposed towards their aspirations was correct. Moreover, their champion's place in Parliament was at stake. Sadler's constituency of Aldborough had been swept away. He had been adopted as Tory candidate for Leeds, a new constituency electing two members. He was opposing two strong candidates. Thomas Babington Macaulay had represented a pocket borough and was already well known as a writer propagating Liberal views. John Marshall was the son of a Leeds flax spinner whose rise to power and fortune had been due to his ruthlessness no less than to his industry. The younger Mar-

[1] A. C. Johnson, *Viscount Halifax*, p. 20.

shall continued in the same tradition. His election was regarded as certain and the struggle was for second place.

The campaign opened long before the dissolution of Parliament. Oastler had been somewhat manhandled in the June of that year, when he sought to extract from the Liberal Marshall and the Whig Macaulay some indication of their attitude to Sadler's Bill. Marshall had replied definitely enough. He believed that so low a limit as ten hours would not be in the interests of the labouring classes. Macaulay was more cautious. Although he had written vigorously supporting Malthusian doctrines—he had written against Sadler, who had refuted that teaching—he confessed that he knew little of local factory problems. He wished the factory children well, and wished them: "Not to work one hour more than what is to their real advantage."[1] Meanwhile, in view of his lack of knowledge of manufacturing, he would await the findings of the Sadler Committee.

It was the policy of the Short Time Committees to extract from every candidate a statement declaring his attitude to Sadler's Bill. With few exceptions, they supported the candidate who promised to support it. They worked for the Tory Sadler at Leeds and for the Radical Joseph Wood at Huddersfield. (Joseph Wood lived at Sandal and was no relation to either John Wood or Charles Wood.) Tory though he was, party labels meant little to Oastler. The Ten Hours men naturally attached most importance to the Leeds contest. Sadler's defeat would mean the repudiation of the Ten Hours principle in a great manufacturing centre, with all that might imply to people in other parts of the country, and it would also leave the movement without a Parliamentary leader.

Bull was active in Bradford and the West Riding. He wrote an open letter to the candidates for the Borough of Bradford in the course of which he said:

> If any of you, Gentlemen, can find it in your hearts to propose a longer period than Ten Hours of the actual labour of young persons, above 9 and under 18, when convicted felons only work ten hours on an average . . . I hope from my very heart that you never represent the Borough of which I am an Elector.[2]

He also questioned Morpeth and Strickland, candidates for the West Riding, at Wakefield. Besides the factory issue, he was concerned

[1] *The Leeds Intelligencer*, 21 June 1832.
[2] Bull, *To the Candidates for the Borough of Bradford*.

about Poor Law questions. Poor Law reform was needed, and the issue was to become a prominent one during the life of the new Parliament. Bull asked the candidates to heed the medical evidence which supported the factory reformers' case and to vote for the Ten Hours Bill. He said that he did not wish to tie their hands or to cripple them, but he hoped that the representatives of the people would take care of the poor. The rich, he added, would take care of themselves.[1] Meetings on behalf of candidates who were in favour of the Bill not only helped them, they kept alive the Ten Hours campaign at a time when it could have been forgotten in the excitement of a historic election.

However diffident Macaulay had been in June, he lost that diffidence as the campaign got under way. Earlier meetings had resembled Eatanswill, but the intrusion into the campaign of personalities made it more bitter still. Marshall was a Socinian, and there had been much discussion between Hamilton,[2] a leading Leeds Independent minister, and the Socinian minister about the Socinians' right to call themselves Christians. Macaulay took pains to affirm that there was no doubt that he was a Christian. But when, in addition to attacking Sadler's Tory outlook and social views, he accused him of hypocrisy, Bull wrote an open letter to him in which he made Macaulay's affirmation the basis of his rebuke.

He began by reminding Macaulay of a meeting at which Hamilton had been a speaker. Although a Ten Hours man, Hamilton supported Macaulay, and the meeting to which Bull referred had been held to support Macaulay's candidature. He had asked the meeting if it was right for a Christian minister to interfere in the cause of charity, to which question the meeting, of course, had replied in the affirmative. Bull said that it was in the cause of charity that he publicly addressed Macaulay.

Having occasion to visit Leeds yesterday, I was informed by a very respectable and excellent man that he heard you say last Tuesday evening, while lecturing at the Music Hall, that Mr Sadler had assumed "a convenient philanthropy" and you added, "You have heard of an animal called the hyaena which imitates the cries of little children that it may lure the unwary traveller to its den", or words to that effect.

---

[1] *White Slavery*, Vol. II. 20 December 1832.

[2] R. W. Hamilton was a well-known Leeds dissenting minister. He was one of Oastler's first associates in the campaign, but worked for Macaulay in the Election.

RICHARD OASTLER

He also told me that on the same evening you vehemently insisted that you were a Christian.

You are a Christian.

Tell me, sir, where Christ teaches you to take advantage of your competitor's absence in a select meeting of your supporters, not only to call his "philanthropy" a convenience, but also to compare him to a certain Beast which feigns the moans of infancy to lure its prey.

He asked him what part of the Divine Redeemer's laws had taught him to impute hypocrisy to a man whose concern for the suffering poor and the helpless infants went back, to Bull's knowledge, seven years or more. Was it in the school of Christ that he had learned to compare to the savage hyaena a man whose heart yearned over "the poor hapless, toiling, Factory Child, whose physical, moral, social and future happiness is sacrificed at the gloomy shrine of heartless and unfriendly avarice"?

The most damaging part of the letter followed, however. He moved from indignant rhetorical questioning to a reflection on the inconsistencies in Macaulay's own position.

Ah, Sir, when I once visited that blood-stained coast, the western shore of Africa, I lived in the same colony where your relative Kenneth Macaulay was a principal merchant and realized much wealth by a wholesale and retail trade, in musquets and gunpowder, and rum, and tobacco, and bar iron and which were sold to the Mandingoes, and Foulhas, and Timmanees, and Bassas, and other native African tribes, and with which they purchased slaves and shipped them off to Brazil and Rio de Janeiro and the South American continent generally—yet members of your family at home, who freighted the ships and shared the profits, were placed at the head of a cause which is dear to my heart—the cause of Negro liberty—but which I will never plead again in connexion with those who rave at the mention of Africa's wrongs, but can see a thousand redeeming qualities in White Infant Slavery, and its inexorable inflictors, when their "vote and influence" lies at their feet. (When you next launch your keen sarcasm at "convenient philanthropy" take aim at such as these and twang your bow-string as hard as you will.)

When, as a missionary, he had lain in bed, heard the "hyaena's frightful howl" and thought of his distant home, it had never occurred to him that a man would call himself a Christian and compare even his competitor to the fiercest and subtlest of the savage tribe. He reminded Macaulay of the sacrifices Sadler was making, for he was losing some of his oldest and most active political friends.

He went on, reminding Macaulay of his Christian professions and of Marshall's claim to be a Christian:

> But what are those who running weeping to the Factories at five o'clock in the morning and who stay there till eight at night and what are they who are pulled out of bed and violently shaken till they wake, who wake but to tremble and to weep? Are these Christians too? And what are they who have their choice either to starve, or else, when Christian Masters so will, must toil in the night as well as the day and who have thus been forced to toil, (I can prove it) 17 hours at one stretch with only *Thirty Minutes rest*.
>
> And which are they like—Christians or Hyaenas—who supposing that "Gain is Godliness" stretch the frame of infancy to the utmost endurance "that they may add house to house and field to field", who regard the labourer as the mere instrument of aggrandisement to be paid as little and worked as much as possible?
>
> Sir, I ask these questions most sincerely—you may not condescend to answer them, but those who read this will answer. And you, sir, proud and ungenerous as you are, will one day stand at the Bar of Christ, whose servant you claim to be, and then you will no longer dare to despise the poor unpitied weakling, whose cry, unheeded by such Liberal politicians as you and Mr Marshall, yet ascends to that God who says. "For the oppression of the poor, for the sighing of the needy, now will I arise", saith the Lord, "I will set him in safety from him who puffeth at him."

The children whose oppression Macaulay was unwilling to relieve and whose friend he traduced, were made in the image of God, and Bull added,

> when next you borrow an image from the Hyaena, apply it to those who amass wealth from protracted infant labour and then use it and the influence it confers to prevent their alleviation from unChristian Thraldom.

He condemned the duplicity of men who labelled "their lips with Christ but exercise tyranny with both their hands". It was vigorously written, but so were most pamphlets and speeches. It was one of the few occasions on which Bull indulged in personalities, but Macaulay had asked for it. It says much in Bull's favour that he had made no mention of the West African activities of Macaulay's family until Macaulay had referred to Sadler so ungenerously. Most candidates and their supporters were quick to make use of knowledge of opponents' interests much less damaging than that which Bull here divulged.

Bull's use of the Bible was usually apt and seemly. He reveals here that he had a clear understanding of the fundamentals of Christian social teaching. What he believed about the origin and nature of Man was vastly different from the Liberal individualism then gaining ground and which was a much watered-down version of Christian teaching about Man. Indeed, it is clear that Bull took for granted those beliefs about him that Christian social philosophers of our own day are trying to recover. Our social problems may have changed but they arise from the apostasy against which Bull prophesied.

Bull was right in his forecast that Macaulay would not reply. Baines replied in his paper. His enmity towards all factory reformers had grown bitter by this time. Party feelings ran high during the election campaign. Added to these considerations, the memory of the Liversedge meeting was still fresh.[1] Baines was therefore ready for battle. He said:

> This pugnacious parson, not content with his achievement at Liversedge and Dewsbury has thought fit to come from Byerley to Leeds and to address a letter to Mr Macaulay on his favourite Ten Hours Bill.
>
> Mr Macaulay likened the Tory Party in Leeds—not Mr Sadler—to a hyaena. (It is) the hypocritical cry of humanity in order to achieve its own selfish purposes. The reverend bruiser, whilst calling out that Mr Macaulay has given an unfair blow to Mr Sadler should have been careful not to strike an unfair blow himself.
>
> Mr Macaulay and his father have, in becoming the most zealous and conspicuous advocates of Negro Emancipation, acted against the interests of their family. Mr Bull, therefore, in this dirty insinuation has overreached himself.

This correspondence is reproduced in *The British Labourer's Protector and Factory Child's Friend*, which Bull edited. Both the Open Letter and Baines's reply appeared, and with the latter his reply to Baines. He referred to his letter and said that Macaulay, not finding it convenient to reply, the Editors of *The Leeds Mercury*,

> as in duty bound, took up the soot bag on behalf of their pet candidate and advertizing friend. These gentlemen possess a fund of "real Billingsgate" and, being now so highly in favour, it is not too much to hope that they will get a patent shortly for this distinguished and superhuman accomplishment. The following is a very moderate specimen of the elegant style of the continental traveller and gentleman—the Junior Editor who, by the way, is a very great religionist—nevertheless and notwithstanding.

[1] See above, Chap. 5.

He quoted the attack upon himself for the benefit of his readers who had not seen the *Mercury* and replied:

> The Rev. G. S. Bull is highly honoured by the vituperation of Messrs. Baines and Son in the *Mercury* of this day. He has long been used to it, and never therefore expects to take any public step, either in defence of a calumniated friend, or in defence of the poor, or in defence of the Bible without being abused by these professedly Christian Editors as "a pugnacious parson, a reverend bruiser, and a dealer in dirty insinuations". The return of such complimentary and polite language is neither suited to the feelings nor to the public character of a clergyman.

He expressed the hope that the Baineses had not forgotten the direct falsehoods which they had propagated about the Liversedge and Dewsbury meetings. He had gone to those meetings, he said, "to protest against the very bad precedent of pulling the Bible to pieces to please anyone—and especially when it assumed the form of an Act of Government". The Bible was relevant to the issue on which he differed from them.

> How did Mr Bull know but what those who would admit of that mutilation might find it convenient for the sake of certain great Liberal Capitalists to expunge the passages which declare God's heaviest wrath upon the heartless oppressors of the poor and of their little children which so sting and gall the professedly Christian editors and the interested admirers of an overworking, cruel and demoralizing Factory System, who grin like Mr Macaulay's beautiful hyaena at a Ten Hours Bill and its Patron? Besides, who could tell whether some Members of Parliament who, as Mr Hamilton has proved, are not Christians, might not like to pull out some obnoxious places which exalt the Divinity and Glory of the Lord Jesus Christ—the Lover and Friend of the poor?

With the Bible in one hand and the forthcoming volume of the evidence given before Sadler's Committee in the other, "we bid defiance to all", said he. "Humanity must triumph."

Dealing with what purported to be a correction of the report of Macaulay's speech, he quoted the report of some actually present at the meeting and asked why the *Mercury* had omitted from its report that portion of the speech. He added:

> Mr Baines, or rather Mr Macaulay, who, of course, sanctioned the elegant article on the Rev. G. S. Bull, "pugnacious parson, reverend bruiser, dirty insinuations", &c., &c., admits that the illustration of the Hyaena was severe

as applied to Mr Sadler. Now let Mr Macaulay remember that he formerly compared Mr Sadler in *The Edinburgh Review*, Volume 52, page 504, to a "Juggler's Snake" whose bags of poison are full but the fang is wanting.

Discussing the reply to his allegations about the West African activities of the Macaulay family, he denied that "the Reverend Bruiser" was wrong. The reply was a quibble. He reminded Baines that the discussion had been about "convenient philanthropy", and that it might be convenient

> to be pocketing Sierra Leone profits from merchandise which was the means of freighting slave vessels and that it might be equally "convenient" to apply to the conscience the "flattering unction" of great anti-slavery zeal at home, and it was very inconvenient for Mr T. B. Macaulay to throw stones at Mr Sadler when his own glass house was so near at hand. It is, therefore, Mr Macaulay's defender who has over-reached himself and not Mr Bull.

After thanking the Liberal Candidate "and his genteel apologists" for advertising him as an advocate of his "favourite Ten Hours Bill", he addressed himself to his readers, mainly factory workers:

> Mr Baines, who presents me to you in this day's paper as a "Parson" with so many genteel names (and people never begin to call vulgar names till reason and argument have failed them) might have had the candour to have told you that I am, and have been for nearly ten years, a poor parson. He might have said that no cursed lust of gold attracted me to your cause and that of your poor children. He knows that you have no fat livings to give me, and I fear he is more ready to put me into the Black List than to to get me into the Grey List.[1] He knows you cannot procure me 1,200 pence a year and I know he cannot deprive me of your prayers and your good wishes and your support to our favourite cause. You like me no worse for defending our Bill nor for being as poor in my station as you are in yours.

The journal was published for the benefit of supporters of the movement, and was read mainly by operatives. He begged his readers to judge the issue from their own experience of factory life if they had any and from feelings of humanity if they had not. If they did, he was certain that no man, "be he Whig or Tory, Liberal or Conservative", "Poor Parson" or "Reverend Bruiser" or "Government Pensioner"— a reference to Macaulay's offices under the Crown—would seduce them from their Ten Hours Bill.

His final words give a hint of the division amongst sympathizers.

[1] Earl Grey was the Prime Minister.

Hobhouse was no longer counted a supporter. It is evident that some friends of the movement still believed that to demand a Ten Hours Bill was a mistake. Bull said:

> listen to no "Eleven Hours" insinuator; if you do, you will surely fall at last into the "Clap Trap" of Sir John Hobhouse's *Twelve* Hours Bill. Cling to your *Ten* Hours Bill as tenaciously as Mr Sadler clings to the Poor Man's Cause or Mr Macaulay to his Liberal paymasters.

The Leeds Short Time Committee plastered the town with posters addressed to the manufacturers and capitalists, written ironically and "signed" "Thomas Babington Hyaena". The whole argument arose out of a bad lapse of manners on Macaulay's part. In spite of the *Mercury's* omission of the offensive passage from its report, this lapse was known through its publication in other papers. Naturally, his opponents made much of it, and Bull's open letter was widely circulated.

Sadler, however, was defeated. Too few supporters of factory legislation had voting rights to join with Tories in defeating Marshall and Macaulay. Many of the new voters were opposed to all that Sadler stood for. His attack on the factory system, on the political economists, and the millowners—the "millocrats" as someone named them—made him a special object of attack. As Parliamentary leader of the Ten Hours movement, he was something of a symbol to both sides. If it was important to the ten hours men that he should be returned to Parliament, it was no less important to the millowners that he should not be. The millowners and their friends were the more powerful, and Marshall, a millowner, and Macaulay, an apologist for the new way of life, were returned. It was a severe blow to the factory reformers, and the elation of the Liberals was justified.

8

THE NEW CHAMPION

OTHER RESULTS in the West Riding added to the depression of the factory reformers. They had kept the issue well to the fore throughout the election, but two candidates to whom they had given official backing had been defeated, and well-known opponents had been elected. Charles Wood had been returned at Halifax. He was a fitting Member for that constituency, where the millowners were most nearly unanimous in their opposition to factory reform. At Huddersfield, where Oastler and the Ten Hours men had worked for Joseph Wood, they had suffered another set-back. Not only was their candidate defeated, but Oastler's support of a Radical led to complaints being made to Thornhill, his employer. Oastler had finally persuaded him that the interests of the factory reform movement cut across party alignments, and that a Radical supporter of the movement was to be preferred to a Whig opponent of it. Thornhill himself was a Tory and, as at that time, "Peel's delusion that he was a Tory" had not transformed the Tory party, he was prepared to accept Oastler's argument that a community of interests united the aristocracy and the factory workers. It was the beginning of a rift that was to widen, however.

It was the loss of Sadler that was most serious. He was the movement's Parliamentary leader, the Chairman of the Select Committee gathering evidence for submission to Parliament. The poet Southey, who was interested in the movement, expressed the view of others like him:

> Sadler, too, is a loss; he might not be popular in the House or in London Society; but his speeches did much good in the country, and he is a singularly able, right-minded and religious man. Who is there to take up the question of our white slave trade with equal feeling?

In his comments which follow, he gives some hint of the success of the movement's propaganda. In less than three years, observers and publicists at some distance from the textile areas had been compelled to take notice of it. The reformers' arguments were known, and the term "White Slavery" had become the normal term to use to describe the lot of the factory child. A passage in the same letter is revealing:

> They who grow cotton are merciful taskmasters in comparison with those who manufacture it. Robert Hildyard (whom you know) told me the other day that Marshall (the Member for Leeds) shewed him one of his manufactories, and upon his remarking on the extreme delicacy of the children, replied they were consumptive, that a great many never reached the age of twenty, and that this was due to the flew with which the air was always filled. He spoke of this with as little compunction as a General would calculate the probable consumption of lives in a campaign. A General may do this under—even a righteous—sense of duty; but I know not where the love of gain appears in a more undisguised form than in a cotton mill. The cruelty is never so excessive as it is in a plantation, but it is more un-mitigated; the system is more uniform and incorrigibly evil. The negroes in a plantation may be rendered happy by kind treatment, and no doubt often are, but I know not how a cotton mill can be otherwise than an abomination to God and Man.[1]

Southey made no mention of the woollen or worsted trades, which were Sadler's first concern. He viewed the matter from afar. That this was so shows that thoughtful people had begun to take notice, and that Sadler's defeat was widely recognized to be a loss. The mention of Marshall serves to show the type of Member with which the supporters of factory legislation would have to deal. Marshall and Macaulay at Leeds, Fenton at Huddersfield, and Wood at Halifax, had all declared themselves to be opposed to it. Men who would form the Government were known to be ill-disposed to legislation "interfering" with industry. These men would strengthen their resistance to it. Wood himself was likely to be a member of it. The entry of men engaged in the trade, and for that reason regarded as "practical men" whose opinion would weigh considerably, certainly added to the difficulties of the reformers. It is astonishing how frequently the nation has been misled because the spokesmen for vested interests have been heeded on the supposition that they had expert knowledge which was

---

[1] Quoted in *The Life and Work of the Seventh Earl of Shaftesbury*, by E. Hodder, Vol. I, p. 46. A fuller version, from which these extracts are taken, is in the Manchester Reference Library.

hidden from their opponents. They had largely nullified the efforts made by Hobhouse, and they had obstructed Sadler. With his defeat, the difficulties facing the reformers were increased, but their determination was in no way diminished.

Oastler strove to maintain the non-party nature of the organization. The Liberal Press and party line had deprived the movement of all but a few Liberals. Some few Whigs continued to give support, but for the most part the leadership was in the hands of Tories and Radicals. He tried to rouse the Tories to become a reforming party. He wished to inculcate into them some of the reforming zeal of the best Radicals. Traditional Toryism, rejuvenated by the Radicals' concern for the ordinary man who lacked political influence, would, he thought, preserve the nation from the sort of class war that seemed to be otherwise inevitable if the Baineses and the Marshalls gathered power. He had twice been to see Wellington, whom he enlightened on the factory problem and whom he tried to persuade that the industrial workers were not opposed to the aristocracy. He

> assured him that the only way the aristocracy and the clergy could regain the affections of the people and save themselves from ruin was that they should use their powerful influence to rescue the working classes from the thraldom and delusion in which money and steam power held them.[1]

On the second occasion, he took Bull to see the great man, and hoped for much as the outcome of these interviews. His hopes were misplaced and had almost petered out by the time that Sadler lost his seat in Parliament. Wellington had received them courteously enough, but he never really grasped Oastler's argument. The North of England was a long way away and mill workers were as a foreign people. In any case, Wellington was by that time a kind of elder statesman and something of a back number. His leadership had been unimaginative when he had last held office. He seemed to be more concerned with defending an untenable position than with moving to a better one. He had nothing to give to the Tory Party but his prestige. The deaths of Canning and Huskisson had left the party with no prospective leader who had any real understanding of the problems raised by the new industrialism, except Peel, who was too closely associated with it. None of them could withstand the new teaching which the Liberals

---

[1] *Tory-Radical*, p. 188. *Fleet Papers*, Vol. I, p. 11. *The History of the Factory Movement*, Vol. I, p. 321. Croft, *Oastler and the Factory Movement*, p. 85.

were propagating. It was only a matter of time before Toryism degenerated into Conservatism, itself a modified version of Liberalism.

At the beginning of 1833, however, there was still a Tory rank and file opposed to the new industrialism on what we would now call "ideological grounds". Its members disliked the change in the nation's way of life, the changing face of the countryside and the irresponsibility of the new rich, while the lot of the poor shocked them. Other Tories supported the factory movement for different reasons. Some did so mainly in order to oppose their traditional opponents, some for humanitarian reasons. Radical supporters, too, were a mixed bag. Most of them regarded factory reform as but one of a number of needed reforms. They threw their weight into the movement because they saw that a united front, although limited to a single issue, was important. John Doherty, for example, although mainly concerned with building up a strong trade union organization, was one of the Lancashire leaders.

A small group of delegates was brought together in Bradford on 11 January 1833 for a conference that was to last four days. Its Chairman was William Halliwell, a leading cotton spinner from Lees, near Oldham; Doherty and Bull were there, in marked contrast to him and to each other. The election campaign had thinned out the Short Time Committees, but twenty-six survived. They sent either a delegate or a letter expressing their views. The Conference had important decisions to make. It was imperative that a new campaign should be launched. The propaganda of the previous fifteen months had made the manufacturers shift their ground. The evidence given before the Sadler Committee had been reported and had made a wide impression. The publication of the Report at about this time was awakening people in other parts of the country to the seriousness of the problem. The manufacturers had largely abandoned hope of preventing legislation being enacted and were concerned to make it as ineffective as possible. It was widely believed that they were behind Lord Morpeth, who (it was rumoured) was to introduce a bill providing for an eleven-hour day. Morpeth meant well. He believed that the dispute would end in a compromise and that to legislate for it would end the agitation, bringing peace to the industry. It seemed to him that the millowners would not concede more and that to legislate for an eleven-hour day would go some way towards meeting their objections to legislation. The Ten Hours men, however, insisted that eight hours factory labour was quite enough and that their demand for a ten-hour day was itself a compromise. Bull, in one of his letters, said that the reformers were often asked why they so obstinately fought about one hour—"what difference did it make?"—"It is the difference between being an hour late for the mail and being in time," he replied.[1] It was, in any case, an argument that cut both ways.

The most important task of the Conference was to find a successor to Sadler. Hardly less important was the task of rebuilding the organization to some extent broken up by the election campaign. The short-time committees had previously been concerned to win support. The time had come to build up a membership organization with a subscription rate. No doubt the selecting of witnesses for the Sadler Committee, carefully as it had been done, had revealed the need for a tighter organization. Delegates would be needed for lobbying Members of Parliament. Their selection must be made with care and with due regard to the susceptibilities of others within the movement. The conference therefore made arrangements for the nomination and election of these delegates.

Bull acted as secretary to the Conference. He it was who carried out the important decisions. The most important of them was to go to London to seek out a person suitable and willing to take up Sadler's work in Parliament and to lead a campaign throughout the country. In spite of the disappointment felt in Wellington, it was to the Tory Party that they must look. Only a Tory could carry with him any considerable section of the party. Without Tory leadership, the movement could easily be made to appear but one aspect of Radical agitation. Only in the Tory Party could they hope to find a leader whose outlook resembled theirs and who would be able to reconcile the rights of the factory workers with his political and social philosophy. Factory reform as a part of the programme of the Opposition for the sake of opposition would not do. The man that Bull must look for must be a Christian, who could be persuaded of the righteousness of the cause. A Tory who regarded all campaigners as Jacobins would be worse than useless.

Bull had no time to waste. If Morpeth intended to introduce an eleven hours bill with the backing of the millowners, it was important that the Ten Hours men should beat him to it. The Ten Hours Bill

[1] To *The Standard*, reprinted in *The British Labourer's Protector and Factory Child's Friend*, 1 February 1833.

required to be moved again in the new House. It would be lost if an eleven hours bill were passed first. Sadler had made suggestions of suitable members whom Bull could approach. He approached them and many others. They were either doubtful of their powers or uncertain about their sympathies, for he received many refusals. He asked Sir Andrew Agnew, a Scottish Member, for help. Agnew was quite right in thinking that he was himself unsuited to the task. He was a Whig of sorts, but too much of an individualist to follow any party line. He suggested to Bull that Lord Ashley, heir to the Earldom of Shaftesbury, might undertake the task.

Ashley was then thirty-one years of age and had been returned as one of the Members for Dorset. He was taken by surprise when Bull approached him. He afterwards recalled his "doubt, astonishment, and terror, at the proposal". He asked for time to consider it, but Bull pressed for an answer. He was haunted by the fear that Morpeth would get in first. Ashley consulted other people, meditated and prayed, and came to the conclusion that he could not refuse to do as Bull asked. In a letter to Bull, he said:

> I dare not refuse the request you have so earnestly pressed. I believe it is my duty to God and the poor. . . . To me, it appears a matter less of policy than of religion.

Later, he said:

> It was a great religious question; for it involved the means to thousands and tens of thousands of being brought up in the faith and fear of the God who created them.[1]

If persuading Ashley to undertake this work had been Bull's only contribution to the social history of this country, he would have deserved to be remembered. In fact, although Hodder gives a full account of these comings and goings, most standard histories do not mention him. Not only did Bull persuade Ashley to succeed Sadler; he also briefed him about the factory conditions. He kept in touch with him and, as one local historian put it, "instructed" him. It is commonly believed that the movement for factory reform began when Ashley set his hand to it. In fact, the manufacturers themselves had largely given up hope of preventing legislation being passed. The demand for it was so insistent that Poulett Thomson was reported to say that although the Government was unwilling to legislate, "the

[1] Hodder, *op. cit.*, p. 155.

feeling outside the House" was such that they must do so. The Sadler Report had shocked the country. Only the most stubborn of the manufacturers failed to realize that the most they could hope to do was to limit the scope of the factory reformers' measure.

Ashley himself recognized how much he owed to the work of Sadler. At a meeting in London on 23 February 1833 he said that it was

> By the diligence of Mr Sadler that the people of England had been aroused from their apathy, and he in return had been assailed with obloquy, insult and reproach, after collecting an amount of evidence which for its importance and accuracy had rarely been equalled and never been surpassed: and yet that was the man who to the great loss of the country had been rejected from that House which he had adorned.

During the course of the same speech, he said that Sadler had borne the burden and heat of the day, and that he himself was entering in "to reap all that abundant harvest that Mr Sadler had sown".[1]

Sadler himself was present. The speeches at the meeting—organized by "The London Society for the Improvement of Factory Children" —make clear that his contemporaries understood the value of his work. Bull never referred to the early days of the movement without paying warm tribute to the part that Sadler had played. It is not "de-bunking" Ashley to stress what he himself stressed. The demand for factory reform had been created when he began his work. Without all that had gone before, and without the work of the Short-Time Committees —especially the Central Committee—it is difficult to conjecture what the course of his life would have been. He himself did not visit the textile areas until 1841, during a later phase of the campaign. By that time, Sadler had died—his labours as Chairman of the Select Committee had taken heavy toll of him—Bull had left Yorkshire, and Oastler was in the Fleet Prison. The first phase of the campaign has been largely lost sight of. As a result, Ashley is credited with the work of those before him as well as with his own great achievements. So reputable a historian as Professor Trevelyan avoids any reference to either Sadler or Oastler in his *History of England* and suggests that the agitation began under Shaftesbury and Fielden later in the thirties, partly in protest against the new Poor Law Amendment and partly

---

[1] *White Slavery*, Vol. VIII.

out of disappointment at the outcome of the Reform Bill.[1] In his *English Social History*, however, he says:

> The passing of the Reform Bill of 1832 was at once followed in the Industrial North by a fierce agitation of the factory hands against the hard conditions of their lives, particularly in the matter of hours. In Yorkshire, it was to some extent a Radical and Tory coalition. At Westminster members of all parties took part in it, and in 1833, the Whig Government gave it legislative form. The principal leaders in the country, Oastler, Sadler and Shaftesbury, were Tories; they were also Evangelicals.[2]

This brief summary is slightly more accurate, although even here no notice is taken of the work done before the passing of the Reform Bill. Moreover, it suggests that the Reform parties were in agreement with the proposals. The previous experience of the factory reformers and the tactics of the Whigs and Liberals in the new Parliament do not support this assumption. Bull's difficulty in securing a new Parliamentary leader, as well as Ashley's "doubt and terror", indicate that the House was more divided than Professor Trevelyan represents. Ashley knew how much he needed active help in the country and the Ten Hours men had no illusions. Twice already they had been disappointed, and they knew how much power their opponents had. Neither the publication of the Sadler Report nor the re-introduction of their Bill would bring success without much careful planning and hard work on their part.

Bull waited until Ashley had given notice of motion seeking leave to re-introduce the Bill before he took any further step. Besides giving guidance and information to Ashley, he had anxiously watched the course of events. He was cheered by the reception accorded to Ashley, for it was warmer and more general than he dared to hope. He knew that Ashley had succeeded in giving notice of motion before Morpeth —though only just—when he wrote to the Short Time committees in the West Riding to tell them of the course of events.

Although less than a month had elapsed since the Bradford Conference, the organization had been greatly strengthened, and it was possible to implement the third important decision of the Conference. Delegates were elected to go to London to help Ashley by lobbying in support of the Bill.

The first weeks of 1833 constituted an important period, therefore.

---

[1] *History of England*, p. 642.   [2] *English Social History*, pp. 541-2.

The gap created by Sadler's defeat had been filled; the Sadler Report had been published and had created a deep impression in most quarters; the organization had been greatly strengthened, especially in Yorkshire, and was likely to be more effective than it had been; and delegates were ready to go to London to help Ashley.

It is not surprising that hopes rose again.

9

SUPPORT FOR ASHLEY

POSSIBLY HISTORIANS' neglect of the early phases of the campaign is due to its apparently regional nature. A violent clash would have drawn the attention of the whole country to the factory problem. But the leaders kept a firm hand on the rank and file, so that there was no need for violent methods of repression. Another Peterloo was unthinkable.

Oastler and Bull—the former especially—came in for much criticism, but their stimulating speaking was intended to stir their followers to press for legislation, not to stir them to violence. Most of them had no political power, for manhood suffrage was still some decades off, and they adopted the best constitutional means of pressing for the redressing of their wrongs that lay in their power. They could hold their meetings and send their petitions pressing for legislation, but the task of enlightening those who voted was hardly less formidable than that of pressing those who governed. The most serious obstacle to the passing of the Ten Hours Bill seemed to them to be the indifference and ignorance of those who were not familiar with factory conditions. The pamphlets and speeches of the spokesmen for the movement were mainly directed to change this. Most people in the textile areas—even those not in the trade—had by this time taken sides one way or the other. Further afield, thoughtful people had begun to exercise their minds about the problem. As Southey's letter, already quoted, serves to show, their knowledge was still slight. The country as a whole was largely unawakened to the appalling conditions, the heartlessness of the employers and the cruelties and inhumanities in the factories.

The Sadler report altered this. Published about the time that delegates of the movement were to meet at Bradford, it drew the nation's attention to the factory issue. The newspaper extracts and comments made readers aware of the nature of its contents. Even *The Leeds Mercury* had to admit that the case for legislation had been made out, though the admission was accompanied by the inference that the *Mercury* had held that view for nearly two years and by the warning that it must not concede all that the reformers asked. It could no longer be treated as a purely regional issue. As Professor Driver says:

> Its publication marked the completion of the process by which the factory question was transformed from a local to a national issue.[1]

Generally, the Press gave support to the reformers as a result of its publication. Sometimes, the support was grudging, but that it was given at all is some indication of the effect of the publication of the Report. It confirmed the charges of cruelty previously made by the reformers and denied or explained away by their opponents. The accounts of factory conditions, previously refuted as untrue or exaggerated, were borne out. The employers' assertion that factory work was good for children—which led operatives to ask them why their own children did not do it—was disposed of by the wealth of medical evidence embodied. Apart from suggestions of exaggeration, no answer was forthcoming to the evidence in the Report or to the conclusions drawn. Here was powder and shot for the reformers. The victimization of some of the witnesses shocked decent people and underlined the ruthlessness of the worst type of manufacturer.

Naturally, the manufacturers' tactics were affected. Some of the pamphlets written at this time were as extreme as any written at the beginning of the campaign. Their writers, chiefly in Scotland and Lancashire, had made no advance since the Halifax resolutions were passed. Some writers paid tribute to the sincerity of the reformers' leaders, but regretted the "impractical" nature of their remedies. A considerable body of manufacturers still advocated the complete application of *laissez-faire* principles. Fiscal policy and Government spending were to blame for the state of the poor, they said. There would be no need for the restriction of hours by legislation if trade were freed. (Eleven years later, Bright was still arguing that the Corn Laws made the Ten Hours men's demands impossible, but he still opposed them after the Corn Laws had been repealed.) All the old arguments about the dire consequences—bad trade and unemployment—were repeated by these writers. The assumptions of the political

[1] *Tory-Radical*, p. 207.

economists were being more widely accepted, and these arguments could be made to appear forceful in consequence. Professor Trevelyan refers to the period 1833 to 1847 as "a period which it is usual to condemn as obsessed with the doctrine of *laissez-faire*". He adds:

> It is difficult to obsess people with a doctrine if once either their hearts or their pockets are touched. A former generation, in anti-Jacobin days, being in a mood to grind the faces of the poor, had chosen out those parts of *laissez-faire* which suited their purpose and neglected the rest.[1]

He is here referring to the period of the factory reform campaign, though admittedly he has the middle eighteen-forties chiefly in mind. Yet it is impossible to read the pamphlets and broadsides of the opponents of factory reform without seeing how obsessed they were with *laissez-faire*. Their hearts were not touched, and their pockets benefited by the application of the principles of *laissez-faire*. Dr Trevelyan says that "at no period was *laissez-faire* in force in all directions at once",[1] but this is so only because it is an impracticable doctrine. Certainly in the early eighteen-thirties every attempt was made to put it into force in all directions. The factory reformers had to contend with men who genuinely believed in it as well as men who found it profitable to accept it. Macaulay could accuse Sadler of "a convenient philanthropy", but the adherence of the more militant and intransigent manufacturers to the doctrine of *laissez-faire* was due to its convenience as a philosophy. Even some who admitted that children were over-worked maintained that legislation would be wrong and harmful.

These die-hards were probably in the minority, however. Most of the manufacturers, especially in Yorkshire, recognized that legislation was likely, if not inevitable. The best of them, like Wood in Yorkshire and Halliwell in Lancashire, were anxious for it. They had improved conditions, but they could not go as far as they wished if they were to compete with less enlightened and less humane employers. Others were determined to make any legislation passed as modest as possible. They tried to steal a march on the Ten Hours men. They were accustomed to bargain in order to buy as cheaply as possible, and they were determined to give as little as possible in bargaining with the champions of labour. They had no need of mass meetings. The Reform Parliament contained so many of their friends and associates that it was

---

[1] *English Social History*, p. 544.

exactly suited to their purpose. They could exercise pressure behind the scenes while they themselves knew every move made by the reformers.

The reformers knew this. They were in a constant state of anxiety for this reason. They knew that they must leave nothing to chance, that their organization must be tight, close-knit, and efficient, and that their pressure upon the country must be intensified rather than relaxed. Besides winning new supporters amongst those only beginning to be awakened to the problem, they must work hard in the lobbies. Only incessant lobbying could counteract the influence of the manufacturers in Parliament.

Ashley's notice of motion was followed within a few hours by Morpeth's announcing his intention to move an Eleven Hours Bill. Oastler and Bull were often critical of this action. The fact that Morpeth had been associated with earlier attempts to secure factory legislation and claimed to be a friend of the operatives caused Oastler to liken him to Judas, the millowners to the bands of murderers who accompanied Judas to Gethsemane and the friendship for the children that Morpeth professed to the betrayer's kiss. This was no doubt hard on the well-meaning Morpeth, but the action could not fail to look sinister to the reformers. Not only was this notice given within two days of Ashley's, but Morpeth announced his intention of moving his motion on 27 February about a week earlier than Ashley was to move his. Besides this, they had a growing fear that the millowners intended to back his measure because it would not only kill Ashley's, but also because they saw a means of lengthening adult working hours although the measure would shorten the working hours of children. This could be done by working children in relays.

Oastler's bitter and virulent letter to Lord Morpeth and, still more, *The Times* editorial,[1] caused Morpeth to write to Ashley to say that

---

[1] *The Times*, 7 February 1833:

"The renewal of Mr Sadler's benevolent measure, the Ten Hours Bill, was undertaken on Friday evening by Lord Ashley, who feels a deep interest in this affecting subject.

"Lord Ashley gave notice immediately on the return of the Speaker from the Lords, and that notice was received with unusual and very hearty approbation from all parts of a House of upwards of 300 members. His Lordship has been requested by the official organ of the delegates' meeting, whose address was recently agreed to, to undertake this charitable work.

"It seems, however, that the millowners, unable to resist the strong tide of he intended no discourtesy. He told him, and later he told the House itself, that he thought that the *Ten Hours Bill* had no chance of being passed and that he thought an eleven-hour bill would be in the best interests of all concerned. This is no doubt true, for he had expressed doubts about the prospects of meeting the arguments of "practical men" when a Ten Hours Bill had first been mentioned. Hobhouse's prediction that such a Bill would not be allowed to go a single stage, so nearly right, had been made at the same time.[1] The reference of the Bill to a Select Committee had been the price exacted for the Second Reading. It is fair to Morpeth to say that he had good grounds for his doubts. His tactics were open to some criticism, however.

Oastler and the reformers were perhaps a little hard on Morpeth, and he was clearly disturbed by the attacks made upon him, especially by the assertion that he was acting in the interests of the millowners. He courteously refused Ashley's offer to leave the Ten Hours Bill to him, and after postponing the moving of his motion more than once, gave up his intention of doing so. The powerful support of *The Times* had much to do with the outcome of this first skirmish of the campaign. For some years to come, *The Times* was to give valuable support to the causes espoused by Oastler and Bull. John Walter, the proprietor, became a close friend of both of them. Bull became a frequent correspondent to that paper, and many articles were clearly his work. Much of the information that Walter acquired about the West Riding came from him. The real beginning of the alliance seems to have been about a year earlier, when *The Times* had poured scorn on the need for a Select Committee and had suggested that its value to the Government lay in the greater ease with which a Committee of twenty-three

public opinion which the force of the evidence before the Select Committee, the result of Mr Sadler's indefatigable labours, has set in motion, have resolved to dole out some niggardly measure of relief to the poor children by the hand of Lord Morpeth, one of the members for the West Riding of Yorkshire.

"His Lordship must have been somewhat forgetful of Parliamentary courtesy when, after midnight on Tuesday and when the House was all bustle, he announced his intention to bring in his—or rather the masters'—bill and in doing so dated his motion for the 27th of February, although Lord Ashley's was previously given for the 5th of March. There can be very little doubt which of the two propositions—that which comes from the sufferers and their friends or that which emanates from the inflictors of that suffering—will meet with public support, as probably the petitions from the country will furnish some illustration."

[1] P. 44, above.

THE 7TH EARL OF SHAFTESBURY, 1801–85, PORTRAIT BY JOHN COLLIER, 1878

During the period with which this book deals he was Member for Dorsetshire and bore the courtesy title Lord Ashley

could be won to the manufacturers point of view than the whole House with its six hundred and fifty-eight members.[1]

Meanwhile, the organization of the reforming forces proceeded apace, and the campaign was carried on intensively. Oastler and Bull divided forces and, in company with other leaders, toured the West Riding. Bull was in some demand elsewhere. Evidence of this, as well as of the widening interest, is to be found in the notices and reports of meetings. One of them announced him as a speaker at a meeting in Newcastle called by the Mayor, saying that he was "resident in the manufacturing district of Yorkshire", that he had been examined by Mr Sadler's Committee, and that he was to be at the meeting "to give what information he possesses".[2]

For many weeks, there was a spate of pamphlets and letters to the Press covering the ground already covered and developing new arguments. Manufacturers issued posters warning their operatives of the loss of work that would result from a restriction of hours to ten—indeed, from any restriction at all. The reformers pressed their point that long hours of labour and a large body of unemployed showed how irrational the system was and how false the employers' argument. The share-the-work plea was constantly to the fore, not only because it seemed to answer the employers' and the political economists' argument, but also because unemployment and loss of wages offends the instincts of both its victims and their well-wishers. It is a problem that recurs. The argument that work should be shared was much in evidence during the slump period between the two wars. It was difficult to persuade people in dire need that we had over-produced. It was no easier a century ago. (Lord Liverpool, it will be recalled, had said that there had been "much over-production".) It is only during times of scarcity that we succeed in distributing work and wages. Labour is then in a "seller's market" and, especially in these days of powerful trade unions, able to see to it that work is shared. Indeed, the present tendency to press for a shorter working week arises from a desire to gain more leisure in which to do overtime. A century ago, the employers wielded the power. The eighteen-thirties were days of plenty, and the volume of poverty was enormous. Labour was in a "buyer's market". The worker had no bargaining power and was unprotected by

[1] 13 February 1833.
[2] See the album of posters and other literature in the Bradford Reference Library.

legislation. The price of labour was low, therefore. Few will deny that
the modern situation was created by the way in which the masters
used their power. Not only their ruthlessness, but the principles on
which they acted have come to be accepted without being questioned.
If labour, like any other commodity, is worth what it will fetch, can
it be wondered at that it becomes costly when it is in "a seller's
market"? The employers followed the teachings of the political economists and exercised their power. Oastler and Bull had little success
in persuading them that the labouring classes are not free agents. So
strong was the influence of the new social philosophy that many who
wished to ease the lot of children were not convinced.

There was another illogicality in the employers' arguments which
the operatives were quick to see. Why should a lessened demand for
their products in foreign countries result in there being less for them?
Why could not work be shared and the home demand increased?
It could not be argued that it was necessary to export surplus quantities
in order to live. The trade surplus increased the overseas wealth of
the finance houses. Many speakers at factory reform meetings questioned the logic of the situation. Wages were low. In some homes, the
few shillings earned by the children constituted the family income.
Workers, especially unemployed workers, could not buy the products
of their own labour. They had common sense on their side when they
argued that lack of purchasing power in the hands of the working classes
was a cause of bad trade. The theories of the economists were against
them. Ricardo's theory of "the iron law of wages" made nonsense of
their arguments, it was said. Only the demand for the Repeal of the
Corn Laws offered them any hope. But that demand sprang from
concern for the capitalists rather than for the workers. Rarely, indeed,
has a campaign been carried on with so much humbug as was that
campaign. Its spokesmen said that the Corn Laws cost two hours of
the workers' day, but they continued to resist the passing of the Ten
Hours Bill after their repeal. The fact is, the employers would concede
no more than they were compelled to concede. Since the workers
could make them concede nothing, they and their friends could only
hope to force the hand of an unwilling Government by appealing to a
wide public on grounds of equity, humanitarianism, and policy.

The manufacturers also argued that it would be difficult to enforce
legislation. It was said that the Acts passed to protect young cotton
workers were largely ineffective. There was much truth in this, for

only the better employers observed their provisions. Magistrates were called upon to investigate infringements from time to time, but large numbers of employers were never charged. None of the Acts had provided for inspection. But it was not a good argument for men who were resisting the passing of legislation to use. If it would not be effective, why were they so fearful? The men most likely to observe the law were on the side of the reformers.

The question of law enforcement caused some difference of opinion amongst the reformers. Yorkshire leaders called for a Time Book, recording the hours of working; Lancashire committees were in favour of a restriction on the working hours of machinery. Oastler and Bull seem to have come to favour this at a later stage, without abandoning their demand for a Time Book. As the greater part of the drive at this stage of the campaign came from Yorkshire, the Yorkshire concern for the Book determined the policy on this issue.

As the time approached when Ashley was to move his motion, the momentum behind the campaign gathered. The leaders visited the textile areas and addressed enthusiastic meetings. New speakers bore a share. Many operatives developed gifts of sincere and moving speech. They began by addressing small local meetings or as class leaders in one of the Methodist connexions; the Primitive Methodists, the Methodists most friendly to the movement provided many of them. By the middle of February, petitions began to pour into Parliament. The Leeds petition bore 16,000 signatures, that from Bradford 12,000; there were nearly 5,000 to the Huddersfield petition, and large numbers from the other textile areas in Yorkshire, as well as large numbers from the textile areas of Lancashire, Clydeside, and other parts of Scotland.

The London meeting, besides introducing Ashley to the London supporters of the movement, showed what an asset the Sadler report was as propaganda in parts of the country removed from the scene of the agitation. Many people accepted it because they agreed with Sadler's politics, and only his enemies denied his disinterestedness. The "platform" included Robert Owen, the Socialist pioneer and himself a millionaire, Sadler, Torrens, the economist, Oastler and Bull. It included another newcomer to the movement in Daniel O'Connell, at that time the stormy petrel of British politics. He had risen to prominence during the resistance to "Union", had led the successful agitation for Catholic Emancipation, and was still the leader of the agitation for the removal of Irish grievances. He supported the Ten

Hours movement for three or four years, then suddenly withdrew his support. Oastler later said that O'Connell was paid £1000 by the masters to withdraw his support and that the Roman Catholic bishop then told his priests to withdraw theirs. Oastler claimed that he was told this by a Roman Catholic priest.[1]

Sir Peter Laurie, the Lord Mayor of London, presided. He said that owners cared for horses and slaves because it was in their interests to do so if they had no better reason. Factory children, he said, were less fortunate. Their employers recognized no responsibility towards them. "The measure of amelioration now proposed is on the principle that by limiting the time in which portions of labour are to be performed, the double advantage would be gained of preventing the over-working of those employed and extending the sphere of employment". Sadler made a moving speech and Oastler one of his best. This fashionable and influential London audience was no less willing to bear a long session of speeches than were the people of the North, for the meeting lasted three and a half hours. Besides these speeches and Ashley's first address to his supporters, Bull spoke at some length. Like Oastler, he was able to give first-hand information of the state of the textile areas. He told of his growing concern and of his present observation. He told of parents who sat up

> a great portion of the night lest their children should be late for work. . . . At five in the morning, sometimes even at four o'clock, they are roused from their weary beds by their anxious parents. . . . In some families, where the parents are too poor to have a clock, it is not uncommon for the children, labouring under the fear of punishment, to start to their work a considerable time before the appointed hour, and the other morning, a stranger found two little girls, crying in the streets of Bradford before 3 o'clock, who had run at that early hour to the factory trembling lest they should be after their time and get punished.

He told of the scanty opportunity given for refreshment, especially when spinning was bad. Then it was frequently impossible to get any refreshment and "they continue from six in the morning till twelve without food or rest". He told of the long hours when trade was brisk, when a machine broke down, or when an order had to be completed urgently. He gave specific instances.

As he frequently did, he referred to the criticisms of himself and his clerical colleagues in the movement, and replied to them.

[1] *The Fleet Papers*, Vol. I, No. 25.

It is said by some that the clergy ought not to interfere in this matter, but he, as a minister of religion, thought they above all others were called upon to interfere and he vowed that so long as he had a heart in his bosom and a tongue to utter the feelings of that heart, he would plead the cause of the poor factory children.

He went on to tell his audience of the long journeys that many of the children had to go to their work, of the day in the heated, tainted, atmosphere, and the weary dragging home of their tired limbs. Many Northern audiences had heard these things, but they were new to the members of this London audience. It is easy to imagine the horror and indignation when he produced a long, heavy strap of leather with a large knot at the end, saying;

There are many parents present. How would they feel if their young and lovely children were cruelly beaten with an instrument of this description? . . . A brother clergyman had received it from a father who had taken his child from a mill where they were punished with an instrument of this description. The overseer used to put the children's heads between his legs and while thus held he inflicted such punishment on them with this strap that they could not rest in their beds nor go to sleep for pain—and this to females too.

He ended by saying that he was sure that those who turned "a ready ear to the prayers of the negro slave would not turn a deaf ear to the wrongs of the factory children".

It is clear that the meeting was moved. Dr Russell, the Rector of Bishopsgate, said that he had intended simply to propose a vote of thanks to the Chairman, but after the call which had been made of the clergy he could not refrain from saying that he would give his utmost support to the proposed measure, and that it could not be supposed that the clergy in general could hear such statements as were contained in the book of evidence without coming forward with a like support.[1]

Besides rallying Yorkshire and stirring people so far untouched, largely drawing attention to the Sadler Report, Oastler toured the textile areas of Lancashire, addressing meetings in the larger towns amidst demonstrations of great enthusiasm. The textile areas throughout Britain were better organized than before. Petitions continued to pour into Parliament. Ashley's Bill was the only bill dealing with the factory problem to be debated, the public conscience had been shocked

[1] A full report is in *White Slavery*, Vol. V.

by the revelations in the Report, and, even more than a year earlier, "the feeling outside the House" was for the Bill.

Yet the manufacturers were able to win time still again. In spite of all their work, their careful and thorough organization and assiduous lobbying, the reformers found that their opponents could rally more powerful support in the House than they could muster. A friendly Government would have tipped the balance in their favour, but the Government was allied politically and ideologically with their opponents. It connived at a further delay, and the cause received another set-back.

This was the Government that historians credit with zeal for factory reform.

IO

THE ROYAL COMMISSION

THE OPPONENTS of the Bill had no great success in their attempts
to influence the public. They tried to discredit the Sadler Report,
saying that it was "one-sided" and "exaggerated". They
created uncertainty in some minds by the threat of reduced wages for
a shorter working day and of unemployment through the loss of overseas markets which a rise in costs must bring. These two arguments
largely cancelled out, of course, for if wages were cut to pay for the
reduction in working hours, costs could not be increased by it. Not
everyone saw this, but some of the reformers did, Bull amongst them.
On the whole, however, the public felt that the report had revealed
an intolerable state of things.

What the manufacturers had in mind to counteract the reformers'
lobbying in Parliament was a matter of conjecture giving rise to many
rumours. For some time, the Ten Hours men's chief fear was of the
attempt to get an Eleven Hours Bill through Parliament. *The Leeds
Mercury* advocated this, but Lord Morpeth was not prepared to fight
for such a measure, especially in view of criticisms of his tactics and the
impugning of his motives.

Their counterblast proved to be a proposal to refer the factory
question to a Royal Commission. A Royal Commission differs from
a Select Committee in being partially composed of people who are not
Members of Parliament while a Select Committee is composed of
Members. It is certain to include "experts" from outside the House.
These were the people whom the reformers feared most. They were
likely to strengthen the opposition because they were opposed to
legislation on principle.

When the idea was first mooted by Wilson Patten, a Lancashire
Member, it was in a tentative kind of way, but the idea caught on and
he found himself getting a good deal of support. Indeed, so well was

the suggestion received that Althorp, who at first had thought the idea a dangerous one, found it possible to withdraw his early advice not to proceed with the motion to appoint the Commission. Some of the opponents of the Ten Hours Bill hoped and believed that it would kill the Bill. They made no bones about it. Others were more cautious, and expressed the hope that the Commission would enable the criticisms of the masters arising from the Sadler Report to be rebutted. This, of course, was nonsense. The only way to rebut the evidence was to cross-examine those who gave it. This had been done by Sadler's Committee, which had not been composed solely of Sadler's supporters. One or two members of his Committee said during the debate that the witnesses had been thoroughly examined and the evidence carefully taken. The House decided, however, by the smallest possible majority, that the Royal Commission be appointed to look at the factory problem afresh.

To say that the operatives were disappointed would be an understatement. They were fiercely resentful. Oastler, Sadler, and Bull all protested vigorously. They voiced the resentment of the operatives and organized a series of meetings at which they and their supporters demonstrated their fixed determination to see to it that the Ten Hours Bill should be passed. Some of the first meetings were hastily organized, but the resentment was so great that news of a proposed meeting spread like wild-fire. At Bradford, for instance, the posters announcing the meeting were not on the streets until the early afternoon, but by the time of the evening meeting the news had swept through the town, and more than three thousand people gathered for it.[1]

The first of these meetings took place at Halifax on Easter Monday. In this hotbed of the opposition, Oastler was in militant mood. He replied to a number of people who had attacked him—in particular, two ministers, Morgan and Godwin—and replied to those who had denied the truth of some of the reformers' assertions and who had defended the millowners. Apologists were inclined to harp on the theme that millowners were respectable and humane men, often very religious men. Many of them won this reputation by their gifts to charity and to their places of worship or by their mode of life outside business. But neither Oastler nor Bull would ever allow that such considerations counted for much in men who grew rich by overworking their employees, including children. Oastler told of one firm which

[1] Oastler Collection and local papers.

imposed fines on children who were late for work, giving the money as the firm's subscription to a missionary society. His audience knew to which firm he referred. He replied to Marshall of Leeds, who had said that there was no slavery in his father's works, by pointing out that it was notorious that few girls who worked there reached the age of twenty-one.[1] This meeting, held in a town whose manufacturers had framed the notorious resolutions, and where conditions were generally amongst the worst in the West Riding, set the tone for the series. It began on a militant note and the militancy grew as the series continued. This was particularly true of Oastler, for Bull was more restrained if no less indignant.

Bull, at this meeting, besides restating some of the former arguments, drew on fresh evidence and new information. It was often said that of the twenty-one medical men who gave evidence before the Sadler Committee and who were in favour of the Bill very few were resident in the manufacturing districts. Bull retorted that medical men could be expected to know what the human frame can bear, but that in fact most of the medical men who gave evidence did live in factory areas. He spoke of the courage of the doctors and of their lack of self-interest. He mentioned particularly Dr Young, a Bolton doctor, who did not concern himself about the reactions of the factory owners, "by whom he was employed and from whom he received fees".[2]

By this time, Bull was a victim of hostile attacks as bitter as those to which Oastler himself was subjected. It was at a meeting earlier in 1833 that he first told the story of his "conversion" to the cause of factory reform.[3] On the same occasion, he had replied to critics who accused him of deserting the cause of the negroes, saying that the two causes were bound up together and that those who were zealous in the cause of negro emancipation, to be consistent, should be concerned for the white slave. Here, again, he referred to these attacks. He spoke of the previous occasions on which he had spoken in Halifax. He had spoken there in the cause of religious truth, he said, and added that he would have been glad to see his clerical brethren whom he had met on that occasion. (Halifax was a parish in which clerical support for factory reform was less than in most others.) He had also been to Halifax to plead the cause of the negro. Bull said, somewhat ruefully,

[1] See Southey's letter, quoted p. 78.   [2] Oastler Collection.
[3] See above, Chap. 2.

that he had never been called names for his exertion on behalf of the negroes. He went on, somewhat more militantly, that he had made sacrifices for the injured sons of Africa that his calumniators never made.

> But charity begins at home. We shall never be allowed by Providence to put down black slavery till we have shown our honest and sincere detestation of white slavery at home.

He was now abused for his exertions for the factory child. *The Halifax Express* and *The Leeds Mercury*, which had praised him when he pleaded in favour of the black slave, now abused him when he pleaded for the white. He had something better to do than quarrel with them, however.

A Sunday School teacher present told of a manufacturer who had said that it was no hardship for a child to go to work at six years of age. The speaker said that he had asked how this agreed with the condition of those gentlemen whose own children could not go to school without attendants. He told of a child in a home lacking a clock who went to work at 3 a.m. and had had to wait, shivering in the cold until 6 o'clock. The child had since died.

Meetings following this pattern were held in all the textile towns and villages. The operatives rallied to express their indignation at the device adopted by their opponents, with the connivance of the Government. They saw that the Government and its majority of supporters in the Reform Parliament was as hostile to their demands as they had feared. The Government, therefore, had to share the opprobrium for this second delay. The remitting to a Royal Commission of an awkward problem is still regarded as the indefinite postponement of its solution. It is sometimes a device to shelve a problem that the Government dare not or will not deal with. To commit to a Royal Commission this question, the answer to which seemed obvious, could only appear to the operatives in that light. Oastler, and indeed most speakers, made clear that it was their view that the Whigs had maintained the same attitude from the outset. It was the fourth time that the reformers had been baulked, and each occasion had increased their distrust as well as their exasperation.

Mass meetings, however, only served to demonstrate the indignation of the operatives and their friends. It was important that concerted action should be taken in other ways. It was most important to determine on the policy to be followed when the Commissioners visited the textile areas. It was obvious that the Short Time committees must all adopt the same policy. Representatives were called together to hammer it out. The operatives had only agreed to co-operate with the Sadler Committee after much persuasion. They had resented it, and no doubt the fact that their champion was its Chairman helped their resentment to be overcome. What could they be expected to do in the face of a Royal Commission, made up as it was of a very different type of enquirer?

As the campaign of public meetings drew to a close, a Conference was held at Manchester. No doubt the representatives of the committees had been affected by their own propaganda as well as by the facts of the situation. Speeches—especially Oastler's—had grown more fiery. Bull himself was forthright, but he never uttered the threats that were implicit in some of Oastler's speeches. Oastler had learned what he could do with a large crowd and the effect on him of an enthusiastic mass meeting was not always happy. By the end of April, when the last of the series was held in the Manor Court House in Manchester, he was thoroughly aroused. If he did not, like Saul of Tarsus, breathe threatening and slaughter, he came very near to it. Bull's indignation was no less than Oastler's, but any hint of unconstitutional conduct by any of his friends grieved him. Crowds did not have the same heady effect upon him as they had upon Oastler, and he was able to speak in language that was telling without being inflammatory.

At this last meeting of the series, he addressed himself specifically to the clergymen and ministers, whose support was being assiduously sought at that time. Evidently, it was Bull's assignment to try to win over clergymen and ministers who were either opposed to the cause or lukewarm towards it. At this meeting, almost the whole of his speech was directed towards this end.[1] Later, at a meeting in Bradford, he spent some time defending himself and his colleagues against those who said that the clerical factory reformers were going outside their proper province. In doing so, he re-stated the Christian sanctions for the movement. He sounded the prophetic note and insisted that a Christian minister could do no other. Indeed, the attacks upon himself and his friends forced him into an aggressiveness he had wished to avoid when he first made his entry into the movement.[2] At Manchester, while he spoke definitely and strongly enough, there was a

[1] See below, Chap. 17. [2] See above, Chap. 3.

plaintive note in his speech as he expressed a certain bewilderment at the inactivity of some of the Manchester clergymen and ministers. Possibly his plaintiveness was simulated, but it enabled him to argue with his colleagues more effectively than he could have done had he been as fiery as Oastler.

The tone of the meeting indicated the mood of the delegates at that time assembled in Manchester. They were in no mood to receive the representative of the Commission with courtesy, much less with enthusiasm, and the Conference decided not to co-operate with it.

It was a decision of great moment, for it left the field clear to their enemies. Even after the Commission reported, the wisdom or un-wisdom of the Conference's decision could not be assessed. If it was unwise, at least it was understandable. The reformers were certain that the Commissioners knew what they wished to find before they began and that their minds were made up in advance. It did not seem to them that anything that they could say would influence the verdict. The Sadler Committee had collected sufficient evidence to prove the case. Men whose outlook and social philosophy made it certain that they would support the millowners were not, it seemed to the reformers, looking for evidence at all. This attitude is not difficult to understand. The masters' argument that only the operatives' side of the case had been put to the Sadler Committee was itself ominous. What answer could there be to the plain facts set out in the Report? They were undeniable. What could a commission find either to strengthen or to off-set them? They could only explain them away or point to some factories in which the workpeople were treated better than they were in most.

The Conference decided, therefore, that instead of briefing witnesses, each local committee should organize a protest when a Commissioner visited its area. The whole movement was involved in this. Bull visited West of England textile areas to help the Short Time committees to organize their protests. A list of eleven instructions was drawn up. In a preamble, it was said that the Commission had been appointed on the false pretence of insufficient and untrue evidence given to the Sadler Committee, "and with a view to the gratification of the Masters of Factories". It was intended to delay or defeat the Ten Hours Bill by this means. The preamble went on:

any voluntary recognition of such a Commission would preclude our privilege of rejoinder, and also because this course is most unjustifiable, as proposing to try the Cause of the Rich before one Tribunal and that of the poor before another. . . .[1]

The Commission was to work in a different manner from the Sadler Committee. A central body in London was to receive the evidence collected in the factory centres by Assistant Commissioners. In Yorkshire, Alfred Power, John Drinkwater, and Dr Loudon had the field work to do. Soon after they appeared, the arguments between them and the Ten Hours men became fierce and acrimonious. They met manufacturers and reformers and explained how they proposed to work. A good deal of their time was to be spent in research in matters which seemed to the reformers to be impertinent. Questions asked of women workers, dealing with intimate details of married life offended many of them and made their friends indignant. Typical of these questions were;

How soon after marriage did you have your first child?
How many miscarriages have you had?

The Times, and many other newspapers, expressed scorn and indignation. It was clear that the evidence of the medical men in the Sadler Report was to be nullified if possible.

In addition, of course, the Assistant Commissioners were to question people on matters relating to factory conditions. They proposed that their investigations should be free from scrutiny of any kind, but that representatives of the Ten Hours movement and a like number of masters should be present when evidence involving masters and men was being taken. Sadler objected to this procedure. He wished evidence taken independently to be verified in public. He asked that the inquiry should be public and that an independent shorthand writer should take down the evidence. His insistence that evidence should be given on oath made the millowners particularly angry. He felt, not unnaturally, that the Commissioners should examine witnesses with the same care that his Committee had done. Sadler, normally a gentle soul, carried on a fierce argument with them. The pamphlets and letters published at the time show how strongly he felt about the method adopted.[2]

Oastler, as was to be expected, had an acrimonious correspondence

[1] Oastler Collection, Reprinted in Tory-Radical, Appendix C.
[2] The Leeds Intelligencer, during May and June 1833, reproduced much of this correspondence. The pamphlets are in the Oastler Collection.

with them. They angered him by saying that his refusal to co-operate
was un-English. They accused him of blasphemy when he invoked
the Name of the Trinity in his condemnation of their activities. To be
fair to them, it must be admitted that the opening of that particular
letter does give the reader something of a shock; only his belief that he
was doing God's work could justify his strong terms. Indeed, even an
ardent admirer of Oastler must admit that he allowed himself to be
goaded into indiscretion. He had cause to be angry, it is true. The
Commissioners accused him of sedition because he had replied to them
that "it is un-English to use the prerogative of the King of England
for the continuance of oppression and murder"—"his prerogative is a
Prerogative of Mercy". He answered by reminding them of the Leeds
Rally, at which Baines had encouraged seditious speeches and had
called for disloyal demonstrations.[1] Baines, of course, was in favour
of the Commission, and the Commissioners were indiscreet enough
to accept Marshall's week-end hospitality on two occasions. Oastler's
retort was not inapposite, therefore.

His remarks about the King's prerogative were in line with one of
the addresses issued by the Manchester Conference. It had issued,
besides the instructions, a protest to the Commissioners and an
"Address", on behalf of the operatives, "to all Ranks and Classes in
the Land". The Protest opened with a declaration "of unfeigned
loyalty and attachment to the King and constitution by law established", and the address repeatedly made the same point:

> We leave our cause in your hands, and implore our fellow countrymen
> of all ranks to petition without delay for the Ten Hours Bill, and that it
> may be passed without reference to a partial, unjust, unnecessary, and
> delusive parliamentary commission, sued out on false pretences, to the abuse
> of the King's Royal Prerogative, and to the hurt and grief of his loving and
> loyal subjects.
>
> We address you as those who revere the constitution of our country.
>
> We honour the King—we respect the House of Commons; but we
> firmly believe that in the matter to which our present appeal refers, the
> influence of the interested and heartless millowners has misled the House of
> Commons, who were induced by gross misrepresentation, to sanction the
> Commission by a majority of one. . . .
>
> We believe his gracious Majesty has been imposed upon; and we have
> ventured to represent the same to our Sovereign. We, therefore, protest—
> not against the exercise of His Majesty's Royal Prerogative nor the authority

[1] See above, Chap. 3.

Approach OF THE Enemy!

*Copy of a Letter from an Operative at Leicester, dated
April 27th, 1833.*

"**You will be surprised to hear that wee have
had the head Commission here to-day, they had got
my name and wanted me to assist them—But I asked
them whether they was come to get Evidence for
the Masters, or what was their errand, for I as-
sured them it was my opinion that they had Evidence
enough already to Satisfy any Reasonable Man, and
as I thought the Commission was uncalled for, I
could not but protest against it, and would not recognize them in any way whatever. They spoke, at
length, to some of the Men in the Factory, and asked
a great many Questions, and told them they should
want them at some Future Period. OUR MASTER
TOLD THEM HE THOUGHT TEN HOURS
QUITE SUFFICIENT FOR THE CHILDREN
TO WORK.—I shall watch their movements while
they stop here. I expect the Comission will be in
Derbyshire on Monday, so that our Friends must be
on the look out.**"   Yours, **J. BRIERLEY.**

RACHEL INCHBOLD, PRINTER, 62, BRIGGATE, LEEDS.

The copy of a letter dated 27 April 1833 expresses the general feeling of
discontent with the inquiries of the Commissioners. This reproduction of the
letter in poster form, as it was displayed in the West Riding, shows how the
reception was prepared for them as they moved about the textile areas.

of Parliament—but we protest against the sordid influence by which both the one and the other have been so grossly imposed upon. . . .

This is not the form of words used by seditious rebels, and the Tory leadership of the movement ensured the constitutional correctness of its procedure. Oastler's indiscretion never led him to sedition. Wood, Sadler, and Bull, were attached to the Crown and Constitution. Both Wood and Bull were occasionally made uneasy by Oastler's inflammatory speeches, but his loyalty they never called into question.

The protests of the leaders were unavailing. They failed to secure any modification in the proposed procedure. The Commissioners began their researches amidst protests of another kind.

On the very day that Sadler had his abortive conference with the Commissioners, special posters were displayed calling factory children to join in demonstrating immediately after leaving work on the next day. Three thousand of them foregathered and serenaded the three commissioners. They shouted slogans and sang catchy verses such as they were accustomed to sing at the rallies organized by the committees, ditties and songs which enabled young campaigners to combine young people's love of being noisy with propaganda for the movement. The operatives needed no great urging to follow the Manchester instructions to arrange meetings and rallies wherever the commissioners went. Indeed, had the short time committees not organized them, ensuring orderliness in doing so, they would have developed spontaneously as disorderly demonstrations. There were meetings for factory workers. There were meetings to which various sections of the community were called. In almost every town, there was a meeting of factory children.

As the weeks passed during which the Commissioners did their work, the factory workers' tempers rose. The reception given to the Commissioners at Leeds was warm enough—though not what is usually regarded as "a real Yorkshire welcome"—but by the time they went to Bradford the mood of the operatives made a vigorous protest inevitable. There were the usual sectional meetings, but the great demonstration was on 6 June. It was one of the most spectacular of the whole campaign. Some reports say that there were as many as twenty thousand people present. Like all the meetings in the Bradford district, its success was due in large measure to Bull's organizing skill. Indeed, he contributed much to the campaign at this period, for throughout the West Riding he was called upon to assist in organizing rallies, while his readiness to speak and his wit and power as a speaker caused him to be called upon to address most of the meetings he helped to organize. When it is remembered that he did his pastoral work, regularly teaching in his schools, it will be realized how hard he worked during the Ten Hours campaign.

One of the interesting sidelights on his work here is to be found in an account of a meeting of children during this phase of the campaign. Few people who are accustomed to address adult meetings or services are "good with children", but Bull was an exception. He was always a draw when billed to speak to them. At the meeting on 11 June, he took the opportunity of answering those who criticized him and more especially those who accused him of teaching children to be disobedient and disrespectful.[1] Apart from the content of the speech, the accounts of the meeting are of interest as evidence of the various groups' readiness to come together to demonstrate their resentment of the Commission's visit and their determination to have the Bill. In spite of the notice being short and the wetness of the evening, over a thousand children, with parents and overlookers, packed the Primitive Methodist Chapel. Everywhere it was the same. The West Riding was the most thoroughly organized area, but in Lancashire, Scotland, and the West of England, something of the same enthusiasm was evident. The Commissioners, wherever they went, were greeted by large rallies and demonstrations.

The "Instructions" had laid upon the Short Time committees other duties besides organizing rallies, however. One of them was to appoint two of their number, picked men, to watch the Commissioners' movements from the time they entered their area until they left it. "The Select Committee", as these men were called, were to see where the Commissioners went, whom they saw and if possible what passed at the interview. If the Commissioners interviewed members of the public unconnected with the factory system, it was the duty of these men to find out what was the nature of the evidence they might have to give and whether they had any personal connexion with any manufacturer. They were to keep watch on the mills to see if they were "spruced up" before the Commissioners visited them and to look for instances of sickly looking children being hidden away. They had to look out for any kind of window-dressing or any attempt to conceal the true facts of the situation in any of the mills.

[1] See below, Chap. 12.

More than this, the "Select Committee" watched the movements of the Commissioners to see with whom they associated when they were not taking evidence. If they dined with prominent manufacturers—and doing so was one of their indiscretions—the fact was quickly known. Even what they had to eat was noised abroad. The sober accounts of situations to which this shadowing led make amusing reading. Some of the accounts, indeed, are not so sober, for the events are related with a gusto and relish which adds spice to them. One tells of an attempt made by the Commissioners to shake off the tenacious shadowing, which, besides being exasperating, enabled a welcome to be prepared at every point. Having tried many subterfuges to lose their escort, they booked coach tickets from Bradford to Keighley, but instead took the night coach to Doncaster. The mounted Ten Hours man who attended the coach overtook them to greet them at the posting inn at which they stopped to change horses. They were treated to a protest against their activities in the small hours of the morning. It did not strike them as funny. But, in spite of the bitterness prevailing at the time, others saw the humour of it. At the same time, the whole business was deadly serious. At almost every mill they visited, a group of workpeople managed to convey to them their dislike of the Commission and their distrust of the Commissioners.

It is doubtful whether the Manchester Conference made a wise decision in deciding to adopt these methods. Perhaps the leaders and the delegates were right in believing that co-operation with the Commission would disable them from making any rejoinder to its findings, but, on the other hand, by not co-operating, the opportunity was lost of ensuring that their point of view was presented and their motives understood. Certainly, the leaders left themselves open to misunderstanding and misrepresentation. The protest campaign was carried out in orderly fashion. The nearest approach to violence was the burning of Drinkwater and Power in effigy after the vast Huddersfield protest rally. Indeed, as at York, the orderliness of the campaign served to show the extent of the leaders' control over the workers and the more radical reformers. The Commissioners, however, noticed the strength of the opposition with which they had been faced and attributed it to the leaders. They gave no credit to them for the restraint shown by a body of exasperated people. Indeed, for some years, official reports blamed them for organizing the campaign, but gave them no credit for its freedom from violence. But credit was certainly due to them.

I I

OUTBIDDEN?

THE ACT OF 1833

Rumours about the contents of the Commission's Report began to circulate before it was issued. Members of the Government said enough to create uneasiness. A fear that the Bill would be amended to enable the children to work in shifts and the working day of adults thereby lengthened was strengthened. It gained substance when Lord Althorp said during the debate on the Second Reading that ten hours was too long a working day for children and that eight hours was long enough. On the face of it, this ought to have delighted the reformers. It did not. They saw in it a danger and an implication.

The danger was that an eight-hour limitation might enable children to be worked in "gangs", as Bull put it; that they would be able to work eight hours at one mill and go to another to work another shift. Some of the witnesses examined by the Commissioners had been questioned about the possibility of this limitation and how it would work. To us, it seems fantastic. In the circumstances of those days, it was not. Millowners had frankly stated their intention of evading the provisions of the Bill if it should be passed. If they could work two shifts of children without breaking the law, it seemed to the reformers that they were certain to do so. It would not be illegal nor, by their standards, would it be unethical. Besides, they would gleefully score off the hated reformers, whose agitation had brought about legislation.

Moreover, the main issue to the Commissioners was the extent to which the operatives, especially the children, could be deemed to be free agents. The millowners had decided it to their own satisfaction. The children they argued, need not work at all unless they chose to do so. The reformers and those who supported them—including the better millowners—said that family circumstances or some other form of compulsion made nonsense of this argument. Nor would the millowners be likely to regard two shifts as unreasonable, for it was not unknown for children to work sixteen hours when the state of trade made overtime seem to be essential.

The implication was that by a shift system the adult worker's day would be fixed at sixteen hours—in practice and with the law's implicit sanction. The Commissioners' known views made it certain that there would be no legal protection of adult workers. They assumed without question that adult workers were free agents. The operatives had good ground for their fears.

Another mutilation of Ashley's Bill that seemed to be certain, judging by the inspired utterances of Government spokesmen, was the omission of the provision that millowners should be sent to "The House of Correction" for a third offence against the Factory Act. In view of the owners' expressed intention of defying the law, the reformers regarded the clause as vital. Fines, they said, would not hurt the offenders enough, and it was held to be of great importance that the manufacturers who defied the law should be made to suffer personally for their offences. The personal punishment clause was as hotly opposed by the millowners as it was defended by the reformers.

In view of the rumours, Oastler, Bull, and the other leaders, decided to organize their biggest rally. They decided that the most suitable place for it was Wibsey Low Moor, just outside Bradford. It was reasonably accessible to most parts of the West Riding concerned with the agitation. During fairly recent years, a main road has been driven from Halifax to Leeds which goes near to the site of the rally, and it is easy to see what an excellent one it was for the purpose of the reformers. Columns from Leeds, from the Heavy Woollen district, from Huddersfield and Halifax could approach through country which was not unduly difficult; columns approaching from the Bradford side had a steep hill to negotiate, but the distance was less than for most of the others. The arrangement made for the Pilgrimage of Mercy was followed. Columns were built up at different centres and set out from those centres, led by a horseman. Bands played, slogans were displayed and banners were at the head of each contingent. Friendly societies' banners were much in evidence. The crowd was too vast to number accurately, and reports differ in their estimate. It seems certain, however, that upwards of 100,000 people[1] foregathered on that 1 July

[1] *The Times* reporter's estimate.

for a final rally to press for the passing of Lord Ashley's Bill.[1] The "hand out" issued to the Press, though written in the sober style of the day, did not conceal a certain exuberance. It told of children who took French leave from their work in order to be there and of some locked in their mill to prevent their attending who slid down ropes in order to join in. Most of the leaders were present and many of them addressed the meeting. Lord Althorp was invited to attend, but, of course, he did not do so.

The occasion was given added importance by the fact that a new-comer to the movement, who was to make a mark in both local and national politics, was present and spoke. He was William Busfeild Ferrand, who for many years served in Parliament as a Tory and was closely associated with Disraeli. He was a staunch advocate of the traditional English way of life and a fierce opponent of the rapidly developing financial-industrialism that came to be known as "Capital-ism". Contemporary literature issued in connexion with the rally refers to him as "William Busfeild".[2] This was his name until six years later, when his mother inherited her family's Bingley estates. His speech and his obvious sympathy with the movement were a source of great encouragement to the leaders. He was one of the better representatives of the squirearchy, with a sense of respon-sibility. He was concerned for the future of English agriculture, which he believed to be of the first importance to the nation. It is easy to accuse him and others like him of "having an axe to grind", but there are to-day many who maintain that the sacrifice of agriculture to industry was (and is) a mistaken policy for social as well as for political reasons. At any rate, whether from pure motives or mixed, Ferrand was a fierce opponent of the way of life advocated by the new Liberal-ism. His support for the factory movement was first won by his finding an exhausted factory child in the snow early one morning as he went through a wood on his own estate. He added strength to the movement, and his membership of Parliament during the next two decades enabled him to exercise influence there on many occasions.

Some differences of opinion amongst the leaders were aired. Bull,

---

[1] The Report of the Royal Commission was presented to Parliament on 28 June. *The Times*, 3 July 1833, was sardonic about its size and uselessness. On 1 July, the day of the Low Moor Rally, it published an extract stating the desirability and the practicability of the double shift system.

[2] *The Times* referred to him as "William Bousfield".

besides dealing with other aspects of the Bill, raised the matter of the personal punishment clause. He quoted Sadler as saying that it would be as effective as a restriction on moving power—a proposal on which there was still difference of opinion—and said that he himself was much in favour of it. He believed in it and urged that the resolution calling for "No Concessions" should be passed. The boast of the millowners that they would disobey the law, coupled with experience of their tactics and those of their supporters inside Parliament, made the operatives determined about this. Bull, from first to last, although he spoke strongly—"roughly" as one of his gentler clerical friends once said—never countenanced lawlessness. He strove to have good laws passed and bad laws rescinded, but he objected to lawlessness. The threat of it made him insist that the law should be strong enough to deter would-be offenders.

John Doherty, the Lancashire trade union leader, was in favour of giving way on the personal punishment clause. He believed that to insist on its retention would cost many votes in Parliament and lose the support of sympathizers in the country. He and James Turner, of the Manchester Short Time Committee, had done most of the lobbying. Having interviewed some two hundred Members, he had some claim to know what was their attitude. He was not himself given to compromise, and only his conviction that the cause would be best served by dropping the "No Concessions" resolution caused him to advocate it. He spoke of Nathaniel Gould, who had won the twelve hours limitation for the cotton workers and of his own part in the agitation since 1819. He referred to his three experiences in prison and said that he was unlikely to feel any tenderness for those who had been responsible for it. He would have liked the employing classes to endure what he had endured. Yet he felt it to be his duty to oppose Mr Bull's resolution, with its emphasis on personal punishment for a third conviction. It would lose the Bill, he said. He paid tribute to Ashley, saying that he had gone to London an ultra Radical with a prejudice against Ashley, an ultra Tory. He had denounced the peerage and had naturally looked upon Lord Ashley with suspicion. But after the frequent intercourse he had had with his Lordship, he had the satisfaction of saying that in no walk of life had he found "so honourable, so straightforward, kind and condescending, and at the same time talented and fearless a person as that young man".

Oastler replied with some of his accustomed vigour, although, of course, he was less hard on those colleagues who differed from him than on his accustomed opponents. He paid tribute to Doherty, Ashley, Sadler, and Wood—"all our friends"—all of whom were willing to drop the clause at that juncture, although they agreed that it must come ultimately. After some discussion, during which James Brook, a Huddersfield stalwart, voiced his support for Oastler, the resolution was carried.

Oastler then made his main speech, in which he gave further evidence of his growing frustration. He told of the casualties to be attributed to the factory system, the recital of which led him to make thinly veiled threats of "blood in another sense". He told of the threats of personal violence to himself and the hatred shown towards him by Whigs and millowners. As usual, he carried the crowd with him.

Bull read the petition which was to be presented to Parliament by George Strickland, who had served on Sadler's Committee. He had consistently supported the movement, if less fervently than its leaders. Bull also told of a gift of £20 from the Archbishop of York "for the benefit of the poor bairns".[1]

Whatever differences of opinion there were on one issue, the movement was united in its insistence that a ten-hour limit should apply to all young people up to the age of eighteen years, and that no person under twenty-one should be called upon to do night work. These were the main issues. The threat of a double-shift system made them even more important, for they would make impossible such a development. Croft, writing in retrospect thought that the Ten Hours men were at fault in refusing to contemplate any compromise,[2] but it is impossible to say what would have happened had another policy been adopted.

The rally made an impression, but it was neither so far-reaching as they believed nor so lasting as they hoped. It might have influenced Parliament sufficiently to enable Ashley to persuade the House to defeat Althorp's proposal to send the Bill to a Select Committee instead of to a Committee of the whole House,[3] but it had too little influence on the debate a fortnight later. By that time, the Commissioners had issued their report and provided Parliament with a way out of the dilemma that some members were in as a result of

[1] *The Times*, 5 July 1833. *The Leeds Intelligencer*, 6 July 1833.
[2] Op. cit., p. 91.
[3] *The Times*, 5 July 1833. Several members supported Ashley's protest.

their desire to safeguard children's interests without acting contrary to current economic and political beliefs.

Although claiming that conditions had improved, and that the millowners were not to blame for the cruelties admittedly perpetrated, the Report in the main confirmed the findings in the Sadler Committee. The Commissioners said that the greater number of cases of cruelty and harsh treatment were to be found in the smaller factories, especially in those in villages and off the beaten track. It confirmed that there was general overworking of the children. It made much of the fact that Sadler had attached great importance to the medical evidence, William Osborne of Leeds having been examined at some length on this. The Commissioners criticized Bull because he had refused to take them to his Sunday School to see the physical effects of the factory system on the children. In fact, of course, it was possible to see the effects of the system on the physique of factory workers until fairly recently, and the Commissioners had to admit that they saw them without Bull's co-operation. They were bound to report that the labour of the children was not "proportional to their strength".

They departed from Sadler and Ashley, however, in fixing thirteen instead of eighteen as what might be called "the age of discretion". At the age of thirteen, children were deemed to be free and responsible agents, and the Commissioners were too far committed to the doctrines of *laissez-faire* to recommend any protection for free agents. They adduced evidence of this by quoting instances where young wage-earners had "kept themselves" out of their wages and had made no contribution to the family purse beyond paying "for their keep".

Bad as the Report was in many particulars, it could have been worse. The Commissioners might whitewash the owners, and they might misinterpret some of the evidence gathered, but they were bound to admit much that was in the Sadler Report. The fixing of thirteen as the age at which adult responsibility begins was monstrous, as the reformers and many commentators were quick to say. *The Times*[1] and *The Leeds Intelligencer* were particularly critical.

When Ashley's Bill was amended to conform with these findings, Ashley resigned his Bill into the hands of the Government. On the next day, he wrote to Oastler:

[1] "The Ministers, however, are, we hear, proud of their victory, and as Waterloo and Trafalgar have their days, are disposed to celebrate the 18th of July as the battle of the spinning jennies", *The Times*, 19 July 1833.

My dear Mr Oastler,

Last night my bill was rejected by a majority of 145. Lord Althorp moved the insertion of 13 instead of 18 years of age. We had nine hours of discussion, and the whole was closed by the support of 93 members to the cause of the factory children. I never, perhaps not even on the Reform Bill, witnessed such unity, zeal, and determination, as was manifested by my opponents. The cheers to every sentiment and every individual on the millowners' side were like rounds of artillery; on mine, a solitary "hear, hear" was the liveliest token of encouragement or approbation.

I refused to bear the responsibility of an altered bill, believing as I do that the government proposals will produce tenfold misery and tenfold crime. I would not, nay *could* not, undertake to accept any portion of them. I threw the Bill into his hands; he may enjoy the merit, if there be any, or bear the blame of such an alteration.

Yours very truly,

Ashley.

As Althorp had previously hinted, the amended Bill limited the daily hours of children to eight. As it was not intended to limit the hours of adult workers, the reformers wondered what device the mill-owners would adopt to keep them at work longer. Althorp provided provision for the modified protection of young people between thirteen and eighteen years of age, limiting their working day to twelve hours, nine on Saturday. No child of less than nine years of age was to be permitted to work in a textile mill and a medical certificate was to be required as evidence of physical fitness and that the child had the appearance of one of nine years of age. No young person under eighteen was to be permitted to do night work. The Act made compulsory the provision of two hours a day education. This was to serve the purpose of ensuring a modicum of education and of preventing the working of two eight hour shifts. It also provided for inspection in order that the law would be enforced, both in the interests of the protected young people and of law-abiding manufacturers.

Government supporters attributed the legislation to the popular clamour—"the senseless clamour outside", said Thomson—forgetting the clamour for the Reform Bill which they had helped to create. To attribute factory legislation to the Liberalism of the Government in power in 1833 is to ignore its reluctance to accept its principle or to facilitate its passing. The 1833 Act was a Government measure only because Ashley's much better measure was unacceptable to the vested interests and to the Government itself. Professor Ramsay Muir

9

admits that the factory acts were opposed by Liberal manufacturers, but implies that the Government improved "Shaftesbury's Bill".[1] The reformers did not think so. Nor does Professor Trevelyan give any hint of the reluctance of the Government to legislate.[2] They are on surer grounds in saying that the beginnings of the factory inspectorate was a real step forward, but this provision could only be effective if magistrates were willing to convict and if the penalties were heavy enough to deter would-be offenders. Neither of these conditions obtained. In Manchester, manufacturers and their managers discussed who should face the courts,[3] and when Oastler publicly reproved magistrates in Blackburn for their refusal to convict, they laughed in his face.[4] It was nearly forty years before the gaps in the law were stopped.

In addition to these divergences from Ashley's Bill, the new Act provided another ground for future dispute. It was the delay in fully implementing the age clause. The thirteen-year-old maximum was to be introduced by stages. Six months after the Act became operative, children were to be protected between the ages of nine and eleven, after another year, from nine to twelve, finally, after a lapse of still another year, the provisions of the Act would become fully operative. Would this be amended when the public clamour had died? It remained to be seen, but here was a likely cause of future dispute.

The reformers could fight on two fronts.

They could criticize the Bill. It left a loophole for law evasion. It did not limit the working hours of adults. They did not believe that the educational clauses would be observed. Their attitude was not improved by the gibe that Oastler and his friends had been "outbidden in humanity". Baines, who was particularly ready with that gibe, and his friends, were inconsistent. If a ten-hour day was unthinkable, how was an eight-hour day of benefit?

The Report itself, upon which the Act was based, was a challenge to the reformers. It contained attacks upon them which they could not ignore. One section reads:

---

[1] *A History of the British Commonwealth*, II, p. 395.

[2] *English Social History*, pp. 542–3. *History of England*, pp. 638, 647.

[3] *The Manchester Guardian*, during the next few years contained many reports of discussions about this. Some manufacturers were defiant in court.

[4] *The Manchester Guardian*, 24 September 1836.

The most active if not the best instructed supporters of this (Ashley's) measure have manifested a spirit of hostility to the progress of the present enquiry, to which we believe that few parallel instances are upon record on a subject of grave national importance. We refer the principal part of the agitation on this subject to that class of men who entitle themselves, unfortunately with some truth, the delegates of the working people, whom the repeal of the Combination Laws released from all restrictions in the disposal of their own property (Labour) and now seek to impose restrictions equally vexatious on the disposal of the property of others. We refer to that class of men who, while stating the present enquiry to be whether children ought to work more than ten hours a day, are exerting their whole efforts for the restriction of adult labour, and for the arbitrary stoppage of the moving power.[1]

This was unjust. Oastler had been campaigning for some time before trade unions joined him. He had begun with concern for the children, but almost at the outset operatives had made it clear that some of them were attracted to the movement because they saw prospects of relief for themselves as well as for their children. There were many derogatory references. Both Bull and Wood were criticized for their refusal to co-operate, and in both cases, partial accounts were given of the circumstances. Almost every reference made to the Ten Hours men was disparaging. Perhaps, as Professor Driver says, their refusal to play any part in the investigation was an error of judgement.[2] Whether or not the refusal to compromise was a mistake, as Doherty had said, is less important. Too many Members welcomed the Commissioners' Report to be won by a compromise on the personal punishment clause. In any case, later events gave support to those who believed the clause to be essential.

The first meetings of protest were concerned more with replying to these criticisms than with future policy. Speakers at the meetings recalled the occasions on which they had declared their desire to limit the working hours of adults,[3] refuting the charge of hypocrisy. These meetings demonstrated the loyalty of the operatives. The charges of hypocrisy made against their leaders led operatives to organize meetings mainly for the purpose of proclaiming their confidence in the

[1] Report. Vol, V, 1833.

[2] Driver, p. 246. Professor Driver refers to the *Bradford* Conference. He means the Manchester Conference.

[3] See above, Chap. 2.

leaders. One of them, at Halifax, on 13 July—before the fateful 18th—
was announced as having been called:

> To disabuse the public mind of malignant misrepresentation and also to
> petition the House of Commons on the subject of the said libel—that the
> agitation was due to the same men (at Bradford and Leeds) who in every
> instance of rash and headlong strikes have assumed command of the dis-
> contented members of the operative body and have used the grossest means
> of intimidation to subjugate the quiet and contented part of the workpeople.

Mr Carter, one of the speakers, poured scorn on this and on the
charge that Ashley's measure was a Tory manœuvre. He called on
mothers—somewhat grandiloquently—who looked for the passing
of the Bill, on the literary men who had written in its support, and on
the "Right Reverend Prelates who (had) nobly stood forth in defence
of the poor Factory Child", to take notice of the charges.

Bull himself was a speaker at many of these meetings, including
some of the most important. A week after the debate in Parliament,
Henry Heap, the Vicar of Bradford, presided over a meeting. He said
that he was always glad to do his duty to the poor and to their children.
A deputation of the labouring classes had waited upon him at his
Vicarage to ask him to preside over the meeting, and, he said, he would
assure them that at his house the poorest man in his parish would always
be treated with as much respect as the richest.[1]

George Wooler, one of the speakers, said that the eight hours
proposal was cruel to children under thirteen. The other provisions
were impossible to carry out. The Reform Parliament had failed. He
called for an appeal to the Lords. John Rand also expressed his disgust
at the mutilation of Ashley's Bill. Bull told of his own connection with
the movement and of the three years' agitation "for the rights of honest
Industry, for the peace of society and the prosperity of commerce." He
quoted the remark he had overheard when he went to the first Bradford meeting he had attended—"What have the parsons to do with it?"
—and replied to scorners of parsons and to those ministers who
shared the view that he and his friends ought not to concern themselves
with the agitation:

> I can prove they have nothing to do with their office, with the Bible,
> nothing to do with the foundation of order and happiness. Nothing to do
> with the sufferings of the poor, with the toil-worn children and youth of

---

[1] *White Slavery*, Vol. V.

the factory, whose painful and aching limbs—whose untutored minds, whose unsocial and undomestic habits, are crying to Heaven for retribution and to man for help!

He was concerned with equality before the law. The rich man's hall was protected from intrusion and spoliation; the poor man's cottage should be also. He argued that the competition for jobs created by the long hours of those who had work caused the bidding down of wages. He deplored the power over people's lives wielded by men like Marshall of Leeds and Ashton of Hyde. He considered that the "administration of the poor laws and in some degree the state of the law itself" caused much mischief. He foresaw the likely nature of Poor Law amendment and objected to the creation of "a flying population". He wished to see the dense population distributed and manufacture on a smaller scale than the growing concerns of the industrial centres. He wished to see land, only half of which, he believed, was cultivated, put into full production. During the course of these meetings, Bull expounded much of his social and political philosophy. No doubt he was thinking aloud and expressing his view of what seemed to him to be fundamental social issues. His mother had died two months earlier, and he had seen a little more of his home country during her illness. He was trying to balance the interests of townsmen and countrymen, for he believed that social health depended upon this balance. He hoped to avoid the lack of balance now deplored as socially and economically harmful.

At the Bradford meeting, he said, dealing with the immediate issue, that the efforts

> to engrave the Ten Hours Bill upon the British Statute Book had been checked by the united opposition of Lord Althorp, the ministerial party and the millowners in Parliament; of which honourable body there are not less than forty-five.

He said that the millowners were accustomed to exercise almost despotic rule over adults as well as youthful labourers, and

> it was expecting too much that they would have the delicacy to withdraw from the jury of the House which was trying their own cause. The Reformed House, anyway, supplied another hundred who are always ready to do as their honourable leaders may command, whether it be to legalize black slavery under the word "Apprenticeship" for twelve years to come, or to vote twenty millions of our good lawful money for the black slave masters

and that before they have proved that they would lose one farthing by setting the captive free. The same worthy men can with the utmost coolness and the most consummate wisdom declare that at thirteen years of age, little girls and boys are free agents, able to judge and act for themselves—adults in fact, and capable of enduring as much labour as it is profitable for the capitalists to impose.

He believed that Althorp's Bill gave protection only to the age of thirteen in order to enable two sets of children to be employed. But his scorn of the Commissioners' findings, embodied in the Act, were best expressed by the peroration of his Bradford speech:

> Whereas it has been reported to us by our beloved Alfred Power and others, that in various parts of our dominions, and especially where the factory system prevails, the children of the labouring classes are in the habit of despising the authority of their parents, demanding to spend their own wages, and to be their own masters and mistresses and whereas our beloved John Marshall, Kirkman Finlay, Joseph Pease, John Varley and certain other of our loving subjects, who are very religious and have many thousands of pounds vested in machinery, must have some excuse for working all above thirteen years as long as may be profitable to them. Be it therefore enacted by the will and advice of the Millowners and the Political Economists, and the Poor Law Commissioners, and the Factory Commission, and the Reform Parliament, that no such young persons shall be considered otherwise than free agents and adults provided always that they have reached the mature, sober and robust, age of thirteen years and one day.

Another important meeting at this period took place at Hebden Bridge, in the Parish of Halifax on 24 August, some five weeks after the debate in Parliament. Its object was not only to protest against the Act, but also to make public some of the inhumanities perpetrated by certain Liberal factory masters in the neighbourhood. George Crabtree, one of the Ten Hours men, had toured the valleys seeking signatures for the petition asking for the Ten Hours Bill. He reported on the tyranny of the masters. Innkeepers had feared to accommodate him because they feared the local millowner. Only at Todmorden, especially at Fielden's mill, which he had visited under the guidance of James Suthers, the secretary of the Political Union, had he found any co-operation on the part of the manufacturers. Fielden was at that time at the beginning of his Parliamentary career and a Ten Hours man. In the parish of Halifax, especially in the valleys, there were some of the worst employers. Clerical support for the Ten Hours men was worse

THE HOUSE OF COMMONS, 5 FEBRUARY, 1833, BY SIR GEORGE HAYTOR, R.A. [LEFT SECTION]

This day Ashley gave notice of his intention to re-introduce Sadler's Ten Hours Bill. Althorp is on front bench, hat on knees; Lord John Russell, on his left, reaches forward

here than elsewhere in the Riding. This was no doubt due to the difference between Musgrave, the Vicar, and Oastler, a few years earlier. Musgrave himself said that it was due to his distrust of Sadler.

The meeting was one of those arranged on the initiative of the operatives. One of them, Richard Sutcliffe, was the Chairman. Bull commented on this, saying that he had often spoken under the chairmanship of a great man and that he was not ashamed that day to speak under the chairmanship of a poor one. He added, "He is more honourable than those who set aside the law of God and legislate for avarice and cruelty." Glendinning, one of Oastler's Huddersfield associates, referred to the possibilities of the machine, saying that he had lately read that it took four hours labour for the labouring population of Great Britain to produce everything necessary for a day's maintenance.

Bull reflected about life in the Todmorden valley a few years earlier. Villagers, he said, would be happily engaged in domestic manufacture. On a fine day, ruddy and athletic youth would be plying the spinning wheel before the cottage door. The children would labour under their parents' eyes and work according to their ability and strength. They would enjoy a plain but sufficient diet "with uplifted hands blessing God for it". A Christian man would gather up his household to worship God night and morning, to acknowledge his bounty and crave his blessing. "Mark the change!" he went on. Instead of working under the control of parents with work proportional to their strength, they were subject to the control of strangers, who were too often tyrants. The weak were compelled to do the same work as the strongest. They had to eat and work at the same time—"a privilege of boat horses". They were compelled to "perform the unceasing service of Mammon's Temple".

Lord Ashley's Bill had been rejected, he went on. It would have provided for boxing off dangerous machinery and the fining of masters who failed to do this. It would have provided that where life or limb was lost, there should be pensions and provision for the maimed. He condemned what was called "inning up", asking if the machine would not make up for the child's sickness, why should the child make up for the machine? The fining of children for being late, practised for the most part more harshly in Halifax than elsewhere, he also condemned roundly.

He dealt with the personal punishment clause, saying that Ashley had provided for the wilful offenders to be sent to prison. He deserved to be sent to prison—even to the treadmill—after a third offence. It was essential that rich and poor should stand equal before the law. Ashley had provided that no manufacturer should act as judge and jury where his own interest was concerned. When he mentioned that at a meeting at Otley, a person had complained that this proposal was an intentional insult laid upon millowners: "What of the squire-magistrate who convicted poachers?" the complainant had added. Bull had replied, "the more shame for such legislation." He referred to Poulett Thomson's cynical remark, made to justify the absence from Althorp's Bill of the clause to provide for the boxing off of machinery, that the injured operative had a remedy at common law. "So," said Bull, "when you have a hand, an arm, or a leg torn off, you must go to common law to set it on again." (The employers' resistance to proposals to protect workpeople from machinery was because they claimed it was an interference with their property—another piece of evidence of the irresponsibility of the new rich.)

Inevitably, the old arguments recurred, sometimes with a new slant. He told of one master who scorned the medical evidence, saying that factory children were healthier than his own children, to which the operative to whom he was talking retorted, "Well, then, master, send them to the factory for the good of their health." The effects of the factory system on social and domestic life was still a first concern to him. "If you wish that the country shall be happy and prosperous," he said, "you must make rich wives for poor people. They must have good hands as well as well-ordered minds. Long factory hours make poor wives."

Bull often had cause to criticize the labouring classes, but when they were attacked, he was their ready defender. Plain speaking between friends is permissible. Besides, he was a priest and pastor, with the duty of rebuking. But criticism from those who visited the factory areas with no great friendliness was quite another thing. The Commissioners had represented the labouring classes as the sworn enemies of society, although their visits had been too short to allow them time to gain full understanding of either the people or their problems. Indeed, their report had contained the admission that the time allowed had been too short to allow them to make an adequate report. Bull denied their charges. He said that an appeal to moral and Christian principles usually met with approval. He gave full credit to good manufacturers, and denied that he and his friends sought to stir up hatred or to bring them into contempt. But he could not forbear to criticize the Cragg Vale manufacturers for their harshness as employers and for their methods in controversy.

They had challenged Oastler and his friends to a "public examination", but, he said, for some reason best known to themselves, they were absent from the meeting. "They are even afraid to put their names on their handbills," he said, "but it is not so with us. Mr Oastler sets his name and address upon it, so that you may know where to find him, but these brave men, like some bold Spaniards I have seen, appear as if they fight best behind a wall."

He said that the Commission was an insult to the British people, to Christianity and to truth. He referred critically to Althorp's breach of his promise not to oppose a Committee of the whole House to consider Ashley's Bill and the departures from it in Althorp's. He expressed the belief that this organized opposition to the Ten Hours Bill by capitalists and political economists was only one part of a great conspiracy against the honourable industry of the Kingdom. In questions which showed his affinity with the social and religious outlook of the Old Testament prophets, he asked, rhetorically,

> Shall we destroy the bonds of society that the great owner of machinery may monopolize orders, destroy his lesser neighbour and depress wages by working youth above thirteen as long as he likes, to the destruction of health, happiness and morality? Shall we pull down the altar of domestic piety and comfort and set up golden calves of avarice and say, "These are thy gods, O Israel?"

The protests were in vain. The Bill was duly passed, and the reformers could only wait for their forebodings to be either proved groundless or justified. The Ten Hours men had compelled an unwilling Government to legislate. Even a bad bill was better than no bill. It was a start.

12

MR EDITOR AND HIS CRITIC

DURING THE years 1832 and 1833, all kinds of publicity methods were adopted. Reprints of newspaper reports, broadsides, letters to the Press and all the methods formerly used, were used more intensively. Some of them had disadvantages. A newspaper discussion depends very greatly of the good will or the fairness of the Editor. Readers of a newspaper whose Editor (or proprietor) has taken sides are often given only one side of the argument. Editors can exclude matter of which they disapprove on principle. Even to-day, people with minority views often find them misrepresented in the Press or find difficulty in propagating them owing to the imposition of what amounts to an unofficial censorship. Some editors treated the factory reformers well, but others treated them unfairly. As the question of factory hours came to be increasingly a party issue, Liberal papers presented a one-sided version of the campaign.

The reformers, therefore, decided to launch a journal of their own to present their case and to report on their activities. Bull's gift of forceful and ready writing caused him to be made its Editor.

The journal, *The British Labourer's Protector and Factory Child's Friend*, recorded some of the later events of 1832 and continued during the 1833 campaign. The editorial principles were set out in the first number:

> To advance the legal restriction of Factory Labour and of Machinery where it interferes injuriously with human labour.
>
> To uphold the cause of the labouring poor against the oppressor, whether he be found in the situation of an Employer, an Agent, or a dispenser of the National Charity.

Party politics were to be eschewed. The Editor was to be unpaid. He was to use his discretion in selecting material, and the publication was to be conducted on Christian principles. It was assumed that it would promote the best interests of the labouring classes, whether in industry or agriculture. The Editor believed that these sections of the labouring classes were not opposed to each other. He added:

> We do not pretend to any extraordinary skill by which we can unravel that which seems to puzzle others nor do we underrate the labours of many who appear zealous in the country's cause. Our view and objects are practical and simple. Our principle is, that whatever benefits the labouring classes benefits the whole community, and that no nation is blessed of God or prospers in itself, where they are depressed.

The early numbers set out the principles and early history of the movement. They told of the attempts of Rand, Wood, and Thompson to persuade their fellow-manufacturers to take voluntary action in 1825. The story of Hobhouse's Bill was told, and how "Lady Avarice's zealous and interested votaries had baffled him", with the result that an innocuous bill was passed. The early correspondence, beginning with Oastler's letter to *The Leeds Mercury*, was summarized and commented on. The Editor made some caustic remarks about Townend's letter, especially his insistence that "abundant time" was provided for refreshment. "Abundant time!" said the Editor. "None for breakfast, half an hour for dinner, and none for drinking." Oastler had told of a West Indian slave-owner who had been appalled by the discovery of an eight-year-old child working a twelve-and-a-half-hour-day. Townend had admitted that the normal working day was 6 a.m. to 7 p.m. but he had added that the labour was not laborious.

The open letter to Macaulay and subsequent comments were reproduced. Accounts of meetings were included, the salient points of speeches being reported. Testimonials from Scottish clergymen and ministers and medical evidence supplied by Scottish doctors reveal how far afield the campaign was developing. The reformers had not forgotten the part played by Scottish manufacturers in the defeat of Hobhouse, and a good deal of work was being done there, especially in Glasgow and Dundee. The new journal reported all this. Varied items dealt with personalities in the movement. The Editor usually found an apt text for quotation. Indeed, the note of Christian prophecy was much in evidence, not only in the Biblical quotations, but also in the editorial comments.

The hostility to the movement and its leaders grew during this

period of campaigning, and this hostility was reflected in a publication
replying to *The British Labourer* and purporting to review it. The
writer was scornful of the inference that the British labourer needed a
protector or the factory child a friend. He criticized the reformers'
programme mainly by attacking Bull. Even for that hard-hitting
campaign, it was a cruel piece of invective. It must have stung Bull,
who was far from being insensitive. As he had told the Sadler Committee, he was not concerned with personalities, and he tried to avoid
them. He had little patience with anonymous writers. He believed
that a man with the courage of his convictions would not hide behind
the cloak of anonymity. One of the taunts in *The Review* was that he
did this when writing editorially. This was unfair. It was well-known
that he was the Editor, and the whole of the so-called "review"
betrayed the fact that the writer knew. In one section, he sketched in
outline the life of a person whom he purported to know. It followed
the course of Bull's early life too closely not to have been a deliberate
cut at him.

> Have you deserted the cause of the Negro? Why are you so soon given to
> change? You remind us of a certain fine lad, a true John Bull, who was full
> of ardour, fuss and fury; he would go to sea; and to sea he went. But in a
> short time he got quite tired of the sea; he became very seriously inclined,
> and would go to convert the heathen. But this good work was soon aban-
> doned; and he resolved to become a quiet, snug, country parson. However,
> his restless spirit would not be content without changing from place to place.
> His plans too were continually altering. One while he was alive for the Bible
> Society; but he left it because he imagined that by associating with Dis-
> senters he would overturn the Church. He also had a fit of zeal for the con-
> version of the Jews, but that work was given up. He would dispute with
> Roman Catholics but on that subject too his zeal evaporated. He would at
> another time emancipate all the slaves in the world, and bawl aloud for two
> or three hours against the planters; of that work he became tired. . . .

The writer went on to refer to his subject's concern for education,
which also passed, he said. The end product was a prematurely ageing
man, who, with his wife and family, "were pining away in solitude,
having reaped no fruit from such labours". He enjoined Bull to take
warning. "Study to be quiet and mind your own business", he said.

If, as seems certain, the course of Bull's life had been the basis of
this sketch, the writer was unjust. He ignored the illness that caused
Bull to leave Africa and the fact that a deacon-to-be often had difficulty

in finding an incumbent to "give him a title". It may be true that young
George had been a restive boy, but in his manhood he showed tenacity
of purpose. He never lost his concern for education, and to the end of
his active ministry he was concerned with it.

It was, indeed, his concern for education that was the immediate cause
of his association with the factory reform movement. If it were true
that he spoke on slavery emancipation less and less, that was because
his former associates in that work were fierce opponents of factory
reform. Oastler, ten years later, expressed himself very strongly about
a claim that the abolitionists had been in the forefront of the campaign
for factory reform.[1]

Bull replied to this frequently-made charge at Bradford.[2]

> Sir, (he said) I shall always love the Negro's cause as sincerely as those who
> never crossed six thousand miles of ocean to instruct him—who never
> embraced a land of the shadow of death (forsaking their native shore)—to
> comfort him, and who have not lingered there as I did, till only the last
> dregs of life remained, so that when by a miracle of Divine Goodness, I
> reached my home again my mother hesitated to embrace me. . . . I am
> loath at present to join my efforts for the abolition of Negro Slavery with
> theirs who label their lips and engross their phylacteries with words of
> liberty, but exercise, or sanction, the exercise of tyranny with both their
> hands.

The Review attacked him on many counts. Sarcastically calling him
"The Chaplain to the Ten Hours Bill", the writer accused him of
subverting the children. Addressing them, he said:

> You are taught by him to consider your parents as unnatural monsters,
> your masters as worse than slaveholders, your overlookers as Brutes, your
> Sunday School teachers as villains, and even the Ministers of the Gospel as
> "utterly unworthy of their office" unless they roar like bulls against mills
> and factories.

This, too, misrepresented Bull's line of approach. He castigated
"degraded" parents who sent their children to work when there was
no need, but he knew too many parents who sent their children to
work with genuine sorrow to speak of them as "unnatural monsters".
He knew too much of the work of Sunday School teachers to call
them "villains", but he had no patience with those who supported

---

[1] *The Fleet Papers*, Vol. I, No. 22.
[2] 19 February 1833. *White Slavery*, Vol. VI, No. 6.

Sunday Schools or taught in them but exploited the children in employing them and resisting reform. The employer who could fine young children for being late (often after a long walk) and put the money in the firm's missionary box would see nothing inconsistent in maintaining a Sunday School while overworking the children who attended it. Such men saw nothing wrong in exacting twelve and a half hours of labour from young children. Their philosophy may seem to have been a convenient one, but its convenience helped to make it appear true.

When these misrepresentations gained currency, Bull took advantage of the children meeting to demonstrate against the Commissioners to reply to them.[1] Besides stressing the value of importunity, reminding the children of the Unjust Judge of Scripture who gave judgement in favour of a widow because of her importunity,[2] he dealt with the inconsistency of the millowners. They were at that time making much of the fact that the Ten Hours Bill would compel them to "pull off wages", but an Eleven Hours Bill would not. What of the money owed for the extra hour the children were working? he asked. They were working twelve and a half hours a day.

The main part of his speech, however, was devoted to refuting the misrepresentations of which those in *A Brief Review of the British Labourer's Protector and Factory Child's Friend* were typical. He said:

Well, my young friends. I dare say you have heard me called a very bad man because I will insist you get your Bill. I cannot help it. I have done what I could and will do so by God's help till we get it. (Punctuating cries of "That's right.")

Nothing is so common as for people to cry out "They say . . . he has done so and so," when they want to blacken a man's character. I use the expression when defending my own, for I cannot hear who says it, only I am told "They say . . . such and such things". Well, they say that I "have been setting children against their parents." Now I have not done so. I have taught you to love your parents—to think of the days of your infancy—of a Father's toils—of a Mother's tears. . . .

I want you and your parents to be more together that they may teach you your duty to God and Man.

Have I ever said one word to make you disobey your overlookers or

---

[1] 11 June 1833. Copies of the pamphlet embodying this speech in the Oastler Collection and in the Bradford Reference Library, entitled *A Meeting of the Children Took Place*.

[2] Luke 18. 1–6.

disrespect your masters? I have even told you to be patient under bad treat-ment and not to be saucy even to a bad master.... As to Master and Servant, the proper bond that should unite them is love. But oppression breaks it asunder.

He told them that he had been a Sunday School teacher since he was sixteen years of age and regarded that work as of great consequence. Was it likely that he should set children against their teachers? He was unlikely to do or say anything that would hinder their work. He felt that by preaching against Black Slavery only he might do so. "I am sure", he said, "that all Ministers must feel that the present factory system is much against us, and by its long hours interferes with our exertions."

Under the pretence of criticizing the proposals that Bull supported, the critic abused him for concerning himself with matters of which he had no knowledge. "It is certain that trade is not your profession", he said. Nor was it literary criticism he offered when he wrote:

It is a fine thing for you to collect a number of lasses and lads around you and talk on your premises to them; what a delightful thing it will be for them to work only ten hours instead of twelve and a half so that they can go to Evening School, learn to write, dance, knit, sew, and be gentlemen and ladies, getting, of course, the same wages.

This was a dig at Bull's concern that girls should be trained for their part in a cottage economy. He had no need to reply to this. His work was answer enough. He went on with his educational work and con-tinued to campaign for better tools and for more time.

The fifth number of *The British Labourer* carried an account of the opening of a school for the children who worked at John Wood's mill. This was typical of Wood's enlightened policy. It was natural that much was made of the occasion. Most of the children lived in the town-ship of Bowling, for the factory was situated in it. Most of the clergy-men in Bradford were present as well as some from farther afield. Some Wesleyan ministers were present as well. It is not surprising that there was some boisterousness. Wood was well-respected by his work-people. He was known to be in favour of the Ten Hours Bill and to be a generous supporter of the movement. He added much to its effective-ness by augmenting its funds, mainly derived from the small contribu-tions of the workpeople. Much of what he did was unpublicized, but generally realized. The opening of his school, therefore, was made an opportunity to honour him. Workpeople, children and their parents, and his friends gathered together. The Bill that concerned him was as much in their minds as the school they were opening. The usual Ten Hours enthusiasm was in evidence, and the natural tendency of enthusiastic children to cheer led them to cheer everyone in sight. Bull, never averse to leading cheering for Sadler, Oastler, or Wood, acted as Chairman. Bull's critic in another number of *The Review* made much of this. He wrote:

> With much pleasure do we meet you, Mr Editor, to congratulate you on the most delightful opening of Mr Wood's factory school as recorded in your fifth number, and we sincerely wish there were such a school attached to each factory. But we were sorry to hear from a friend who was present that the clergy of the Church of England and the Wesleyan Ministers who addressed the meeting soberly and religiously retired and that the Chaplain of the Ten Hours Bill destroyed that "pious feeling" by making the children clap and cheer Mr Wood, Mr Oastler, Mr Sadler and himself. How singing hymns, praying, and religious instruction, can thus be joined with clapping and shouting we cannot tell. Much less can we tell how "The Ten Hours Bill", political subjects connected with it, and irregularities of various sorts, can be introduced into a pulpit and within consecrated walls. We are well assured that though the two Archbishops and the Bishop of Lichfield and Coventry, with the other Bishops and Clergy, would gladly advocate the interests of the factory children in every prudent way, yet such would not desert their own cures and make use of such weapons as you, Mr Editor, and the Chaplain of the Ten Hours Bill do.

We are not here concerned with the pastoral work of Parson Bull, but it can be said that his work in Bowling left a lasting impression. There could be no question of his neglecting pastoral work for political agitation. He mentioned, in another connection and almost in parenthesis, that the Archbishop of Canterbury had commended him for his work in the factory movement.[1] Indeed, the casual way in which this was mentioned adds to the value of the remark as evidence of his good relations with the hierarchy, of their concern for the movement and as confirmation of what ought to be obvious from the work he did in Bowling—that he was a diligent pastor, concerned for his people's well-being. A letter to his parishioners at Christmas 1831,[2] written long before he edited *The British Labourer* shows how deeply he cared

[1] See below, p. 188.
[2] Oastler Collection and Bradford Reference Library.

for his people. He encouraged them and understood their difficulties. His entry into the Ten Hours movement was due to his concern for them.

The Review contained much more that was critical of him. The value of that publication in a study of this controversy lies not only in helping us to see Parson Bull through the eyes of his opponents, but also in showing something of the outlook of those opponents. The writer spoke of those ministers of the Gospel who worked amongst the people "with a very small salary not equal to many a mechanic" and "without the chance of a Chaplaincy of any kind, or a fine dinner at a rich man's house". Considering how small was Bull's stipend as the Curate of a church without a parish, the suggestion that he was well-off was unfounded, while the inference that he derived some benefit from his work for the movement was slanderous. Whoever called him "Chaplain to the Ten Hours Bill"—whether they did so in derision or esteem—acknowledged his concern that the Bill should become law and that he worked and prayed to that end. He had much more support than is commonly supposed, but he seems to have been regarded as the spearhead of clerical support for the movement. But although he often expressed regret that all clergymen and ministers were not active in the cause, he did not accept the credit of being the only parson active in it.

Bull's critic seems to have been a devout person. Probably his devotional life was of high standard, but he clearly belonged to that section of the Christian Church which believed in the separation of things secular from things sacred. His appeal to labourers and factory children is revealing:

> Your chief best friend is God. He is indeed the friend of the poor. It is he that maketh poor and maketh rich. He has said that "the poor shall not cease out of the land"—"To the Poor is the Gospel preached". . . . Be assured that those ministers best fulfil their office who spend and are spent in promoting your eternal welfare. But be assured that those who save your souls are your best friends as it respects this world.

This was the attitude largely taken up by Dissenters, a section of the Methodists and some Evangelical Churchmen. Both Oastler and Bull complained about it. Many of them were enthusiasts for slavery emancipation and prominent in works of charity. It has been the misfortune of the Church that their attitude has been represented to be

10

typical. The outstanding example of this inconsistency was the great William Wilberforce. He was a good man, rightly honoured for his leadership of the emancipation movement. Yet his attitude to the social ills of his own country was in complete contrast to his attitude to the evils of slavery. As Professor Basil Willey puts it:

> When Evangelical religion has become so other worldly that a Hannah More can regard poverty (like niggerhood) as "ordained" or a Wilberforce can oppose reform on the ground that the existing order "combines the greatest measure of temporal comforts and spiritual privileges" and can encourage the poor to submission because "their situation, with all its evils, is better than they have deserved at the hands of God",—when things are thus, the neglected work will be done by secularists and infidels.[1]

Professor Willey, himself a Christian, writes this without approval. He shows that Thomas Arnold disliked the attitude of the Evangelicals and Puritans because it meant "the handing over of all temporal concerns to the devil or to the operation of natural laws". Arnold, incidentally, disliked the attitude of the Tractarians, just beginning their work at this period, for, he said, their attitude meant a "retreat into priestly inutilities". We are not here concerned with the second of Arnold's strictures—although most Puseyites in the West Riding seem to have been in the factory reform tradition—but as to the first, he was right. Oastler, Sadler, Wood, and Bull were Evangelicals. Three of them were Churchmen. Sadler seems to have combined Churchmanship with Methodism, as did others at that time. They constantly regretted the failure of Dissenters and some other Evangelicals to help in the cause. They found it distressing that so many whose support they would have valued wished to leave social and economic matters to the operation of "natural laws"—laws very different from the "Natural Law" which had been the core of the Church's social teaching. There is small wonder that the gap between the reformers and the pietists widened. It is a great pity that later writers have overlooked the part played by religious men—clergymen, ministers, and laymen— in winning some of these first social reforms. Even Churchmen are inclined to be too apologetic. The pietists and the humbugs have been regarded as typical of that day. But the Church militant was much in evidence.

[1] *Nineteenth Century Studies*, p. 133.

I3

A SET-BACK FOR TRADE UNIONISTS

AFTER THE first few meetings of protest, there was little the
reformers could do to influence the course of events. They
could only protest that the Bill was not their Bill and that it
would not work. Even the prospect of being able to say at a later
stage, "We told you so!" did not please them. Their discomfiture
was increased by the gibe of Baines and their opponents that the
Government had "outbidden them in humanity".

Believing that the campaign must be renewed when the faults in
Althorp's Bill became obvious as its provisions were applied, Oastler
hoped to keep some kind of organization in being. Without the impetus of an immediate and definite aim, there was little chance of
doing so, however. He succeeded in forming a Factory Reformation
Society, through which he hoped to inform the middle classes of the
situation of the factory workers and of the conditions in which they
lived and worked. This was the modest outcome of a conference held
at Birstall, in the Heavy Woollen District.

The movement disintegrated rapidly after the passing of Althorp's
Bill, and this was made the more serious by division amongst its
leaders. A personal difference between Oastler and Foster, a keen
Ten Hours man, who had owned and edited *The Leeds Patriot*, divided
Radical supporters. By the time this breach was healed—and Foster
himself was never reconciled to Oastler—another unfortunate episode
created further division. Captain Joseph Wood, who had contested
Huddersfield at the Reform election, was invited to fight it again in
the Radical interest when the sitting member died. As he had become
a Roman Catholic, he decided that he had little chance of election.
After some vacillation, he was persuaded to accept nomination, but
in the meantime Sadler had been persuaded to stand as a Tory candidate.
His late decision lessened Sadler's chance, who had agreed to stand in

the belief that he would gather Radical as well as Tory support. Although Oastler had advised Sadler not to stand, he had given way when Wood had insisted that he himself did not intend to do so. The Ten Hours men who were Radicals were divided. There was no Ten Hours movement to hold them together, and the Toryism of Sadler did not outweigh his past services at an election at which factory hours were not a live issue. Some of Oastler's speeches and pamphlets attacking Wood were as bitter as any attacking opponents of factory reform. The political truce was over. The Tory reformers' hopes of developing a political philosophy that would commend itself to Radicals and the labouring classes were receding. Many Radicals remained loyal to Oastler, but there were many splits in the ranks of the Ten Hours men by the end of 1833. Some of the dissidents said that the Ten Hours movement had been a Tory trick to curry favour with Radicals and the labouring classes.

This was the state of things when another working-class movement began to develop. Some of the reformers who had been associated with the Ten Hours movement as part of the total effort to benefit the working classes began to organize the various groups in a national body. Owen led the movement. He had never ceased to preach his doctrine, and it seemed to him that the end of Capitalism was at hand and the day of Socialism about to dawn. The trade union movement had been gaining strength since the repeal of the Combination Act but the unions were still mainly local in character and limited in scope. Owen sought to unite them in a "Grand National Consolidated Trades Union" with local and provincial lodges leading to a national council. In Lancashire, where John Doherty's work had made the cotton spinners' union the strongest, the idea of a Grand National Holiday—proposed by Owen—was readily received. John Fielden, the Todmorden manufacturer, and Doherty formed the Society for Promoting National Regeneration, associated with the national movement. Fielden had been the leading Ten Hours man in his district, Owen had supported the movement because it embodied some of his principles, while Doherty had regarded it as one part of his work and had carried with him his trade union followers. As John Fielden's brother said,[1] the new society arose from the failure of the Ten Hours movement. Another factor was the disappointment felt at the outcome of the Reform movement. Many had clamoured for Reform expecting wider

---

[1] *The Bradford Observer*, 6 March 1834.

THE HOUSE OF COMMONS, 5 FEBRUARY 1833, BY SIR GEORGE HAYTOR, R.A. [RIGHT SECTION]

This day Ashley gave notice of his intention to re-introduce Sadler's Ten Hours Bill. Ashley is third on row behind Wellington (wearing Garter ribbon); O'Connell is starting forward on front bench; Cobbett is on his right

suffrage. Others had hoped that newly qualified members and those returned with the backing of the newly enfranchised would accomplish needed social reforms.

Parliamentary reform had done nothing for the poor. They were ready to win something for themselves by industrial action. A Conference in Manchester, which Oastler and Bull decided not to attend, passed a resolution thanking them for their efforts for the working classes, but asking them to desist from them.[1] The Conference had declared aims of a more far-reaching nature and hoped for their support in furthering them.

One of the aims of the Society was the securing of an eight hour working day. As the Ten Hours leaders had often said that ten hours was too long a day to work in a factory, it was hoped that this support would be forthcoming. An eight-hour day would lessen the danger of a shift system being imposed upon children. The Society was to press for wages to remain at the same level, at least, an advance made as soon as possible, and "a system of daily education to be carried on by working people themselves, with the gratuitous assistance of the well-disposed of all parties who may have time and inclination to attend it".[2] The principle of the division of labour was to be properly applied. The workers were to be enabled to produce the best of every article in the shortest time "in those branches of industry they are (or wish to be) engaged".[3] They said, as Bull so often said, that women in manufacturing districts were so lamentably lacking in the ability to wash, bake, brew, make or mend clothes, and other domestic habits as to disgrace the age. They wished this to be changed.

John Fielden, who was Cobbett's fellow-member of Parliament for Oldham, wrote to his colleague to ask for the aid of his "powerful pen",[4] for Cobbett was in the forefront of the "Grand National" movement, and the Lancashire Society benefited from this. Cobbett gave a good deal of help; his vigorous writing was one of the Society's most valuable assets.

It was hoped to achieve the Society's aims with the willing co-operation of the employers. Althorp and Peel had both expressed the hope that the workers would not seek to achieve their aims by political action. They had used the current argument that it was futile and wrong to try to interfere with the natural working of economic laws

---

[1] *White Slavery*. Local papers.   [2] Ibid.   [3] Ibid.
[4] *White Slavery*.

and had said that the workers should come to terms with their masters. It was hoped, therefore, that the masters would co-operate. If they refused, the workers were to give notice that they would declare a National Holiday on 1 March 1834. It was believed that if the workers' offers of co-operation did not bring the employers to terms, the strike threat would.

Propaganda was carried on outside Lancashire, where the Society's chief strength lay. Most of the meetings in Leeds, Huddersfield, and other Yorkshire towns, disappointed Oastler by passing resolutions in terms similar to those of the Manchester resolution. He insisted on standing out, even when his Factory Reformation Society voted itself out of existence, the members joining the Regeneration Society.

There were three meetings at Bradford in connection with it. There was only a moderate attendance at the first, and it was decided to adjourn and to go into matters further. Bull presided, making it clear that he was not committing himself. He wished to hear what the speakers had to say. *The Bradford Observer* gave an account of the meeting. It summarized the objects of the Society, without mentioning the Society's emphasis on co-operation, which was one of the chief justifications of the Society's name. The *Observer* dismissed the project as "benevolent, visionary, and absurd".[1] The writer went on to refer to the "foolishness of rejecting the well-established principles of the most eminent political economists to embrace the incoherent theories of Mr Fielden and Mr Grant". In spite of his sneers, however, the Editor regarded the threat of industrial action as serious.

Bull presided at the second meeting. He was clearly uncomfortable. He said that he was taking the Chair because it was an adjourned meeting and no more suitable person had come along to preside. He wished that some master manufacturer were there to do so.

It is clear from the reports that there was deep-seated disaffection amongst the workers and their friends. Bull said that he shared their interest in securing shorter hours. They knew how he had worked to that end. So far, they had a common interest. He had pressed for a curtailment of the hours of factory labour on religious grounds; commercial men were asking for it on other grounds. He asked for it in the name of God; they asked for it in the name of Mammon. Fielden, one of John's brothers, and Philip Grant, both of whom addressed the meeting were optimistic enough to believe that the em-

[1] *The Bradford Observer*, 6 March 1834.

ployers would co-operate in securing the objects of the Society. Fielden gave some statistics to show that the industry could bear even increased wages if working hours were reduced. Philip Grant stressed the fact that they were adopting lawful means and deplored "turn outs", but agreed with Peter Bussey that they might have to resort to them. He did not believe the movement to be strong enough to win by means of local strikes. Another delegate said that most employers would not listen to operatives who approached them with the Society's proposals, but would discharge them out of hand.

When one delegate, named Rawnsley, asked if any improvement could be achieved if the Whig and Tory aristocracy were allowed to continue and the existing system of government not overturned, Bull asked the meeting to appoint another Chairman. He would not preside over a seditious gathering. All parts of society were bound up together, he said, and the Constitution was perfectly compatible with the just interests of all. When another speaker went on in a seditious strain, he put it to the meeting that he should vacate the chair. After some confusion, the first count being challenged, the motion was lost. There were no more seditious speeches.

Some delegates were not convinced that "shorter hours for the same pay" was practicable, and there was no general agreement that fewer hours for less pay would be generally acceptable. There were heated remarks concerning misrepresentations about the previous meeting in *The Bradford Observer*, but Bull, who had himself no cause to be well-disposed towards that journal—although it had only recently been launched—stopped the discussion. He said, "It would be better not to moot that question"; he had no doubt there was no intention to misrepresent. Some person said that Mr Oastler was there— "skulking"—and the audience called on him to express his opinion about the new Society. The *Observer* report said that Oastler had asked the operative to draw attention to his presence—which would have been unlike Oastler—and that he made a long, vague, and irrelevant, speech which it was impossible to report. (This drew from Oastler a short but vigorous reply asking if it were not enough that *The Leeds Mercury* should persistently malign him without *The Bradford Observer* doing so.) The room was crowded, and Bull said that the temperature was 81 degrees by his pocket thermometer. He acknowledged the thanks accorded to him. He added that he cared not a straw for public opinion. He cared more for his own conscience than for all the gold that had been made in Bradford. He did not mind if every man with a good coat turned up his nose at him "as if they were passing a dead carcase".

The Bradford Observer reported the meeting with as much animosity towards Bull as *The Leeds Mercury* was accustomed to show towards Oastler and his friends. Even Bull's refusal to allow seditious speeches to be made was an opportunity for a sneering remark. The Editor said;

> It is only due to Mr Bull to state that when Mr Rawnsley began to talk about doing away with "government power", he, Mr Bull, began to quake.[1]

After quoting Bull's reply to Rawnsley and adding a sarcastic reference to his "lacerated feelings", he added that Mr Bull would be "better employed feeding his sheep at Byerley than presiding at Regeneration meetings". He described him as a "descendant of the family of Wrongheads" and as "a muddle-headed ecclesiastic".

This piece of rudeness was later dealt with by Peter Bussey,[2] whose respect for Bull outweighed their political differences at a time when political differences impaired friendships all too easily. After two meetings at which the aims of the Regeneration Society were expounded, Bull made up his mind to have nothing to do with it and set out his reasons in a letter, which he sent to the third meeting held by the Society at the New Inn. It was referred to by *The Bradford Observer* when describing the proceedings.[3]

> Mr Bull did not attend. We understand that he pleaded important business as detaining him. After an hour, a solitary individual made his appearance. On being asked why Mr Bull had not come he answered that he had just come from a person who had come from him and he had some important business to attend to and could not come. He thought it very strange; it must be something very important that kept Mr Bull from his *duty*.

The reporter went on to say:

> The absence of Mr Bull appeared to throw quite a damper on the spirits of the regenerators of mankind; they were a body without a head; they seemed perplexed what to do.

A sign of the times is discernible in the reported refusal of the innkeeper to allow another meeting to be held at the New Inn. He had

---

[1] *The Bradford Observer,* 13 March 1834.
[2] *White Slavery,* Vol. V. *The Leeds Times,* "To the Friends of the National Regeneration Society".
[3] *The Bradford Observer,* 27 March 1834.

been led to believe that the meetings were to be of "respectable people". Another indication of the state of industrial relations was the fear of many of those present of having their names reported as speakers during the discussion. Subsequent issues of the *Observer* contained protests from Bussey about the alleged unfairness of the reporting and the reporting of speakers' names. The report mentioned the letter from Bull, which Bussey had refused to read unless the reporter undertook not to report it. The reporter said that he must report it if it were read. Because Bussey thought that the report left the impression that the letter was in some way discreditable to Bull, he decided to make it public. He sent it to *The Leeds Times*, with a covering letter which showed something of the influence Bull exercised over the better sort of working man and on those concerned to improve his lot. Bussey wrote:

> Sir,
> We request you as friend of the operatives to insert a letter addressed to us last Monday evening by the Rev. G. S. Bull. We do this because this letter was mentioned by the Editor of *The Bradford Observer* in a way that may lead some people to suppose that it contains something in some way discreditable to Mr Bull; as such, we publish it, although we must confess, that it contains truth not very creditable to the operatives, yet we confess it is true and we only wish it were not so.
> Sir, as the Editor of *The Bradford Observer* is pleased to call Mr Bull "a wrong head" we can only wish the Bradford right heads were all as wrong, and if Mr Bull is "mad" then we wish he may bite all the parsons in this neighbourhood, and then we believe there would be more respect for both Religion and Morality among the operatives. But Mr Bull is well able to defend himself; we hope, however, that he may meet with gentlemen of better manners than the Editor of *The Observer*.
> We are rough, to be sure, we working people—but we do not apply the word "beast" to each other; however, that is a question of good manners and we are only uncultivated people and not judges of gentlemanly manners.
> Sir, the letter is as under, and I remain for the Committee,
> > Yours truly,
> > > Peter Bussey (Chairman).

The purpose of the meeting was to form a Committee, as decided at the previous meeting. It was hoped that Bull would again preside, but he sent the letter instead. He said that he did not intend to become a member of the Society. He approved of its avowed objects, for, he said, he could make good all their statements about the deplorable effects of long hours and consequent over-production upon the financial and social condition of producers. He was in favour of the eight-hour day if it could be secured, and he acknowledged the right of every man to bargain for the right to work and for equal pay. He went on to say,

> I have done what I could to bring the matter under discussion and have had more reproach cast upon me than you are aware of, but think it my duty to employers and workers, and I might add, to myself. For as a Religious, Moral, and Literary Instructor, I have at present no fair chance of exercising the office I sustain amongst the Manufacturing Population.

He was disappointed by the lack of unity amongst the operatives.

> Most of you (he said) would not give up one hour's occupation, comfort, or the price of one glass of ale to save your class from distress and ruin. . . . Where there are two men who will unite, there are twenty who will fawn on an oppressor and cringe to him; some will even give up their children to him without a sigh, to be destroyed by excessive labour.

He blamed them because they would not trust each other and allowed their enemies to foment and increase their jealousies. They were often jealous of their best friends. They talked of "Tory tricks", of "Whig tricks", to discredit the motives of their friends. But what of Mr Clegg and Mr Fielden? he asked. They were Ten Hours men and leaders of the Regeneration Society. They were also Radicals. He demonstrated the short-sightedness of their faith in the ballot-box and in Republicanism:

> Suppose you had universal suffrage and Vote by Ballot and along with it the long hours and scanty wages of American operatives, what better would you be? Don't you know you might live in absolute and horrid slavery under a Republic?

He pointed out that in the Free States of America, there was no National Debt and no Corn Laws, which many regarded as the cause of Britain's ills. Moreover, America had an abundance of raw material to hand, and it was untaxed, "but yet," he added, "there is one tax, and that is a tax upon everything that you, the British operatives, make and send there".

In a Republic, he said, it was possible to have "most horrid and active slavery" as well as sweated labour for supposedly free men. To those who looked for a classless society and the end of the Aristocracy in a Republic, he said:

> Yes, my friends and there is a Republic and an American Aristocracy. Yes, and a very proud Aristocracy of Money, though not of Blood. Here we have both, but believe me, I would much rather be the slave of some English duke than a Factory Lord's Freeman. One is proud and says he will do what he likes with his own, but yet loves to see his peasantry happy, and some of them have told me that he contrives to make them so, though perhaps when the fit takes him, he turns out a score or two; but on the other hand, the Money Aristocrat is no less proud, though well cloaked with the guise of Liberality.

He added a plea that they should exercise forbearance and keep their "political playthings quiet while great practical issues are at stake."

His fourth reason for standing aloof was their failure to persevere in anything they undertook, and their addiction to intemperate and immoral habits.

> I know there are good men among you, of noble spirit, and of exemplary self-denial—but where there is one of this description there are, how many, who would not sacrifice a thimbleful of intoxicating liquor to save the West Riding. Now if this is not a fact, then make me happy by proving me mistaken. How glad I should be!

He reminded them of the help he had given and of Oastler's undaunted friendship for them; he told them of the disappointment in them of both. He said:

> Cast away all the self-imposed slavery of your ungodliness, your intoxicating cups, your dissolute habits, cease to rob your own families and your own breasts of comfort and peace, cease to suspect each other—be united— exercise forbearance—be steady and zealous in your own cause, and there will be some encouragement to disinterested men to work with you.[1]

There was a practical reason for his decision, also. Oastler and he were obnoxious to the masters. Perhaps his association with it might prejudice the employers, and stand in the way of the co-operation for which the Society aimed. He was with them in all reasonable and lawful measures for bettering conditions. He wished, as "a Religious Instructor", to take advantage of the Eight Hours Bill, and hoped they

---

[1] *White Slavery*, Vol. V. *The Leeds Times*, "To the Friends of the National Regeneration Society".

would settle the matter as Lord Althorp, Sir Robert Peel and Mr Fielden
—representative of all three parties—had suggested. After summing
up and underlining the social principles which he had expressed, he
ended:

> Cast off your self-imposed Slavery of intemperance and ungodliness—
> Love your families, Conciliate your masters. Obey the Law and may God
> prosper you.[1]

The Society's hopes were soon dashed. The small local strikes
which had begun to take place in 1833 were quickly broken, and the
number of broken strikes increased throughout the early part of 1834.
Most masters refused to employ union men or men who refused to
undertake not to join a union while in his employment. There
was no hope of masters co-operating voluntarily, as both Althorp and
Peel must have known, and the workers lacked the strength to coerce
the masters, as Philip Grant had told them at the Bradford meeting.
They lacked the unity and strength of purpose to stand together, as
Oastler and Bull had said. Besides, the spirit of the times was against
them. The Government sought to curb the growing power of the
unions. The Royal Commission had declared them to be unrealistic.
Like the Ten Hours men, they were deemed to be foolish as well as
dangerous in seeking to contravene the "laws" of political economy.
Some judges gave decisions in keeping with Government policy—a
lapse from the customary high standard of English justice—and helped
to set back the development of trade unionism for some years. The
most notable of these decisions was the sentencing of six agricultural
labourers of Tolpuddle, in Dorset, to seven years' transportation.
They were charged with administering illegal oaths to would-be
members of a local lodge which was being formed, and which was to
join Owen's Grand National Union. They were respectable men, of
good repute and behaviour, but Williams, who tried the case, was a
newly appointed and ambitious judge, and acted as he thought was
desired of him.

This was on 18 March, when Bull was in the midst of his discussions
with the National Regeneration Society. It was a judgement that
shocked most people. Even *The Bradford Observer*, although opposed to
trade unionism, especially to the pressure exerted on men to join the

[1] *White Slavery*, Vol. V. *The Leeds Times*, "To the Friends of the National
Regeneration Society".

unions, thought the sentence severe. The Editor, while not blaming Williams said:

> Whether or not the Act (37 Geo. iii C 123) on which the unionists were tried—an act ostensibly referring to seditious meetings—was applied to its legitimate construction in the matter of the six labourers at Dorchester is another matter and may perhaps admit of doubt.

He added that it was a matter for lawyers.[1]

Bull wrote one of his most telling pamphlets, in which is implicit his love of justice and his passionate belief that there should not be one law for the rich and another for the poor.

Written in satirical vein, it is called *The Entire Demolition of Trade Unions by the recent discharge of an old Rusty Parchment Blunderbuss*. He referred to some measures restraining sedition during the French wars, of their falling into desuetude and being unknown to later governments and law officers. He referred to two Liberals who had drawn "Lord Lamb's" attention to this weapon and said that "Sergeant Williams", who had just "been given a new suit of regimental ermines" was "bursting with gratitude for favours received". "He was," said Bull, "a worthy descendant of Corporal Jeffreys." He referred to the Duke of Sussex's Freemasonry and to the Duke of Cumberland's member-ship of an Orange Lodge. Towards the end, he became more direct and largely abandoned the satirical style in which most of the pamphlet was written. He said:

> These simple men had been taught to mimic their betters, the Freemasons and the Orangemen, and this was all their fault. They were trying hard in the mud and the puddle (poverty is often there) to get a little more than 7/- per week or at least to avoid taking less, but however, though they had not been rick burning, nor refusing to pay taxes like "Fitzmilton" and exciting people to "stop supplies", though they had never dressed the King in petticoats, nor the Queen in breeches (as the Whigs did in 1831), though they had not made a procession like Baines at Leeds during the Reform agitation consisting of an executioner with a bloody axe and representations of the King's crown falling off his head—they would have scorned to propose three groans for the Queen as that prince of good breeding, young Neddy did before 60,000 people in 1831[2]—and finally though the Church parson of Toll Puddle, where they lived, gave them a certificate of good character as quiet, harmless, and religious men, yet Williams was not to be moved—let go—and down all six went, for seven years, into Botany Bay.

[1] *The Bradford Observer*, 27 March 1834.   [2] See above, pp. 28-9.

He referred to the practice of planting spies amongst the unionists and the friendly societies, writing of "spy oil" and "spy lamps", and to the help that the trade unionists had given to the Whigs at the 1832 election. The pamphlet did not bear his name, being attributed to the "old rusty parchment blunderbuss", but he was known to be its author. He used the same simile in speeches on the subject.

Petitions against the carrying out of this sentence streamed in from all parts of the country. Many people less closely concerned than were trade unionists—or even than Bull, who was closely associated with the working-class movement—joined in the protests. But the sentence stood.

14

POULETT THOMSON'S AMENDMENT

FOR A year or two after the passing of the Althorp Act, the
Ten Hours organization was inactive if not completely moribund.
Other problems, more pressing, pushed factory reform into the
background. The issue was raised here and there in speech or letter,
but there was little to be done.

Bull himself was concerned in one or two controversies related to it.
He found himself in bitter controversy with Dissenters who resented
his sturdy defence of the Church against their attacks and whose bitterness was increased by his activities in the movement. Indeed, the year
1834 found him engaged in controversy on a number of issues arising
from his Churchmanship and his social activities.

If little could be done to change the law, a good deal was done
to see to it that the best was made of the Act. Its operation was studied
and evasions denounced. It became clear that it did not provide the
protection it was supposed to provide. On the other hand, some of its
provisions were capable of being beneficial. Reformers noted them and
sought to see that they were observed.

The inspection provided for by the Act, for instance, could be a real
benefit. Whatever may be said against the Act, this beginning of one
of the most beneficial of social services is embedded in it. There was
a long way to go before the factory inspectorate became the highly
respected body of men and women we know it to be today. Workers,
knowing the outlook of the inspectors and the sponsors of the Act,
had reason to fear that they would be unfriendly towards them.
Rickards, the Inspector for Lancashire and Yorkshire, issued a first report on the state of the working classes which did nothing to allay
this fear. He followed the line taken by the Commissioners, blaming
the workers for allowing themselves to be led, or as he implied, misled.
He wrote of:

The intelligence, energy, activity of many of its members, with the coarse, low habits of the general mass, from want of sound moral and religious education, the slaves of Vice, prejudice and passion, easily excited by factious clamour as to real or supposed grievances, and formidable in all such cases from their numerical and united strength: the bond of union between masters and servants feebly knit. Such is the apparent state of the manufacturing population of these parts, a population where the vicious propensities of the many keep pace with their augmented means of gratification (drunkenness, it is said, being on the increase), a population, therefore peculiarly fitted to be the instruments of seditious incendiaries and whose means of organized association are too well known to be lightly estimated.

Bull constantly condemned the sins of the poor and the rich alike, as some of his sermons of this period testify. He rushed to the defence of any class unjustly attacked. He defended the Throne and constantly asserted his belief that nothing in the Constitution stood in the way of achieving social justice. In the same way, he defended the poor against misrepresentation when they were attacked. Those of the working class whom he tried to recall to better things were not typical. Moreover, he knew their plight and the handicaps under which they lived. Rickards's report drew from him a protest against its partiality.[1] His experience had taught him that those who had "vicious propensities" were hard to enlist in a well-organized movement. Rickards, in any case, was much too sweeping. In a defence of the working people of Bradford and the manufacturing areas, Bull pointed out that, if as applied to the worst section of the working class, what Rickards had said were true, many employers set a bad example. Throughout the discussions on factory conditions, cases of seduction by overlookers and employers were often quoted. Some showed a callousness to the women only possible in men with no regard for the dignity of a woman, or of any human being, of another class. It matched the indifference that many of them showed to all the people in their employment. Bull had good ground for his retort:

Are there no extraordinary moral evils in existence amongst the masters? No drunkenness? No vicious propensities?

In a piece of what might be called "pre-Churchill Churchillism", he described them as:

a race whose whole wisdom consists in that cunning which enables them to devise the cheapest possible means for getting out of the youngest possible

[1] *The Manchester and Salford Advertiser*, 29 November 1835.

workers the greatest possible amount of labour, in the shortest possible amount of time, for the least possible amount of wages; a race which you find difficult to manage with all your despotic powers; a race who hate you as heartily as they do me, and finally a race of whom Agur would have said: *There is a generation, oh how lofty are their eyes! and their eyelids are lifted up. There is a generation whose teeth are as swords, and their jaw teeth are as knives, to devour the poor from off the earth, and the needy from among men.*[1]

While deploring the attitude of mind revealed by Rickards, it must be admitted that there were difficulties in applying some clauses of the Act. It was difficult to secure trustworthy information about the age of children, for there was no system of registering births. The inspectors could only accept a medical certificate that a child had the appearance and strength of a child of nine. Some of the attesting medical men were unqualified, and the safeguards provided by the Act were difficult to apply. Unscrupulous masters and the worst kind of parents adopted various means of evading the age regulations, with the result that the task of conscientious inspectors was made more difficult. Inevitably, standards varied. Fielden complained that in some places standards of height and weight were too low.[2] Besides this, many magistrates showed their contempt for the Act by imposing trivial fines on law-breaking employers. The reformers, however, recognized some of the possibilities in the system of inspection. Improvements in the law were necessary to ensure its benefits. The practice of working children in relays underlined the need. The shortage of children old enough to be employed made impossible the working of two relays, but by "staggering" children's hours, it was possible to use the available children throughout the adults' working day. This meant that the children were on the premises for the greater part of the day, if not for the whole of it.

The provisions made for education varied. Some employers, John Wood being the most notable, provided good buildings and appointed a good schoolmaster. Matthew Balme, whom he appointed, was a devout and influential Churchman. He played a prominent part in the life of Bradford and Bowling, succeeding Bull—who had taught him at Byerley—as Secretary of the Short Time Committee. But not all millowners made such excellent provision. Some gave the educational work to an almost illiterate workman, pushing it into some odd corner

[1] Proverbs, 30. 13, 14.
[2] Letter to *The Champion*. Reprinted in *The Times*, 22 October 1834.

of the mill premises. But the many reformers concerned about education realized that here, too, possibilities had been opened up.

These two provisions did not redeem a bad Bill, however. Neither was being satisfactorily carried out. In any case, the Act was no more satisfactory than it had been from the first. When it was seen to work badly, and various groups of people railed against it, the reformers came in for much blame. Those who wanted no legislation blamed them for forcing it, and some who did not like the effect of the Act were persuaded to blame them. Liberals forgot their gloating that the reformers had been "outbidden in humanity" and clamoured for the amendment of the Bill.

Their influence and that of the millowners, brought to bear upon dissatisfied groups of workers, led to some petitioning for the repeal of the Act. Overlookers, who found the supply of children's labour lessened, and spinners, who had to pay more for the labour of the children who helped them, were amongst them. Some parents were opposed to the restrictions because the family income was reduced. Many millowners encouraged the holding of meetings in their factories. Some organized them, bringing in outside speakers to persuade their workpeople to petition for the repeal of the Act or for some modification in its provisions. In some cases, barristers were briefed for this purpose. The main demand was that children over the age of ten should work the same number of hours as adults. Ten Hours men were put on the defensive.

At first, their replies were isolated, personal utterances. As pressure grew, they began to reform their local committees. The Bradford Committee issued a protest against the proposal to lengthen the hours of children's labour. They replied to those who blamed them for the situation that had developed that they had forecast the outcome of the Act, but they had been told that they had been outbidden in humanity. They had said that its supposed benefits were delusive and impracticable. When this had proved to be so, they were blamed, and care was being taken to inculcate this falsehood into the minds of children and parents. The protest repeated that this was not their Act, and quoted Stuart, the Glasgow Commissioner, who had spoken of a millowner who supported the Act because he did not believe it would work. The Committee said that Lancashire opponents were pressing for a twelve-hour day and Yorkshire opponents for an eleven-and-a-half-hour day—though they too meant twelve hours. "They ask that we should all agree on eleven, but will give no written pledge." They revived the argument that Bull had used—that if the masters were sincere in saying that an eleven-hour day would mean no reduction in wages, then the young people had been robbed in the past. "The hole and corner" nature of mill meetings was contrasted with the reformers' open meetings.[1] When Oastler or Bull or any of the practised campaigners spoke at meetings, they did not speak as men on the defensive. They enlarged on these points, speaking with the old vigour.

During 1835, the heat and bitterness began to return. When a number of clergymen and ministers sent a petition to Baines, who had succeeded Macaulay as Member of Parliament, he retorted that he did "not blame the petitioners, but he would prefer that petitions should not be forwarded by clergymen and persons not connected with the trade, and who could not know what the required hours should be". Together with Boddington and their Wesleyan friend, Jabez Smith, Bull replied in the form of a petition supposedly addressed to Parliament. They justified their concern. They were instructors of youth and must be deeply concerned; they were surprised by assertions that Christian ministers ought not to be. This was a question of humanity no less than trade, and one affecting the dearest interests of Christians. It was a system that was fraught with extreme danger to the temporal and eternal interests of many thousands. The petition went on to say;

That your petitioners protest against that sort of Liberalism which, at the bidding of Mammon, would seal the lips of a Christian Minister. In the case of Negro Emancipation, your petitioners were never thus bidden to be silent except by the interested upholders of Colonial Slavery, and yet those very persons who in that case cheered us on our way now tell us, when home slavery is the theme of our reprobation, to hold our peace.

From a most solemn conviction of the mischievous effects of the present Factory System, regardless of our inconsistent reprovers, we once more entreat your Honourable House to amend the present Factory Act by substituting an effective Ten Hours Bill, thus enabling us with good effect to affect literary and Christian Instruction to the Children and Youth under our care. . . .[2]

During this phase of the campaign, the growing rift between the movement and official Methodism was widened by the refusal of a millowner-trustee to allow Oastler the use of the Methodist School

[1] 19 February 1835. Local papers. Oastler Collection.
[2] *White Slavery*. Local papers.

at Oldham, where a meeting had been arranged.[1] Oastler expressed regret, and outlined the reformers' position. He re-told the main events of the campaign, seeking to establish how unwillingly legislation had been passed. He sought to establish that the reformers had been obstructed by telling of the evasive measures taken by the Government and its supporters. He reminded his audience of the reformers' objections to the Royal Commission:

> This Commission, which Mr Sadler and others protested against, was appointed at the instigation of the owners. Mr Condy published a pamphlet to prove its illegality; my much respected friend, the Reverend G. S. Bull, a most excellent Episcopalian Minister, published his protest against it.[2]

Largely on the initiative of the leading Ten Hours men in Lancashire, the efforts to revive the campaign became more co-ordinated. Doherty again brought with him the support of his union, still the strongest in the industry. Owing to their longer experience of law evasion, Lancashire reformers had always tried to persuade their Yorkshire colleagues of the importance of the restriction of moving power.[3] When they called a meeting at Preston, in August 1836, to decide on future plans, it emerged that much had already been done to do so. The Lancashire Short Time leaders had asked Charles Hindley to sponsor a new Ten Hours Bill in Parliament. He had been associated with the movement since 1832. He was a manufacturer and, since the Reform Election, a Member of Parliament, calling himself Liberal-Radical. He had thought Ashley wrong to abandon his Bill when it was amended in its important clauses. Possibly this was a reason for the Lancashire men by-passing Ashley, though possibly Ashley's Toryism was by that time regarded as something of a liability, and certainly the fact that Hindley was a manufacturer was held to discount one of the criticisms of the Ten Hours leaders.

John Fielden had been made Treasurer of this Lancashire organization, and a decision had been made to launch a new campaign early in 1836, just before Parliament re-assembled. The Conference was not

---

[1] See Chap. 17 below. *White Slavery*, pp. 185-6.

[2] Lancashire Press. Oastler Collection. Bull's Protest: Appendix A.

[3] The Lancashire factory reformers were concerned to restrict the hours during which the machinery might run rather than to restrict the hours of the workers. Their experience of the Peel Acts led them to believe that the manufacturers would find means of evading measures which only dealt with the hours of workpeople.

a happy one. It marked a cleavage of opinion between Hindley and the leaders. Bull represented Oastler, and defended Ashley's action when Hindley repeated his criticisms of it. He would agree to no compromise on the Ten Hours principle, but would agree to a clause restricting moving power if that principle were not abandoned. Some of Hindley's fears about the probable effect of the Bill on the export trade did nothing to increase confidence in him. He wished to secure legislation by easy stages so that its effects could be observed.[1] His tendency to bargain did not suggest the forthrightness needed in a leader. As Professor Driver says, he was inclined to look upon Parliament as a kind of glorified Stock Exchange, "where deals were to be made, and bidders could not be expected to clinch with the first offer".[2]

The new campaign was launched at a big meeting at Ashton, in Hindley's constituency. Here, for the first time, Joseph Rayner Stephens associated himself with the movement.[3] He was to be active in it as well as in the anti-Poor Law campaign. His activity as a Chartist caused him to be better remembered in history than either Oastler or Bull. He added a militancy to the movement that made a great deal of difference to it. The effects were not wholly good, though he brought to the movement great ability besides much fervour.

Press propaganda and pressure exercised within the factories had created in the workers a demand for an amendment to the Act that would lengthen the hours of children's labour and lower the age of protection. The demand for an eleven-hour day was becoming general. The reformers had to work hard to convert many of the operatives, therefore. They sought for support for a Ten Hour Bill which would also embody improvements of the good points in the Althorp Act. They had limited success, however, and they had good reason to fear that the operatives, especially the overlookers, would support the owners, and that the Bill would be defeated in consequence.

This was changed by Government action. Poulett Thomson, President of the Board of Trade, announced that the Government intended to sponsor a bill amending the law and reducing the age of protection to twelve. Children of twelve would then be permitted to work twelve hours a day instead of eight. Thomson had opposed restrictions from the first; he had only tolerated it because "the senseless clamour

---

[1] *The Manchester and Salford Advertiser*, 9 January 1836.
[2] *Tory-Radical*, pp. 311–12.   [3] Ibid., p. 315. *White Slavery*.

outside" made it inevitable. His announcement caused the old enthusiasm to be re-kindled. The movement became alive again. Meetings
were well attended and enthusiastic. Bull did his share of speaking
and a good deal of the planning. Like Oastler, he condemned the hole
and corner meetings of the opposition, the latest Government threat,
and, hardly less, the parents who supported proposals to lengthen
children's working day. The old arguments about the dangers to the
export trade were advanced again and as vigorously refuted. The
question they posed was: Should the issue be determined by considerations of what Professor Tawney has since called "political arithmetic"
or by considerations of humanity? The prophetic note was again
sounded, and the adherence of Stephens added to the prophetic fervour.

The Press was sharply divided. *The Leeds Mercury* and *The Manchester
Guardian* led the attack on the reformers, while *The Leeds Intelligencer*
and *The Manchester and Salford Advertiser* hit back. *The Times* thun-
dered daily, and other national newspapers took sides. Oastler came
in for bitter denunciation, especially from the *Mercury* and the rest of
the Liberal Press. He was the arch-enemy, a mischief-maker and incendiary. Other leaders came in for abuse, Bull hardly less than Oastler.

The campaign of abuse led to a public difference with a brother
cleric. Bull and his friends sought to get clerical support for the Bill.
When they called on William Gillmor, Curate of Illingworth, he
asked if the Vicar of Halifax had signed it. He was told that they had
called on him, but he had not been at home. Gillmor signed the petition,
but when Musgrave refused, regretted it.[1] He wrote a strong letter to
The Halifax Guardian, attacking Bull for his activities and for consorting
with the rabble. Some of his charges were wild and ridiculous, especially
his reference to "Bacchanalian orgies". Bull was used to attacks by
Dissenters, but an attack by a colleague let down both the Church and
the cause. He replied in a long letter in the *Guardian*. He recounted the
circumstances of Gillmor's signing the petition, refuted Gillmor's wild
assertions, and stressed that he was not the only parson in the movement.
He said:

> A stranger would suppose that no clergyman "the incumbent of Bierley"
> excepted, had ever taken an interest in the matter, and that he alone had done
> himself the honour of pleading the cause of the oppressed factory workers.
> But, sir, be it known to this ignorant brother that I have no such exclusive
> honour. I share it with sixty-eight clergymen who signed the requisition to

[1] *The Halifax Guardian*, 9 April 1836.

the County meeting in 1832, and with thirty-four who signed the petition to which Mr Gillmor so considerately affixed his name, but which, after a conference with the Vicar, he so sorrowfully repented himself for signing.[1]

It was an unhappy episode.

When the debate in Parliament drew near, the reformers were fearful of the result. They could not measure the success they had had in nullifying the manufacturers' propaganda. The debate covered familiar ground, except that the Government was faced with the difficult task of reconciling the Commission's findings—previously accepted—that children should be treated as adults when they reached the age of thirteen with their proposal to treat them as adults at the age of twelve. The manufacturers and the theorists were able to argue that the needs of trade were more urgent than considerations of humanity and justice. It seemed likely that the Government would win. There was general surprise at the result of the voting, for the Government motion was approved by a majority of only two. *The Times* leading article said:

(Mr Thomson) is a political economist, indifferent to everything but scientific and pseudo-scientific relations between certain causes and certain consequences, ignorant of all that lies beyond that specious theory of which "production" is at once the subject and the idol—of that exclusive and so far narrow and mischievous problem, of which the solution is how to increase to the utmost pitch the materials and the amount of "production". A political economist is an animal with limited brains and no bowels. With moral principles and resolutions he never ventures to trouble himself. Duties, affections, virtues, vices, happiness, affliction, are all the same to him. To trace to them, to develop in them, any element of production is beyond his faculties. He therefore carts them away bodily, as so much surplusage; they have no place in his enquiries as a student or in his policy as a statesman; the human race with such a philosophy are but necessary incumbrances to spinning jennies.[2]

A majority of two was as eloquent as an award of a farthing damages in a law court. The Government dropped the proposal shamefacedly; Hobhouse and one or two other members confessed that they were ashamed to be associated with it.

After this, efforts to get Hindley's Bill through Parliament were redoubled. The reformers grew more militant in the face of the owners' militancy and the partial administration of the law by magistrates.

[1] Oastler Collection. *Halifax Guardian*, 23 April 1836.
[2] *The Times*, 11 May 1836.

At a meeting outside the Court House at Bradford, supported by Walker, Rand, Oastler and Fielden, the five thousand people present cheered enthusiastically when the visitors talked of strike action if Parliament failed them.[1] At a Conference in Manchester five weeks after Thomson's defeat, the operatives were sufficiently on the warpath to say that they would shorten the working week for themselves if Parliament did not do it for them.[2] The masters answered these threats by threatening to close the mills for three months to force the Goverment to change the law. When Oastler and Stephens joined forces at an Oastler Rally at Ashton,[3] they began a personal association which caused the fervour of both to demand action more direct than the movement had previously contemplated.

When Hindley sought leave to introduce his Bill, the reception was so chilly that Ashley and Fielden persuaded him to withdraw it. For some months, pressure was exerted to secure enforcement of the existing law more than for its amendment. Bull was more moderate than Oastler and Stephens, whose fiery speeches became the outstanding feature of this period of campaigning. It is hard to blame them. There was much to anger them. The law was being flouted and magistrates were contemptuous of it. This, indeed, was the cause of Oastler's greatest indiscretion.

He went to Blackburn to address a mass meeting in the theatre. The town was agog because magistrates had refused to hear a complaint against a local magistrate-manufacturer who had broken the factory laws. They were notorious for their unwillingness to convict on such charges, and the Short Time Committee asked Oastler to refer to this. One of the magistrates had said, "That is Oastler's law. We have nothing to do with that. Take your complaints to him". Some of them occupied theatre boxes at the meeting, and during his speech, he asked them if he had been correctly informed. They laughed at him. When he pressed his question, they laughed the more.[4]

Already worked up by his own fervour and the enthusiasm of the meeting, he was infuriated. He reminded them that the Factory Act

[1] Oastler Collection. *The Bradford Observer*, 26 May 1836, thought Fielden impertinent for daring to advise Bradford business men.

[2] Oastler Collection.

[3] *The Manchester and Salford Advertiser*, 27 August 1836.

[4] Accounts of this meeting, as well as Press attacks on Oastler, are to be found in the Oastler Collection. His pamphlet, "The Law and the Needle" like the Oldham speech which followed, was a development of his idea of the rightness of sabotage.

was part of the law which they had sworn to administer. They relied on the law to protect their property, and this law was intended to protect the lives of factory children. He said that it was their duty to inquire whether children's lives or manufacturers' spindles were most entitled to the law's protection. Turning to the audience, he said:

> If after this your magistrates should refuse to listen to your complaints under the factory act and again refer you to me, bring with you your children and tell them to ask their grandmothers for a few of their old knitting needles which I will instruct them how to apply to the spindles in a way which will teach these law-defying magistrates to have respect even to "Oastler's law" as they wrongly designated the Factory Act.

There was a howl from the Liberal newspapers. *The Manchester Guardian* made much of it, without mentioning the provocation which had led to the outburst. "Freedom of speech" did not secure for him space for replies to the frequent attacks which the *Guardian* made on him. Apart from a letter answering the first attack, no further space was allowed him. He was unrepentant, however, and developed the theme at later meetings.

The sad feature lay in its effect upon Oastler's friends. Wood had always regretted his extreme language, and the more recent phase must have grieved him. The Blackburn speech caused a breach between them. Although Wood continued to support the movement, both by his work and by his generous gifts, his friendship with Oastler was ended. Later, when Oastler was committed to the Fleet Prison for default on a debt due to Thornhill, Wood was not one of his visitors. It says much for him that he joined with Walker and Fielden in clearing off a debt on *The Fleet Papers* when they undertook to clear it. Hindley vowed that he would never speak alongside Oastler again, although in fact he did so. Bull publicly dissociated himself from Oastler's incitement to sabotage. Oastler's letters and speeches indicate that the incident created something of a rift between them. If so, it did not last long. Bull was loyal to him throughout his life, in spite of differing from him about this and similar excesses.

In any case, the campaign for the Ten Hours Bill was forced into the background. The defeat of Thomson's motion—for its withdrawal was an acknowledgement of defeat—was the only success of that year, and the reformers had to be satisfied with it. Oastler had a breakdown in health which kept him out of action for some time. When he recovered, another issue was being faced.

15

THE NEW POOR LAW

BOUND UP with the factory movement during the lull in the activities of the Ten Hours movement was the resistance to the New Poor Law. It was inevitable. Bull had said that the opposition to factory legislation and the proposals for Poor Law amendment were part of a conspiracy against the working class.[1]

Poor Law amendment was needed. The Speenhamland system, which augmented wages in relation to the size of the family and the price of bread, might have been tolerable to meet a local situation in wartime, but when it became the norm in agricultural areas, it was scandalous. The cost of poor relief became an intolerable burden. It became a subsidy, augmenting wages. Employers benefited: ratepayers and the poor suffered.

A commission was set up in 1832. Its composition caused foreboding amongst those who were opposed to the views of the political economists. The Report increased the foreboding, for the nature of the forthcoming legislation became clear. The Act of 1834 justified it.

Bull lectured about the Act as soon as its provisions became known. He was concerned with its principles. His first important ground of criticism was that the Act took from the poor an inalienable right. He reviewed the history of the principle that "the poor had a first mortgage on the land".[2] He quoted Moses, Saint Paul, and the Acts of the Apostles, and said:

> If any man could take up his Bible and say that the Book did not establish the divine right of the poor to relief by well-requited work when able to work, he would say that man ought to go and read his Bible again, for (he

---

[1] See Chap. 11 above, p. 119.

[2] *The Bradford Observer*, 1 January 1835. Reprinted with the title: *A Lecture upon the New Poor Law Act, falsely called "The Amendment"*. Bradford Reference Library.

thought) if any one thing was more clearly established than another throughout the whole book, it was the divine right of the poor to relief.[1]

This was recognized by English law. The lands and possessions of
the Church had been divided, a portion being reserved for the poor.
Church and poor had been dispossessed by Henry VIII, who had given
the possessions of the poor to his favourites. "This act of flagrant injustice and oppression the politicians of that day had found it inex-
pedient to meddle with, and the poor had found it impossible to
endure", he said. The state of the country had rendered it necessary for
Elizabeth to pass an Act entitling the poor to relief out of the produce
of the soil. This had been the basis of subsequent legislation. The poor
had not abused the Poor Laws, and the fact that others had done so was
no reason for taking away their inalienable rights. He maintained that
it was unconstitutional to deprive the poor of relief or to grant it as a
loan. He quoted Lord Eldon, a former Lord Chancellor, in support of
his contention. Indeed, Lord Brougham, the Lord Chancellor of the
day, when introducing the Bill into Lords, had said that the governing
principle of legislation had been that the poor had the first mortgage
on the land. He had added, however, that previous legislators had not
enjoyed the benefit of the teaching of Malthus.[2] In view of later
criticism of Bull, these high legal opinions are important. Bull's opposition was justified, it seemed to him, by his belief that the Act was
unconstitutional, denying a fundamental right.

He held it to be unconstitutional also because it gave wide powers
to the Commissioners. They were empowered to issue rules, orders,
and regulations, having the force of law. They could alter or rescind
them according to their discretion. The poor were left unprotected,
dependent upon the Commissioners.

Moreover, the Act provided for too much centralization. Not only
was power vested in the Commissioners, but it provided for the union
of parishes and even townships to make larger administrative units.
This was wrong, Bull maintained. Rates were raised locally and
should be spent by locally elected bodies. Officials should be appointed
locally instead of being appointed and dismissed by the Commissioners.
This was a point pressed by many people. They held local

---

[1] *The Bradford Observer*, 1 January 1835. Reprinted with the title: *A Lecture
upon the New Poor Law Act, falsely called " The Amendment"*. Bradford Reference
Library.

[2] *The Times*, 22 July 1834.

administration preferable for many reasons. It was less soulless. It was less expensive. One correspondent to *The Times* pointed out that a saving of expense was secured by "the simpler and cheaper apparatus of a resident local and (of course) no pluralist hierarchy instead of those lay commissioners and endless expenditure".[1] Bull often tilted at the pluralism which permitted a highly-paid Poor Law official to be a factory inspector also. The writer of the article, who might well have been Bull—for it is known that he was a frequent contributor—said that the by-passing of the clergy was deliberate, and was done "that there may be one argument less for an established Church".

The working people were alarmed at the proposal to stop paying out-relief to the able-bodied, sending them into the union workhouses. What they thought of these places is indicated by their calling them "Bastilles", for the Bastille was the symbol of tyranny. Bull spoke of the administration of Poor Law by Lowe, which the Commissioners commended. Lowe was a clergyman, evidently of the Malthus school, a fact which made Bull "blush for his profession". He had forced every applicant for relief into the workhouse, refusing out-relief and had caused the man to be separated from his wife and both from their children. He had boasted, said Bull, that labourers were glad to get work at twelve shillings a week, "the whole parish being better off in consequence".[2]

This became the accepted principle of Poor Law administration. Workhouses looked like prisons and were administered like them. If a man saw his wife at all, it was in the presence of an official, in prison-like conditions. Paupers were subjected to regimentation and prison-like rules. It was the admitted intention to make workhouses less attractive than the homes of "independent" labourers. Food was made unappetizing. Mr Christopher Hollis did not exaggerate the bitter absurdity of it all when he wrote:

> If the pauper was to be given an allowance less than that of the labourer, it would be both less troublesome and less hypocritical to leave him to starve. However, it was thought a solution to give him the same quantity of food, but to serve it in less appetising fashion. But how? and so, for the first time in the history of mankind, the salaried servants of the Government were turned to the strange research of discovering ways in which the inadequate food of the poor could be rendered artificially more nauseous.[3]

[1] *The Times*, 16 January 1836.   [2] *Another Lecture on the Poor Law Amendment.*
[3] Christopher Hollis, *The Two Nations*, p. 109.

Bull said that the Act was one of compulsory emigration. A man out of work was out of bread. "Capitalists, land-holders, owners of steam-engines throw the labourer out of work, and the Poor Law Commissioners were going to see to it that a rigorous workhouse system drove him to the waterside."

At one of his public lectures, he referred to his previous activities, he expressed his disappointment that so many of his hearers had not helped him in his efforts for factory reform. He went on to say that he was

> fully convinced of the necessity and justice of immediate emancipation. But instead of this, they passed a law for the gradual emancipation of the Blacks, which law is intended to effect the gradual enthraldom of the whites.[1]

A constantly recurring complaint was that the bastardy clauses, which left the unmarried mother unprotected, were unjust and cruel. Immorality was rife. Seduction by employer or overlooker was not infrequent. Parish clergymen and social workers were concerned and maintained that these clauses were unjust. It is true that when the Act was in operation, some clergymen—although opposed to the Act on other grounds—thought that it effected a drop in the number of illegitimate births by these clauses. Generally, however, Bull's criticism of them was supported by social workers.

The niggardly medical provisions provided further ground for criticism. Medical attention could only be given at the public expense when sanctioned by the overseer, who was often tardy about doing so. Moreover, the fee of half-a-crown a case was fair to neither doctor nor patient. A writer to *The Times* gave instances of prolonged treatment given to patients for which this fixed sum was paid. Some of them involved the doctor in long journeys. Medical experience was gained at the expense of the poor. The writer cited the case of a young doctor "who effected a perfect cure of stricture of the bowels by killing the poor woman, whose case he treated improperly".[2]

When the Act was put into operation in the South and East, criticisms on the score of principle were strengthened by experience. Opposition newspapers recorded daily instances of harsh administration. *The Times* was much to the fore in this, although not a Tory paper. John Walter, its proprietor, was Member for Berkshire and was persistent in presenting petitions and in telling of the way the Act

---

[1] *Another Lecture on the Poor Law Amendment.*   [2] *The Times*, 16 January 1836.

operated. Henry Phillpotts, Bishop of Exeter, was equally busy in the House of Lords. He incurred the displeasure of Melbourne, who reminded him of the privilege of being a member of the House and inferred that bishops should show their gratitude for being allowed to exercise the privilege by being supporters of the Government.[1]

Bull maintained that the Act was one of expediency.

> Poor rates, it was said, were an intolerable burden, but what of taxation? Why take the poor man's one ewe lamb and leave their own fat sheep? If capitalists were bound by law to provide maintenance for the poor, out of selfishness they would care for their interests lest they would have to keep them.

Newspaper reports support his contention, for there were many instances of harsh treatment which could only be justified by an appeal to expediency. *The Times*, for instance, reported that a woman told the Brentford magistrates of the small amount given in relief to her and her four small children—an occasional shilling. (The "bastille" had not then been built.) The overseer said that he had a duty to the ratepayers. The magistrates were powerless, but warned him that if death from starvation ensued, he would be awkwardly placed.[2] Poverty was not relieved. Only those in a state of destitution were relieved. When the workhouses were built, even that relief was at the expense of family life. Only indoor relief was offered to the able-bodied.

The Commissioners' rulings, communicated to guardians by Edwin Chadwick, became a sort of case-law. The working out of the Act in practice was based upon the principles laid down in the Report, but these communications added much to the anger of opponents and to the vigour of their opposition. One of them was a reply to the Petworth Guardians, who objected to a ruling that "no relief be given to children of the able-bodied unless all go into the workhouse". They argued that they knew local conditions best and would not accept such a ruling. Chadwick replied that when wages in the Petworth union were insufficient, workers should migrate to the manufacturing districts of the North. Relief should only be given in extreme cases which could not possibly be provided by their own exertions.[3]

Similarly, the ruling made when the Vicar of Eastry, Sandwich, asked for permission for the paupers to worship in the parish church

---

[1] *The Times*, 3 January 1837.   [2] *The Times*, 16 January 1836.
[3] *The Times*, 8 August 1836.

created a precedent to be followed, besides reiterating a principle. Chadwick said that it was "important that workhouses should be less attractive than the home of the independent labourer". He added that prayers were said in the workhouse. *The Times* expressed surprise at this edict, and asked "what Lord John Russell had to say in defence of such a Bull of excommunication by the Poor Law Pope and his Cardinals of Somerset House?"[1] This issue recurred frequently. In 1837, there was a prolonged argument about it. It was from this that the sharp words between Melbourne and Phillpotts arose.

Bull's first lectures, in 1834, were an examination of the principles of the Act. "The rod," he said, "is hung up." He wished it to be removed. The events of 1836 caused the Poor Law issue to be pushed into the background in the North, especially as the Act was not being applied there. In the South, the opposition came from various groups of people. There were those who said, "We never did this before." That, to them, was sufficient ground for opposition. There were others whose social outlook was rooted in the social teaching of Christendom. They quoted the Bible—and their quotations were relevant—but they owed much to inherited assumptions. The new Poor Law seemed to them to be based upon the wrong beliefs about Man and Society which were displacing those inherent in Christian teaching. Oastler, Bull, and the large number of protesting clergymen, were of this outlook. The clergy, much concerned with poor relief, were in the forefront of the opposition. Others opposed for party reasons. J. B. Atlay, writing of Brougham's part in the controversy, says:

> The revolution which it affected in English life is an enduring monument to his work as a legislator, though for years to come the New Poor Law was a most effective stick with which to belabour the Whig dog.[2]

It was customary to attribute party motives to those who defended the politically powerless. Factory reformers were so misrepresented from the first, and for the most part they were opponents of the New Poor Law. In January 1832, when the Whig-Liberal Press said that the Leeds rally of factory reformers was a Tory meeting, *The Standard* said that this was a great tribute to the Tory party in view of the care taken to keep the movement free of party entanglements.[3] The reply

[1] *The Times*, 20 June 1836.   [2] J. B. Atlay, *Victorian Chancellors*, pp. 327–8.
[3] *The Standard*, 14 January 1832.

was apt. Unfortunately, so far as the New Poor Law was concerned, the gibe paid an undeserved compliment to the Tories. The most influential of them supported it. When Oastler sought to enlist Wellington's leadership in opposition to it, he found that both he and Peel were pledged to support it.[1] Oastler could persuade Thornhill of the rightness of the factory campaign, but Thornhill ruined him because he disapproved of his resistance to the Poor Law Commissioner. It was in its support of this Act that the drift of Toryism began to be in evidence.

The Times differed from the Government on this issue as well as on the question of factory reform. Brougham had been indignant at the suggestion that the Commissioners would be so cruel as to separate husband and wife. When it became clear that it was the policy to do so The Times said: "Lord Brougham was believed and we were disbelieved. Events have proved that we, not Lord Brougham, spoke the truth." The Government had been guilty of deception. It was "the most disgraceful measure that ever emanated from a Christian legislature".[2] The Government threatened action against critical editors. The Times noted the threat and added, "We know our antagonists well. They slander and insult the peers. They starve and crush the poor."[3] The Editor carried the war into enemy camp, being in no apologetic mood. He poured scorn on the claim that the administration was economical:

> The soup is made weaker, the bread blacker, the cheese harder, offal is given for meat, and the quantity of each is diminished to starving point in order that a few shillings and pence may, for appearance sake, be divided amongst the ratepayers, while many thousands of pounds are distributed to Government hangers-on who are called Commissioners.

Brougham was the main target. He believed that all forms of poor relief should be swept away. They were contrary to his Malthusian beliefs. He believed them to be bad for the poor and an impoverishment of the rich. In his speech in the House of Lords introducing the Act, when illustrating a point, he supposed that he were "a Westmorland pauper" and added that he soon would be unless existing poor laws were changed. He was never allowed to forget this. When he ceased to be Lord Chancellor soon afterwards, there was much dis-

---

[1] The Fleet Papers, Vol. II, pp. 221–2.   [2] The Times, 24 August 1836.
[3] The Times, 2 September 1836.

cussion about his £5,000 a year pension. It was "out relief". Feargus O'Connor, who associated himself with the opposition, made much of the way he would treat "the Westmorland pauper":

> I shall be sorry for Lady Brougham. I know no harm of her. But I will have no pity for him. "No. No. Harry", I will say to him, "you may not go with my lady. This is the way for you. Otherwise you might breed."[1]

When the Act was operating in the agricultural areas of southern and eastern England, the Commissioners turned their attention to the North. They began there early in 1837. They sent as Assistant Commissioner the same Alfred Power that had been one of the field officers of the Factory Commission. It was a tactless appointment. On 31 January, at about the time that Power was beginning his work, Bull addressed a meeting in Christ Church Schoolroom, Bradford.[2] He said that "when wicked men contrived and mistaken men have been induced" to support such a law "which tends to oppress, to demoralize the poor, to lower their wages", he cared for neither the threats nor the entreaties of the politicians, but would protest against it with every power he possessed, stopping only at force.

He restated the grounds of his objections, stressing the power of the Commissioners and the limited powers of the guardians, who could neither appoint nor dismiss their officers. "The Commissioners can and do prescribe the scale of diet, even to an ounce of bread and a spoonful of skilly, and the guards cannot add a spoonful more", he said. He thought it degrading to any man of good sense and feeling voluntarily to place himself at the disposal of three men in London, "who are armed with such powers for punishing the poor". It was delusory to be elected guardians, he said, because they agreed "to accept office of mere agency under a false designation, and the soft sweet word of 'guardian' is to soothe their consciences, to screen their characters, and to lull the suffering poor and the indignant public into a false security." He challenged Mr Assistant Commissioner Power to correct him.

> An Act of Parliament is a powerful gun, especially when it is loaded with hard measure for the poor, and as long as men who have the power to pull the trigger when they please are invested with more discretionary power than the King himself. We remember the poor farmers of Dorchester who

---

[1] Quoted by Cole and Postgate, *The Common People*, p. 272.
[2] *The Times*, 8 February 1837. Local papers.

were blown to Botany Bay by an old rusty blunderbuss which was kept loaded and had been laid aside for a score of years, and yet when it served the Government to intimidate the working men and to break up their unions, they brought out this musty Act of Parliament which had been passed to put down the friends of democracy twenty years before and by its power the present Government transported the poor Tollpuddle farmers for taking illegal oaths, which they took unwillingly and by which they were united to keep their wages from sinking below 1/5d. a day, and for this heinous crime they were transported and all the secret orders among the great who had equally transgressed the act were left unmolested.

He called for Mr Assistant Commissioner Power. "Is he here?" he asked. "We are old acquaintances. I once saw him at the Talbot Inn when he was 'commissioning' our poor factory children. As he was one of the enquiring commissioners who recommended the new Poor Law, he knew it before he was born. Failing him, is Mr Factory Superintendent and Poor Law Agent Robert Baker here?" he asked. He was to be responsible for importing paupers from other areas. Bull described the pitiful scenes in their country home, during the journey, and on their arrival. They were forced to sign, binding themselves to some millowner, "as ever a traveller forced to give a purse to a highwayman". He said that it was worse than highway robbery and pressed that every man should be free to serve whom he would when he arrived. He interspersed passages from the Psalms and from Amos, for he believed himself to be speaking what God laid upon him.

To the plea that the Act should be given a fair trial, he replied:

> I ask you, will you be responsible to the poor for the acts of the three new kings in London? How dare you say, "Give it a fair trial?" without considering the poor? At 15½ pence a week? Give the three despots a fair trial. Let us have the crowns plucked from the heads of these usurpers. Restore the clauses giving power and responsibility to the guardians.

He called for the removal of the clauses that relief should be a loan to be repaid when the recipient was again able to work, for the removal of the bastardy clauses and for the right of appointment and dismissal to be restored to the ratepayers' representatives.

> The ratepayers of England have not chosen these despotic men to manage their affairs and we will not have these kings to reign over us.
> Sir, there is in this Act a spirit of malignity, of malice, not only towards the living pauper, but even, I say, to the dead.

He told of a girl who, he had been told, had been flogged on her naked back, of the straits to which the poor had been driven to bury their dead, and of William Minto, who had so much dreaded the Bedlington Union that he had hanged himself. He told of a widow at Heywood, who, with her seven children, was bound to a millowner for three years. When paid less than agreed upon, she had left, and the Manchester magistrates had sent her to prison for two years. "Independent labourers indeed!" he exclaimed. He quoted Wakley, Member for Finsbury, who had stated the precise amount of the weekly diet: 42 oz of bread, 15 oz of beef, 8 oz. of cheese, 24 oz. of potatoes, 4½ pints of soup, and 19½ pints of gruel. The claim that savings had been effected he dismissed by saying that they were being effected before the Act came into operation, but, in any case, "saving in defiance of the commands of God to piety and care for the poor is a deadly loss".

He told of the treatment of some of the clergymen who had led the local agitation against the Act, particularly Maberley, of Great Finsborough in East Anglia. His name was associated with the opposition to the Act there as Bull's was to be in the West Riding. Maberley had been the object of ministerial disapproval. Bull, referring to this, said:

> If it is come to this that the Secretary of State is to set our bishops upon us to harass us, there will be an end of Church and State, and it becomes every man who wears a gown to stand up for his order. I am quite sure that this system and the Bible cannot stand together. One must fall, and with all my heart, I say, perish the Poor Law and let Christianity live and prevail.

The seconder of the motion condemning the operation of the Act, Mr Brook of Horton, a working-man, expressed the gratitude of his class, adding, "I love my wife as well as the greatest noble in the land". In spite of the opposition of William Byles, whose firm published *The Bradford Observer*, the motion was carried by an overwhelming majority.

During the following weeks, petitions from parishes and townships in the West Riding and Lancashire were added to those from other parts of the country. Trade was bad, short time prevalent, and foreboding grew into alarm. The clergy presided over meetings, and joined together to send petitions through Parliamentary supporters. Ten Hours men were to the fore, but new names are to be found amongst the opponents. John Sharp, of Horbury, who was to make his mark as a Tractarian parish priest, was one of them. He had supported his father, the Vicar of Wakefield, who had been prominent in the Ten Hours movement, but he was able to play a bigger part in the Poor Law agitation in view of his increased responsibility as Curate (and first Vicar) of Horbury.[1] Jabez Smith, Bull's Wesleyan friend, continued to work with the opponents of the Government, in spite of the tendency of prominent Wesleyans to identify themselves with Liberalism.

Bull was called upon to address meetings farther afield, but he was most prominent in Bradford. He addressed a rally at the end of March outside the Court House there. He was mainly concerned to persuade the meeting not to elect guardians. They were guardians of the Commissioners, he maintained. They should have power to administer the locally raised funds because they knew local people and local conditions. The Commissioners received £2,000 a year, not 15d. a week. The pensioners were kings and the payers vassals. He criticized the type of workhouse master and relieving officer being appointed, ex-N.C.O.s, an occasional officer or metropolitan policeman. He poured scorn on the workhouse uniform, and when his sardonic humour caused some laughter, he said: "I am glad you are in merry humour, but I see not much to laugh at".

Burrows, a working man from Lancashire, expressed his wonder that there should be "mountains of wealth, yet nothing but prison for poverty in distress". He pointed out that Brougham, "the Westmorland pauper" "received £5,000 a year for his pauper pay—out-door, you know"; for him there was no 15½ pence per day and no Bastille.

Byles, who was a Bradford version of Baines, was seen at the edge of the crowd, but slipped away when he knew that he had been seen. His paper was supporting the new Act as vigorously as it opposed factory legislation, trade unionism, and the Church. It was one aspect of the Liberalism which was gaining ascendancy.

If the agitation in opposition was engineered by people like Oastler and Bull and widely supported by clergymen, it was because it sprang from a way of looking at things to which they were opposed and which they believed to be anti-Christian. That was the bond between them, not political affiliation.

[1] *The Times* of this period reports many meetings in the West Riding and in Lancashire. Local papers give fuller accounts of the proceedings. In Yorkshire, *The Leeds Intelligencer* was the journal which supported the anti-Poor Law movement at this stage. So did the Radical journals.

16

BULL ANSWERS BACK

A T FIRST, the resistance was unco-ordinated, the spontaneous expressions of indignation and alarm, but a few days after the January meeting, the Short Time delegates met to consider the renewal of the Ten Hours campaign. They decided to turn their organization to the resistance of the New Poor Law instead.[1]

They decided to follow the plan of 1833, when the Factory Commissioners had been greeted with a series of hostile demonstrations. So Power was met with organized protests and petitions. In some places, the Guardians were prevented from appointing a Clerk. In others, where opponents of the Act were in a majority, they prevented an appointment being made. Without a Clerk, the Act could not be worked. Power said that he was concerned to apply the new Registration Act, for the Clerk to the Guardians was to be Registrar. Opponents regarded this as a subterfuge and said so in various terms, none of them unmistakable.

A rally, similar to the York and Wibsey Rallies during the factory campaign, was organized on Whit Tuesday, 1837. It was at Hartshead Moor and was bigger than either of the others. Fielden estimated the numbers at 200,000. In addition to local leaders, Fielden, Stephens, Owen, and Feargus O'Connor were present. Bull took no part in it, although he had helped to call it. Some London speakers wished to make the rally an occasion for advocating universal suffrage and other views held by groups which were to found the Chartist movement, views with which Bull had no sympathy. *The Bradford Observer*[2] belittled the meeting, saying that many of the crowd present—100,000 was the figure given—went for a picnic. It mentioned Bull's refusal

[1] Local papers. The Oastler Collection. *Tory-Radical*, in which is a graphic account of the events at Huddersfield.
[2] *The Times*, 18 May 1837. Local papers.

to be associated with the views the visitors wished to propound and told of the invitation issued by Bell of London, asking people to remain for another meeting to discuss those issues. Fielden pleaded that the meeting should concern itself with the issue for which it had been called.   Most of the speakers did so, but even without the suggested diversions the speeches were lively enough, especially those of Oastler and Stephens.

As the year passed, the controversy grew fiercer. At Huddersfield, Oastler and his supporters prevented the election of a Clerk. Power's every move was anticipated. Guardians in favour of the Act feared to follow their convictions. At Bradford, a Clerk was appointed, but the Guardians were not called together until 30 October. The Anti-Poor Law Committee sent out a crier to inform the townspeople, and a large crowd demanded admittance to the meeting. On being refused, they rendered business impossible. The Board slipped out of the Court House and went to the Sun Inn. Matthew Thompson, who had been an opponent of the Act but had joined the "give-it-a-trial" school, persuaded the Board to return to the Court House and appealed to the crowd to allow the meeting to proceed. It was useless. The meeting was wrecked and Power was mobbed. A fortnight later, feeling was so high that it was deemed unwise to attempt to hold a meeting. Power asked for protection and more troops were made available.[1]

The meeting was held on 20 November and the crowd was again refused admittance. When it attacked the Court House, the Riot Act was read and the soldiers were summoned. Even the Hussars' sabres did not cause the crowd to disperse, and reinforcements were sent from Barnsley. The troops escorting the Guardians to their homes were attacked. It was remarkable that of the many casualties none were fatal. A week later, the Board met again to finish the business, but reinforcements of troops were standing by at Barnsley, Burnley, and Rochdale. No doubt the presence of a large number of troops already in the town kept it quiet, for the Board finished its inaugural meeting unmolested.[2]

Bull was not present at these riots. He believed that the presence of troops would be an incitement and that the swearing-in of special constables would have been better. The importation of police from

---

[1] *The Leeds Intelligencer*, 24 November 1837.

[2] *The Times*, 24 November 1837. For several days, *The Times* reported and commented on the events in Bradford. Local papers.

THE COURT HOUSE, BRADFORD

London had been resented. The fact that some of them were in plain clothes was an added aggravation. The Hussars had arrived at 11 p.m. on the Saturday evening, when the town was full of people. It was in a ferment throughout Sunday, therefore. The *Observer* shared Bull's view of the unwisdom of this. It is true that there were many rumours and that the authorities did not know how much force the crowd might use to prevent the meeting being held. Oastler denied the truth of a rumour that he was to march on Bradford with five thousand men. It is certain that there was no sign of such a force being gathered, and Bull would have dissuaded Oastler from such action.

At the public meetings that followed, Bull and others protested against the imposition of such a law by the muskets and sabres of the military. Speeches and petitions remained as the only means of protest. The battle was lost so far as Bradford was concerned. Resistance continued for some time at Huddersfield, and Fielden, with Bull's help, secured further delay in East Lancashire and at Todmorden. Indeed, in 1838, Fielden closed his mill in order to prevent the Act being applied at Todmorden.[1] Bull continued to lecture, to quote instances of harsh treatment and to declare the Act iniquitous and unconstitutional. He pressed for its repeal, for a real amendment of Poor Law legislation based on "43rd Elizabeth," and for the Ten Hours Bill.

These activities led to trouble with Parliament. The Commissioners, through Chadwick, challenged him about the accuracy of some of his statements. He was called upon to submit the name of a cripple who, he had said, "had been mercifully delivered from a union workhouse in the South, and the name of the friend who had rescued him". He replied that the cripple's mother was in receipt of "the single loaf", and the power of the Commissioners was such "that even if they promised to continue this relief, the law allowed them to break their promise, to rescind all their own orders". He added that he was not young enough to be caught in that trap. He required that the cost of the weekly loaf should be invested in the nearest savings bank in the name of the widow, "or they will get no name from me", he said.

He was asked the name of the young woman in a union workhouse who, he alleged, had been stripped and flogged on her naked back like a soldier. He replied that he was prepared to disclose her name and "to open the way for—not a Poor Law Commissioners' investigation, nor a Board of Guardians' investigation, with closed doors and to the

[1] *The Times*, 10 July 1838.

exclusion of the Press, but", he said, "I am ready to promote a British legal investigation."

> Let them give me legal and appropriate security that the perpetrators of that barbarity shall be prosecuted in the Court of the King's Bench with a view to afford redress to the injured party, and I am ready to give my authority for my statement.

In referring to the Minto case, Bull had said that the oppressors of the poor who had been responsible for driving him so hard should have a verdict of "wilful murder" returned against them. Chadwick asked whom he so designated. He replied, "The Commissioners; they are the individuals, whether under the old act or the new act, who, by a series of hard and oppressive measures towards Minto at length drove him to suicide." He said that Sir John Walsham, the Assistant Commissioner, had ordered the Guardians to form a commission to investigate the case. "The result of the investigation will doubtless be that the Guardians will acquit the Guardians."[1]

He shared the indignation felt by the working-classes at the practice of forcing countrymen to the manufacturing districts to be "bound hand and foot by agreements to certain avaricious masters at reduced wages". Ashworth of Turton, Bolton, often advocated the removal of more labourers from one county to another to "stop turn-outs and to equalize wages". James Kay,[2] Manchester doctor turned civil servant, complained that people were unwilling to uproot, and that this attachment to their own neighbourhood must be broken. He was himself an Assistant Commissioner, facilitating these migrations. Indeed, Kay provides one of the best instances of a good man obsessed with the economic theories of the day. He had himself written of the appalling conditions of forty years earlier, when pauper children were sent to be

---

[1] *The Poor Law Inquisitors and the Reverend G. S. Bull.*

[2] Dr James Kay was Medical Officer of the Ancoats and Ardwick Dispensary which he largely founded; Secretary of the Manchester Board of Health 1832.

"His philanthropic efforts on behalf of the poor, his experience among them, and his grasp of social science, brought him to the notice of the Government as one well-fitted to locally introduce the New Poor Law of 1834. He was Assistant Commissioner, first of Norfolk and Suffolk, then of the Metropolitan district."
                                        —*Dictionary of National Biography.*

He became Secretary of the Privy Council Committee for Education and a pioneer of the national system of education.

On his marriage to Miss Shuttleworth, of Gawthorpe Hall, Burnley, he changed his name to "Kay-Shuttleworth". His son was the first Baron Shuttleworth.

apprenticed to manufacturers. He had told of their working alternately night and day, alternating in their beds as well as in the mills—infant Boxes and Coxes.[1] Yet, in addition to opposing factory legislation, he lent himself to the policy of the Commissioners. This aspect of the administration was resented by countrymen, who hated both the uprooting and the compulsion, and by townsmen, who saw the depression of their wages to the satisfaction of men like Ashworth.

Attacks on the Act were widespread, and Parliament appointed a Committee of each House to consider the working of the Act. The House of Commons Committee was composed mainly of Government supporters, although Wakley, a critic, and Fielden, an opponent, were on it. When Bull was called, he was examined about the riot. He was not present, he said, but he blamed the authorities for it. He said that Bradford, a town of 30,000 people, had been kept in order by five or six policemen; no soldier had previously been needed. In answer to questions, he said that the opposition to the Act was general, and that even some of the magistrates were opposed to it. Thompson, for the sake of peace had said, "Give it a trial", but had denied that he had changed his mind about it. Asked about the ground of his own opposition, Bull replied that the Act was unconstitutional, that it separated husband and wife and, moreover, it was harshly operated. Asked if there had not been great pains taken to excite the people against it before it was introduced, he replied that there had been no need to do so; the resentment was there without being aroused. The Chairman tartly told him that was not the question; had there in fact been efforts to excite the people? Bull replied:

> There have been great pains taken to explain to the people what I conceive to be the real character and tendency of the law; and I have no doubt that those statements and representations have tended to excite them against the law; nor have I any hesitation in saying that I feel it my duty to excite anyone to a legal and constitutional opposition to a law which I conceive to be founded in opposition to the principles of justice and Christianity.

Replying to questions about the Hartshead Moor meeting, he said that, although he had signed the requisition, he had taken no part in it. He had disapproved of attempts to introduce such questions as universal suffrage and annual Parliaments, to which he was opposed—a reply

[1] Quoted in *The Millocrat*, Manchester Reference Library.
See his *The Moral and Physical Condition of the Working Classes employed in the Cotton Manufacture in Manchester* (2nd Edition, 1832).

which surprised some of the members. He told of his own administration of relief. In his district, there was a work test for able-bodied men. There were some three thousand cases, many being immigrants. Some of the men cleaned out the Beck—known as "t'mucky Beck" to many generations of Bradfordians. Payment was made at the rate of a shilling a day.

After being examined about some of the cases that he had quoted, he was told that he was wrong in the matter of Mary Howes of Nottingham. The workhouse official had said that she had been an inmate under the old law. He replied that he did not care under which law she had been an inmate, the treatment she had received should be condemned. In any case, he would not accept the evidence of Poor Law officials; their testimony was given in their own defence and was not given under oath. He had always made what investigations he could to verify the facts in cases he had raised in public, but he lacked facilities for thorough investigations. Pressed, he replied, "If this, that or the other case was untrue in particular detail, there were many that were authentic." "The Commissioners have the advantage of every person who may bring evidence against the system which they are working," he added. When it was suggested that he had believed newspaper statements if they had gone uncontradicted, he said that he had done so if they appeared to be analogous to statements which had been authentic. He pointed out that *The Globe*, which supported the Government, had reported cases of scandalous treatment of paupers.

What was his knowledge of the Minto case? he was asked. Had he read the evidence? Could he justify speaking so strongly without? He insisted that the case was widely reported, and that it was consistent with the attitude of officials towards the poor they should serve.

Bull followed up his evidence by continuing his investigations in the cases he had quoted. He was able to justify himself fully in regard to some of them, but he had to modify what he had said about Jane Adams, alleged to have been stripped and flogged.[1] She had been severely slapped by the mistress and "subjected to arbitrary confinement in a black hole". In his letter to the Chairman of the Committee, he said that the fact that the earlier story was widely believed in the area where the incident occurred was some measure of excuse for his informant. It has been said that he was ready to believe anything if it discredited the Act and the Commissioners, but the newspapers

[1] A worse case came to light later.

were full of cases analagous to those he had quoted. In any case, the Commissioners' directives betrayed their total lack of sympathy with the poor.

A Select Committee of the House of Lords, under Lord Wharncliffe, examined him shortly afterwards. It covered much the same ground. Asked if he and clergymen like him were justified in holding opinions about the Act differing from those held by the Bishops of Chester and London, he replied that no bishop was infallible and that not all bishops shared their view. When asked why magistrates did not intervene if the administration was so harsh, he replied that the Commissioners were so sensitive that the magistrates dare not offend them. Questioned further, he pointed to Chadwick's letter to him, as well as to other instances. Both committees arose from this sensitiveness.[1]

Before the House of Lords Committee sat, he had been criticized in the House in respect of the Jane Adams case. His letter to the Chairman of the Select Committee of the House of Commons had been used to discredit him, and he was referred to in scathing terms. He was not the kind of man to allow them to go unrefuted, and when he was not allowed to present fresh evidence at the Committee's enquiry, he presented a petition to the House of Lords.[2]

He wished to vindicate himself in view of the censure, he said, for it was prejudicial to his character "as a clergyman of the Church of England and as a loyal subject of the Realm". The Poor Law Commission was "derogatory to the Crown and dangerous to the liberty of the subject, as well as opposed in its operation to the principles and institutions of the Christian religion". It was a sacred part of the Constitution that power to exact statutes was vested in the three estates of the Realm, and it was the prerogative of the Sovereign to exercise them. He maintained that it was not competent to the legislature to transfer to any other body the power to make Rules, Orders, and Regulations, having the force of laws. He quoted Locke's dictum that "the legislature is empowered to make laws and not to make legislators", nor is "the executive to govern otherwise than by promulgating laws, not to be varied in particular cases, but to have one law for rich and poor". The Commissioners' powers contravened this principle.

[1] The proceedings were reported in *The Times* during the later weeks of 1838.
[2] *The Times*, 5 July 1838.

Moreover, he argued, "the combination of legislative and executive powers in the same body had been held by high legal authority to be the essence of tyrannical government", and (quoting Blackstone) "where these two are held together, there is an end of public liberty". "Your petitioner therefore views the existence of the Poor Law Commission as dangerous to public liberty," he said. He referred to Brougham, "its most powerful and enthusiastic advocate". He had admitted, Bull said, that "the larger discretionary powers; an arbitrary discretion, ample and unconfined" might "without contradiction be designated as unconstitutional".

The Act appeared "to beget mistrust in the people at large in the ability as well as the fidelity of the legislature", for it appeared to be "an admission of its own incompetency to apply appropriate and constitutional remedies to existing evils, and that in the opinion of your humble petitioner, the tendency of such a course is injurious to the character of Parliament". He believed it to be derogatory to the Royal Prerogative.

He deplored the prison-like conditions, the cropped hair, the uniform, the diet, and the refractory wards. He quoted a case of a young woman, awarded £60 damages when a law case had been brought on her behalf against the official concerned. He would not accept as justification the answer that unlawful practices were perpetrated under the old Act, for "no invasion of the liberties of subjects can be justified any more than it can be shown that twenty bad statutes make a good law or three arbitrary Poor Law Commissioners make a constitutional Board". He did not claim to be proficient in the Law, but he understood that Christianity was part and parcel of English law. Coke had said that it was neither safe nor wise to pass statutes that were utterly void.

Nor could he be expected to tolerate a statute permitting temporary divorce. He had been ordained and empowered to solemnize marriages. His authority was sanctioned by the State, and this aspect of the Act must concern him. He said:

> That those cannot cherish one another who are parted asunder—the man cannot protect his wife who is removed from his sight—the wife cannot comfort or obey her husband who is taken from her embrace, nor can they virtuously bring up their children to lead a godly and a Christian life (a sacred duty which in great measure cannot be delegated to others) when upon pain of destitution their children are taken from them.

Poverty, which is not a crime, was being treated as such by the breaking up of the cottage home and the disposing of the cottagers' goods for the benefit of the parish, inflicting upon such as had a right to be deemed "the best and most meritorious members of society a set of barbarous regulations which have the effect of a penal statute". He had undertaken before the Bishop to care for the poor, and he objected to their relief being given by the torture of their best feelings and the deprivation of their liberties.

He protested against Brougham's description of the poor as "an improvident, lazy and self-gratifying class". They had not been heard in their own defence, he said. There were bad characters in every class. "Your petitioner conceives that if anyone should condemn the whole body of the Aristocracy as an infamous race of Gamblers and Cheats on account of the conduct of individuals which has now and then been brought to light, the censure would have been equally just or unjust." He was indignant at the condition of the poor and ready to agree to any sound plans for restoring "43rd Elizabeth" to practical operation. Industry was the test of that Act, but the underlying principles were different. Arguing as he had often done, and as Oastler had argued with Thornhill and Wellington, he said that the feelings of the industrious classes were daily "being more and more alienated from their natural allies, the Aristocracy". Attempts were being made to estrange the masses from constitutional monarchy; the rights of the poor were being invaded, and the golden links of society were snapping in consequence.

He called attention, on oath, to specific instances of harsh treatment. A man at Deptford had been refused permission to see his dying wife; a woman at Bridlington had died of starvation. A woman at Woburn had taken her life, and the Foreman of the Coroner's Jury had said that her insanity had been brought on by the Guardians. A young woman of unsound mind had been beaten—the officials said "the beating had done her good"—but by the exertions of Fendall, the Rector of Great Bucknall, the master had been fined for assault.

He said that he had no wish to be concerned about matters not concerned with his professional duty, nor had he concerned himself with public questions that did not interfere with his clerical and pastoral province. For all his deference, however, he was not entirely on the defensive. He said that he might be told "that the Poor ought to be thrown on their own resources". Where were those ample resources?

he asked. He quoted Brougham's speech, in which he had said that the poor were to blame for "forsaking every habit of frugality, taking no care to provide against the ordinary calamities of life or the inevitable infirmities of old age". This, he said, was:

> an argument that cut two ways, and ought never to be used by men of lucrative professions who can earn in one day more than the average yearly income of the Clergy, but "who have not taken care to provide against the ordinary calamities of life or the inevitable infirmities of old age", or else have eagerly grasped at a retiring pension from the public purse under a morbid fear that "their own resources" will not avail, without having some out-relief from the public coffers to keep them from the irksome condition of the pauper.

The petition was more than a retort to the criticisms of himself; it was a statement of some of the principles which in theory ordered British government and underlay the Constitution. Bull had no academic education, but there is much evidence that he read widely and tried to master the subjects he spoke or wrote about. Certainly, the references made in this document to recognized social philosophers and even to legal authorities shows that he had given some study to his subject. It is true that many people were able to talk with knowledge about the ancient principles governing poor relief; "43rd Elizabeth" was referred to by most critics of the new Act with a familiarity similar to a later generation's familiarity with the Highway Code. Bull seems to have been familiar with some of the principles on which social philosophers of our own day have had to lay much stress in the face of totalitarian threats, for they are the principles which must be adhered to if dictatorship is to be avoided.

His devotion to the Constitution was genuine. It was not a cloak covering his "rabble-rousing", as his enemies described his public activities and his leadership of causes concerned with the welfare of the poor and the politically powerless. When, in a few months time, the failure of the anti-Poor Law movement led to the strengthening of the Chartist movement, Bull did not follow his friends who joined it. He adhered to his belief that it was possible to right wrongs in a constitutional manner. The genuineness of his Toryism was well enough known in his own locality for him to find it necessary to stud his parsonage door. He was not against electoral reform, but he had no good reason to believe that at that stage of the nation's life universal suffrage was necessarily in the interests of the working folk themselves.

In spite of the apparent failure of the anti-Poor Law movement, it gave rise to many modifications in the administration of the Act, although it was not until 1847 that a series of scandals led to a Parliamentary enquiry. Its findings justified the charges made by those who had attacked the administrators, and the Commissioners were dismissed. Many of its evils have gone long since, though, alas, delegated legislation has become a feature of the nation's life.

17

WHAT HAVE THE PARSONS TO DO WITH IT?

WHEN BULL attended the Bradford meeting at Christmas 1831, he overheard the question, "What have the parsons to do with it?" Social historians, especially anti-clerical social historians, leave the impression that they had nothing to do with it. Even Church historians have overlooked the period before Ashley began his work, and it is generally assumed that such support as the Church gave to factory reformers was in retaliation to anti-Church legislation promoted or threatened by Dissenters. Here and there, Bull is mentioned as the exception whose work serves to show up the failure of the rest of the clergy. It is true, of course, that the movement received nothing like a hundred per cent support from the clergy. But this lack of unanimity ought not to lead to the conclusion that the Church was opposed to factory reform, as secularist speakers and writers so often affirm. No person who has sought to present the Christian Faith to a haphazardly collected or hostile audience—in the open-air, for instance—has not been faced with that gibe at question-time. That the Church was opposed to factory reform can flatly be denied. It is possible to go further and say that the movement owed much of its impetus to the Church. Its leaders were Churchmen and they were well supported by the clergymen in most textile areas.

In these days, when laymen are bearing a greater share in ordering the Church's affairs, it is not necessary to point out that the work of her laymen in the life of the community is part of the Church's witness. The deepening sense of the Church's responsibility and corporate sense, expressed in the saying that "The Church must be the Church", adds to the force of this. The work of Oastler and Wood arose from their hold on the Christian Faith gained as Churchmen. They were outstanding examples of which there were many, as a complete and documented history of the movement would show.[1] There were others, such as Fielden, whose religious allegiance belonged to some other Christian body, but it remains true that Church laymen played a considerable part in this campaign. The gibe that the Church is "the Tory party at prayer" was less a gibe when Tories held the views of some of these men.

The question that Bull overheard was based upon the belief that the conditions of factory labour had nothing to do with parsons. Throughout his active association with the movement, Bull was constantly dealing with the charge that he, and others like him, were interfering in matters outside their province. Many of his speeches contain some reference to this charge. Indeed, it is ironical how often contemporaries complained of Bull and his clerical colleagues for their part in the campaign in view of the assiduous propagation by later writers of the idea that they were opposed to it.

Mr Maurice Reckitt has said that in the Middle Ages, if anyone had said that the Church had nothing to do with the social order and its problems, he would have been regarded as either a heretic or a lunatic. The assumption that the Church, particularly her ministers, have no business to be concerned with social and political problems became common gradually. The successors of Richard Hooker who were influenced by his social teaching were still following him at the time of the Revolution of 1689.[2] They sought to relate the Church's traditional social teaching to the changed conditions of that day. Richard Baxter, a Puritan, taught on similar lines. Certainly, neither school of thought would have agreed to the later belief that the Church's work was confined to "churchy" affairs and moral problems, with a limitation to the meaning of both words. It is a belief that owes little to the Church's teaching. It arose partly from the pietism of some groups within the Church, but more to the default of some influential sections of the Church. But she was never left without witnesses to her concern for the social order and for social righteousness. It is true that the silencing of Convocation and the frequent failure of the bishops to say or do anything arresting or prophetic suggest no very effective witness. Actually, even of this there was more to be said than has been said, as will be shown. But in any case, the Church's

---

[1] Dr J. T. Ward's forthcoming thesis will provide this.

[2] *The National Church and the Social Order*. A report by the Social and Industrial Council, published by the Church Information Board.

13

witness is often made by unofficial groups, by courageous men and women, or by isolated parish clergymen. If this is true now, it was much more so a hundred years ago.

The readiness of many of the clergy in the factory areas to join in the campaign was due to the fact that the Christian conception of social duties and corporate responsibilities had not died. Then, as now, criticism came from vested interests and from people who differed from them in their views. Bull, like many after him, found that some of the people whom he tried to serve attacked him, but this was due to misrepresentation by his opponents and to misunderstanding of his position. Because he was the outstanding clerical supporter of Oastler and the movement, he was most often attacked, as well as most bitterly. In replying to Gillmor, he pointed this out, and in disclaiming any right to this distinction he gives some evidence of the extent of clerical support in the West Riding.[1]

From the first, Oastler found clergymen interested. He told of one who sought to verify his charges by going round a factory and was refused permission to do so.[2] Most of the clergymen and some of the dissenting ministers in the Huddersfield district supported him in varying degrees. At the first public meeting there, one of the speakers was Richard Oglesby,[3] an Anglican priest. Later, Wyndham Maddock, who went to Woodhouse, and J. C. Frank, Vicar of Huddersfield, spoke at meetings and gave support to the movement. At the second meeting, not only was Bull an unexpected speaker, but J. C. Boddington, Curate of Horton, was one of the main speakers. He took an active part in the campaign, although, apart from the York Rally, there is not much record of his activity away from Horton and Bradford. No doubt Wood first interested him, but that he genuinely shared the outlook of Wood and the other leaders is to be gleaned from letters he wrote to Oastler some years later. One of them is particularly relevant. He said:

> The population of my village is upwards of 18,000 souls and chiefly of the
> working classes. I have seen many poor, miserable, and unhappy creatures,

---

[1] See above, Chap. 14, p. 266.   [2] *Tory-Radical*, p. 148. Oastler Collection.
[3] Oglesby must have been at Woodhouse in a temporary capacity. One contemporary account described him as "Curate of Christ Church"; another describes him as a Dissenting Minister. The archives at the Borthwick Institute, York, show that he was Curate of Attercliffe, from 1826, when he was ordained, and that he went to Skipton in 1835.

starving in the midst of plenty and almost dying from the lack of the common necessaries of life. My house has literally been besieged by them—they naturally look to the clergyman as their common friend and benefactor, and so they ought, but, alas! what can some of us do? My heart is sometimes overwhelmed at the misery and wretchedness which surrounds me and my inability to remove it and which can only be partially relieved. . . .

I am a Tory of the old school. I despise the term "Conservative". It is only a dilution of a pure principle. A Tory must be a Conservative. . . . He would destroy all oppression, cruelty, tyranny, and Malthusianism and have a sound and Christian legislation based upon that old-fashioned book, the Bible.[1]

Bull became the spearhead of Church support. At Keighley, he had the backing of the Rector. At Dewsbury, Reyroux, the Curate, was a speaker at the mass meeting. Indeed, the clergymen there consistently supported the reformers. At the beginning of 1833, at the time that Bull was seeking a successor to Ashley, Buckworth lent his schoolroom and gave the meeting his backing.

Dr Fawcett, the Vicar of Leeds, not only gave the movement much encouragement, bringing all the influence of his position to bear, he gave it active support. He was at York, and as the active Chairman of the Leeds Committee gave a lead to the clergy and middle class people of Leeds. In view of the powerful opposition and the fact that there were already more than enough divisions in the religious life of Leeds, Fawcett's constant support and unremitting work for the cause of factory reform called for no small measure of courage. If he was not the great figure that Hook, his successor, was, he lacked neither courage nor a sense of social justice. Hook himself gave his complete support, in spite of doubts he seems to have had about the accuracy of some of the evidence given before the Sadler Committee. He did not go to Leeds until 1837, so that he was associated with the movement during its middle period. The Leeds clergy, under their Vicars' leadership, gave steady support.

Bradford parsons were probably the most active of any. Newspaper reports tell of many meetings in their schoolrooms, addressed by them. A report, typical of many others, tells of a meeting at Idle, now a part of the city, but then a nearby village. Referring to Edward Hall, the incumbent, it says:

Having readily granted the use of the Old Chapel and attended personally to sanction the good cause, the Reverend Gentleman in most appropriate

[1] *The Fleet Papers*, Vol. II.

addresses, both before and at the close of the meeting, declared his real concern at the immense barrier which the factory system imposes between the Factory Child and its Teacher, its Minister, its Sabbath, and its God. The company who were present will not undervalue, nor can forget, the emphatic remarks of this clergyman as the Ministers of Christ should do, and that most freely, heartily and fearlessly, to plead the cause of the poor. He distinctly declared that it is monstrous to entertain for one moment any extension of actual labour beyond the Ten Hours after the decisive Medical Testimony on that point.[1]

David Jenkins, Incumbent of Pudsey, was chairman at a similar meeting during the same phase of the campaign. He said that no ministerial duty could be more sacred than the one he consented to perform—the promotion of the Ten Hours Bill to protect the children of the poor. The evils of the factory system had grieved his heart for many years, he said. It had interrupted his ministry. These men were typical. William Morgan, of Christ Church, Bradford, critical of Oastler in some matters, supported the movement. He was a close friend of Patrick Brontë, and both of them were close associates of Bull in many activities. Morgan spent nearly forty years in Bradford and had been there twenty of them when the factory movement began. (His wedding, some years earlier had been something of an occasion. He married Jane, the daughter of John Fennell, at that time Head of the Wesleyan Academy at Apperley Bridge, later ordained to a curacy at Bradford Parish Church. Brontë was the officiating clergyman. He married Maria Branwell, Jane's cousin, at the same ceremony, Morgan officiating.[2] Brontë himself played a greater part in the events of those days than most writers about the Brontës suggest.) Christ Church was at the top of Darley Street in those days, and the schools were in Westgate. Being central, they were much used by various groups in the town. Bull spoke there on many issues.

Three successive Vicars of Bradford figure in the records of the movement. When Henry Heap presided over a meeting on 5 July 1833, a reporter said that he had "often stood by the cause when others forsook it and fled although professing to be its friend".[3] Dr William Scoresby, whose policy in ecclesiastical matters was to be the cause of

[1] *The British Labourer's Protector and Factory Child's Friend*, 1 February 1833.
[2] E. C. Gaskell, *The Life of Charlotte Brontë*, p. 34. Cudworth and other local historians record the incident. Morgan baptized the Brontë girls.
[3] *White Slavery*, Vol. V. See also Chap. 12 above.

Bull's departure from Bradford, was a supporter of the movement. The chief ground of his support was the bad moral effect of protracted factory work amongst young females. Burnett's work came at a later stage of the campaign.

Bull's reply to Gillmor tells of the support given by the West Riding clergy to the York rally. Many of them were present. John Graham, Vicar of Holy Trinity, Micklegate, for many years, and Benjamin Maddock, Vicar of Tadcaster, are two who deserve mention. Maddock was Perpetual Curate of Holy Trinity, Huddersfield, from 1826 to 1830. There can be little doubt that his interest began then. In the West Riding, the most tardy support came from Halifax. Some of the parsons there were sympathetic, but did not feel that they ought to intervene. Some of them did. Some signed petitions. Others stood aloof. Possibly the lead given by Musgrave had much to do with this. Gillmor's attack stands out as an isolated instance of clerical opposition. It took Bull by surprise. Some years later, when Gillmor figured in the local Press in another connection, he was described as a Puseyite, but this is unlikely to be the cause of his bitter attack on Bull. Other Tractarians worked with Bull, notably Hook, and Sharp[1] of Horbury. Bull's dislike of Tractarians grew later, when the ritual controversies developed. Even then, he paid tribute to their service to the Church in much of their teaching. Gillmor had worked at Earlsheaton, in the Parish of Dewsbury, under Buckworth, a supporter of the movement, and at Halifax under Musgrave, who was not. He was appointed to Illingworth by the latter. Gillmor's attitude to the movement was well known, for when he later chided a Dissenter about dissenting opposition to the Bill, he was asked why he should take exception to opposition to a Bill of which he had so poor an opinion.

When George Crabtree made his journey through Cragg Vale, in the Parish of Halifax, he found that he got a mixed reception. Custance, the Curate of Ripponden, was willing to sign a petition, but not to organize one. William Bull, George's brother, who was Vicar of Sowerby, thought the less the clergy had to do with the matter the better. Rogers, a dissenting minister in another village was quite

---

[1] It is important to remember that the sharp differences between Tractarians and Evangelicals developed later than this period. The Evangelicals were sound in their churchmanship. The activities of Bull and his friends in other fields, not dealt with here, show how they adhered to the Church's teaching. Their social teaching grew out of it.

bellicose. The Bill was a foolish measure, he said, and the evidence in the Sadler Report exaggerated. He was quite satisfied that factory work was pleasant and easy to those engaged in it. He thought that the manners and morals of factory workers surpassed those of agricultural workers, taking all in all. The masters were good and humane men; one of them had built the chapel. Devine, the curate in another village, was glad to see him and his companion, and was whole-heartedly with them. In spite of the dominance of the hill-side villagers by the local millowner—the innkeeper at one village dare not put Crabtree up for the night—some of the parsons openly declared their sympathy and incurred the enmity of the millowners. If some sympathizers refused to be active in the cause, they can hardly be blamed in the circumstances. The local millowner was usually opposed to the Church, the people depended upon him for their livelihood, and it could not be easy to be active even if sympathetic. There were some who felt bound to take the risk. Crowther, one of the Cragg Vale curates, was well respected by the operatives and hated by the mill-owners in equal measure. At the Hebden Bridge meeting that Bull addressed, one of the operatives told of Crowther's being called "a lying priest" because he had told of factory conditions. He had "in-treated with tears" for the factory children, said the speaker. He added, "They laughed at him".[1]

If the appeals of the reformers to "the clergy and ministers" and to "ministers of the Gospel" give the impression that support from them was poor, two things must be borne in mind. The first is that as the campaign proceeded, and opposition became more unscrupulous, the moral and religious aspects were to the fore increasingly. Clerical support came to be valued because these were the aspects of the problem on which the parson and the minister could speak with authority. Men like Bull grew critical of their brethren who stood out-side. Bull's attitude to them was very different at Manchester in 1833 from that he had adopted in January 1832, at the Keighley meeting. The reformers sought a hundred per cent support from ministers.

The second point to be remembered is that many of the remarks addressed to "the ministers of the Gospel" were intended for dissent-ing ministers. There were more of them in manufacturing areas than there were Church parsons and only a small minority of them were supporters of the movement. Some of the most downright letters

[1] *White Slavery*, Vol. V.

written in criticism of the reformers were from dissenting ministers. From a letter signed "Verax" in October 1830,[1] in reply to Oastler's first letter, throughout the campaign, this continued to be the case. Dissenters shared the Liberal outlook. Some, like Hamilton, retained their political affiliations while continuing to support the Ten Hours men, but there were few of them.

Oastler was brought up as a Wesleyan, becoming an Anglican some time after going to Fixby. He was disappointed by the lack of support that Dissenters gave to him. Even the Wesleyans disappointed him. They did not regard themselves as Dissenters at that time, and did not campaign against the Church as did some of the other dissenting bodies. Indeed, when Stephens joined in the demand for disestablishment of the Church, he was suspended from his ministry in the Wesleyan Church for doing so.[2] The drift of Methodism towards political Liberalism had begun, however. The intervention of a leading Methodist in support of Macaulay and attacking Sadler—himself a Methodist —had caused a stir in Leeds and a division amongst the Methodists. Professor Driver discusses this, pointing out the affinity between the prominent Methodist millowners and the new Liberalism. He quotes with approval E. E. Kellett, who said:

> The fact is, that within the small realm of Methodism there were, as in the larger realm of England, Disraeli's "Two Nations", and there was between them the same misunderstanding as in the wider world.[3]

The leading Methodists gravitated towards Liberalism, especially, at first, the leading laymen. Poorer Methodists joined the Radical parties. Many of the factory reformers' meetings were held in Primitive Methodist chapels and schoolrooms, for this was the dissenting body giving most consistent support. It was the poor man's Methodism. Apart from them, the relations between Oastler and Methodism grew steadily worse. At Oldham, when he was refused the use of the school

---

[1] *The Leeds Mercury*, 23 October 1830.

[2] The confusion amongst Methodists is illustrated by two separate items in *The Leeds Intelligencer* of 26 July 1834. One reports a conference of Welsh Methodists deploring the agitation for the "severing of the National Church from the State"; the other tells of Earl Fitzwilliam's reply to a petition of Wesleyan Methodists calling for it. He expressed astonishment that Wesley's "nominal followers" should class themselves amongst the Dissenters.

[3] *Tory-Radical*, p. 110.

after the meeting had been advertised to take place there, he spoke with grief of the treatment accorded to him, especially in view of his own family's services to Methodism. He protested that he was trying to persuade preachers to say that the love of money is the root of all evil, as he himself was doing, but that he was beng discarded by them for it. He confessed that he was a Tory—a stiff Church and King man— but that he found it a sad circumstance to be shut out by this Church, to be banned their places of worship, and to have the contempt of the Wesleyans, whom he respected. The rift widened during the weeks that followed, but at that time it was possible for him to say that the ministers were privately with him, for one Methodist minister had recently sent £11 to the Ten Hours Committee for expenses.[1] That the gift was sent in this way suggests that Methodist lay people were against the reformers. The social witness of the Church has often suffered as a result of the attitude of lay people, and it seems that the drift of Methodism towards Liberalism was proceeding.

G. J. Holyoake, quoting Francis Place, when writing of the adherence of Stephens to the movement, said: "After these Methodists had made the movement into a great cause, some of the nobler sort of Church-men came into it—as the Rev. G. S. Bull and the Earl of Shaftesbury."[2] One of the Methodists referred to was Oastler, who had become a Churchman ten years before he began his agitation. Stephens did not join it until 1836, five years after Bull had become one of its leaders. Sadler, the other Methodist referred to, retained his membership of the Church. Place and Holyoake were aggressively anti-clerical and rarely referred to the work of Churchmen fairly. Place was far re-moved from the scene of the agitation and was largely ignorant of it, except at second hand. Later writers have formed their impressions on such comments, however.

In most of the textile areas, especially in Yorkshire, the local parson was usually in sympathy with the reformers. Perhaps in Lancashire the support of clergymen and ministers was less complete. The Lancashire parsons were concerned that existing laws should be enforced, and it is possible that they were less active in the Ten Hours campaign than were their Yorkshire colleagues. This led to one of Bull's most challenging speeches being made. Its partial reporting by later writers has helped

[1] See the report of the Oldham meeting, 14 March 1835. Oastler Collection and Lancashire papers.

[2] G. J. Holyoake, *The Life of J. R. Stephens*, p. 73.

to perpetuate the legend of the Church's indifference—soon exaggerated to be represented as opposition.

When Bull addressed the Manchester "clergy and ministers" in 1833, after a few telling but general remarks about the factory system, he went on:

> But leaving the senator, the capitalist, and the monster for others to deal with, I shall direct my earnest and respectful appeal to those who like myself profess to be Ministers of that Divine Redeemer who went about doing good, and to whom the speaking countenance and the imploring eye of misery were never lifted in vain. My object in selecting for observation the conduct of the Manchester ministers respecting the Ten Hours Bill is not to exalt myself in comparison. Sincerely do I assure you that I am, or have been, more deserving in the same condemnation. Hard work, loss of rest, and comfort since have expiated only a small part of my guilt. I want to learn how it is that in this dense population among whom perhaps nearly 70 ministers reside, only two have appeared in public as advocates of this humane and righteous cause.[1]
>
> It cannot be that like Moses, they are slow of speech, for I have myself heard, seen, or read, the fervid eloquence of your Stowells, your Newtons and your McAlls at Bible, Missionary, Tract, and Anti-Slavery meetings, to which I wish God Speed.[2]

Now, of course, two out of seventy is a poor proportion, but it is important to remember that Bull lumped together ministers of dissenting bodies and Church clergymen. While he was a stout supporter of the establishment and adhered to the distinctive teaching of the Church, he deplored division between the Church and Dissent on this issue. The purpose of the reformers seemed to him to be so clearly a part of Christian social work that there was no room for division amongst Christians about it. The greater number of ministers in the area were Dissenters, and Manchester was the home of the economic doctrines to which the reformers were opposed on social or religious grounds. *The Manchester Guardian* was exerting its influence against the reformers. Moreover, while many local clergymen and some of the ministers were concerned about factory conditions, they were not converted to the Yorkshire view that the immediate aim must be "Ten Hours and a Time Book". The volume of clerical support in Lancashire grew, but Bull's remarks must not be taken to mean that

[1] Oastler Collection.
[2] Quoted in part, J. L. and B. Hammond, *The Bleak Age*, p. 201.

the Manchester parsons were indifferent at that time. To him, the Ten Hours Bill represented the minimum concession that reformers could make. Many Lancashire reformers wished to consolidate what they had won: others doubted the effectiveness of legislation. The agitation leading to the elder Peel's Act of 1819 had strong support from Lancashire clergymen[1]—a fact which further disproves the Hammond's assertion.

Still less can it be argued that what Bull said of Manchester clergymen can be taken as evidence of the attitude of clerics elsewhere. Support came from all parts of the country. The signatories of the petition calling for the Newcastle meeting included Armstrong of Wallsend, and Russell of Bishopsgate supported the cause in London. There was influential ecclesiastical backing. The Hammonds isolate from its context one sentence in Bull's speech. They use his reference to the apparent indifference of Manchester clergymen and ministers and his plea to the most notable of them in order to justify their statement that "the Churches were cold to this cause in the thirties" and that the Church later gave support to it because Dissenters had backed the Repeal movement. They ignore what he went on to say:

> It cannot be for want of example. The clergy of the Church of England might be edified by the noble and virtuous example of the venerable Archbishops of Canterbury and York, who are, and have been from the first, hearty friends of this cause, and the former of whom told me that I was in my duty as a clergyman to stand in the gap for the poor factory child. The Wesleyans have the edifying pattern of William Dawson, that plain honest Christian, and surely Dissenters might safely copy Hamilton of Leeds, and John Wilks, of London, who are both our friends.

Howley's speech in support of the Rochdale petition was sincere and telling.[2] Harcourt, Archbishop of York, wrote to the Leeds Committee pledging his support in 1832. In the same year, Ryder, Bishop of Lichfield and Coventry, in his diocesan charge, commended both the Truck Act and the Factory Bill. The latter, he said was

> now committed to a new legislature. Of the factory problem, he wished the manufactory might prove, instead of a hotbed of moral mischief, a seminary of all that is useful and laudable.

---

[1] This is borne out by Professor R. G. Cowherd in his pamphlet *The Humanitarians and the Ten Hour Movement in England* (Baker Library, Boston, Mass.) "On 6 April 1818, Peel presented a petition signed by 1,731 persons including twenty clergymen and thirty physicians and surgeons," p. 4.

[2] See above, page 55.

He added:

> The ever memorable instance of the Scottish manufactory in the vale of
> Dale—where in twelve years, out of three thousand children successively
> employed, only twelve died and not one was brought before the magistrates
> for any serious offence—should satisfy us that such a consummation is not
> a mere dream of benevolent enthusiasm.[1]

Here, the bishop was not only giving his backing to two important
pieces of legislation; he was also recognizing the worth of a social
and industrial experiment carried out by a man whose views he most
certainly disliked intensely. It is on partial statements such as the
Hammonds here set down that we owe the commonly held belief that
the Church has been against social betterment. Many Churchmen wish
that the Church's social witness had been better and that more of her
members had maintained her social tradition. Bull deplored the lack
of a hundred per cent support, but there is abundant evidence that
Church clergymen, in the main, were good supporters in most of the
textile areas, particularly in the West Riding.

Not long after this phase of the campaign, when Bull had left
Bradford, Hook took a deputation to see Longley, the first Bishop of
Ripon. He expressed his sympathy with the movement and promised
to give it his support. Years later, when he was Archbishop of Canterbury, he recalled it. Burnett, the Vicar of Bradford, had written to
ask him to contribute to a testimonial fund for Matthew Balme, and
Longley's reply—and tangible enclosure—showed that he had not lost
interest.[2]

3 June 1863

My dear Dr. Burnett,

I look back with deep interest to the successful struggle which took place
when I presided over the Church in the Diocese of Ripon for securing to the
working men in the manufacturing districts the great boon of the Ten Hours
Bill.

No one could rejoice more cordially than myself in the success of these
efforts, and by none would the loss of those efforts be the more regretted.

I perfectly well remember the name and I feel sure I could recognize the
presence of Mr Balme were I to see him again. I know how indefatigable he

---

[1] Derby, August 1833.

[2] Balme Collection, Bradford Reference Library. This collection contains a
letter from Longley to Hook concerning the deputation. There is also a letter
from Hook accompanying a subscription of a guinea.

was in his exertions on behalf of the working men of Yorkshire in that severe contest for their benefit, and I am sure he deserves an acknowledgment of these persevering services at the hands of those who either profited by his services or approved of them. I beg to send five pounds towards the memorial in his favour, as a token of my unabated interest in the welfare of the operatives in my first diocese.

Believe me, my dear Dr Burnett,

C. T. Cantuar.

The Hammonds say that the support of the Church had no warmth until the forties, and mention "the Vicars of Leeds, Bradford, Wakefield, Huddersfield, Dewsbury, and of many smaller towns", implying that their support was not given until then. It is true that Lancashire clerical support was more marked in the forties, but it was not lacking earlier. Canon Wray of Manchester—then in the Chester diocese— and Irvine, Vicar of Leigh, were associated with the movement before 1840. The support grew, however, and *The Burnley Bee*, as the Hammonds say, complained of the leading part taken by the Church in the agitation.[1]

The Hammonds are justified in saying that those parts of the textile areas less active in the cause at first grew more so during the forties. During the agitation in 1846, when *The Burnley Bee* deplored the clerical activity in support of the Bill, even Halifax clergymen were active enough to arouse comment. A manufacturer, writing in answer to Akroyd—still a bitter opponent of factory legislation for the betterment of the workers' lot—was able to say that the operatives had gained the support of the clergy, the magistrates, the medical men— "indeed", he added, "I may say of the whole community except that small party amongst whom I am sorry to see Mr Akroyd."[2] The newspapers of this period show that there was almost a hundred per cent clerical support for the factory reformers, Gillmor being the outstanding instance of opposition. Even he commented on the strength of dissenting opposition, earning for himself a well-merited rebuke.

From the outset, the opposition to the New Poor Law was led by clergymen. *The Times* reports, from 1835 onwards, make this clear. Long before the Act was applied to the North, clergymen of eastern and southern England were protesting against its operation in their parishes. Much of Bull's early information came from them. Most

---

[1] *The Bleak Age*, p. 201.   [2] *The Ten Hours Advocate*, 26 September 1846.

of them had little contact with factory reformers, but their social outlook was the same.

Bull left Bradford in 1840. He had built Saint James's Church, at the Bradford end of the township of Bowling. Wood had paid for it and appointed Bull as first incumbent. A dispute arose between Wood and Scoresby about surplice fees. It was part of a dispute that Scoresby had with one or two benefactors who built or proposed to build churches in the ancient parish. Wood, therefore, closed the church, and Bull went to Birmingham as Vicar of Saint Matthew's, Duddesdon. At his farewells, the local clergy took opportunity of demonstrating their solidarity, for they gave him a send-off at which their regard for him was movingly expressed. His brother, William, had by that time moved from his position of cautious neutrality and spoke of George's great work. Patrick Brontë was another member of the group which testified to the worth of his leadership in more than one cause, but chiefly in the two so closely touching the lives of the poor.

What had been begun continued, but it is only by ignoring the early days of the factory movement that it can be said that the Church supported factory reformation in retaliation for the Repeal agitation. On the contrary, Ferrand declared on one occasion that "the enemies of the Church" and the supporters of Repeal had made a compact that the latter would press the attack on the Church in return for the repeal of the Corn Laws.[1]

The fact is that there were many influences at work, but one of them was certainly the dislike of many Churchmen for the new way of life and the growth of "the money power". The growth of an alien culture and the transfer of power from men with a tradition for exercising responsibility to men whose social beliefs imparted to them no sense of social responsibility seemed to many Churchmen to be an undermining of the Christian basis of society.

Bull occasionally dealt with the principles which seemed to him to justify his activity, quite apart from the obvious practical reasons. At the Manchester meeting, in the speech already quoted, he did so. He quoted the Bible with telling effect. One neat illustration that could only have been used by one who knew his Bible well is worth quoting:

The ministers of religion know that when Jacob returned to the land of his fathers, when he was urged by his appeased brother to hasten his company,

[1] Manchester Reference Library. *Political Tracts* (P3752).

he said: "Let my lord, I pray thee, pass over before his servants, and I will lead on softly, according as the cattle that goeth on before me and the children be able to endure. . . ."

But they know that the possessors of wealth, too often, unlike the patriarch, disregard what the children can endure and only calculate what the spindle can produce.

He quoted the Bible in condemnation of usury, of "a land of unparalleled plenty, whose merchants are princes and dwell in palaces ceiled with cedar and painted with vermilion".

He deplored the fact that:

This land, the queen of nations and the perfection of beauty, has now in the nineteenth century of the Christian era to legislate "between too much work and too little to eat", to quote Gisburne, the coal owner. The ministers know that the political economists of Egypt conspired to deal wisely and à la Malthus with the superabundant and redundant Israelites by throwing the babies into the Nile and working the adults to death. Jehovah himself demanded satisfaction for their wrongs and taught Egypt's despot at length to set the captive free. . . .

The Lord of Glory Himself made it a chief part of his work while dwelling among us in the flesh to unmask the hypocritical Pharisee. It is better for the rich to give the hireling his due than adorn fifty subscription lists with large sums of money wrung from the sinews of tender infancy worn down with unwholesome toil. The number of institutions for the relief of the indigent clearly proves the existence of a vicious system. I hold the view the best charity of all is to put the labourer in a condition to help himself and to excite him to honest industry by due reward.

Here is a view of social justice based on Christian teaching about the nature of Man and his needs. Charity and social services do nothing to heal a sick society. They provide ambulance work. Such a view is not "reactionary". It is held by many people who have pressed for better social services because they were necessary. No doubt they always will be. But we should regret the need. Bull and those who thought like him—and they were many—probably did not foresee the development of the Welfare State, but they saw its beginnings in works of charity which were done to help the victims of an unjust social system. The campaign for factory legislation and the opposition to the New Poor Law was not the work of men who accepted the view that poverty and oppression were in the nature of things and that all that one could do was to accept them and minister to their victims.

The leaders of both movements—who were the same people in the textile areas—were prompted by their sense of social justice much more than by pity for the poor, although their compassion gave added force to their appeal.

If George Stringer Bull is the central figure of this book, this is because his view was representative of the large body of clergymen and Church laymen who supported him and the still larger body who resisted the New Poor Law. One or two writers refer to him as an exception contrasted with whom other Churchmen show up badly. In spite of his criticism of his colleagues who were inactive in the cause, Bull would not agree that this was true.

His work in Birmingham gave him fewer opportunities for sharing in this work, but the local papers in 1846/7 and the *Ten Hours Advocate* show that he kept in touch with the movement. After the passing of the Ten Hours Bill in 1847, his long and courageous association led to his being one of the most highly commended of all the people who had helped to bring success, but many others were commended besides him.[1]

Bull was active in other fields throughout his ministry, but this book is concerned with his contribution to the Church's witness during one phase of the Industrial Revolution. He did notable work in Birmingham as Vicar of Saint Matthew's and as Rector of Saint Thomas's, Holloway Head. He was Rector of that important parish from 1847 to 1864. He was a tired man when he left there to go to Almeley in Herefordshire, where he died on 22 August in the following year.

[1] See Appendix B.

APPENDIX A

PROTEST

OF THE REV. G. S. BULL

Addressed to the Commissioners for Factory Enquiry.

GENTLEMEN,—Having been summoned to give Evidence before the Select Committee on the Factories' Bill, I esteem it my duty upon your arrival in the Neighbourhood where I reside, to present to you, in respectful terms, my Reasons for disapproving the Commission, which you have been induced to accept.

To the Royal Authority, I bow with due reverence, and to that of Parliament, when constitutionally exercised, I would render cheerful obedience. But at the same time I would never resign or fail to exercise the privilege afforded me by the Constitution of my country, to disabuse my Soverign when I believe him to be imposed upon, or to petition against what I considered an oppressive act of the Legislature.

Believing as I do in my conscience, that the course adopted by the King's responsible Advisers in the matter of this Commission, is of the character above described, I have discharged my duty in uniting with others to Address his Majesty and to Petition Parliament against the same.

1. *I protest against this Commission as one of the Witnesses before the Select Committee.*

The course thus adopted by the avowed Enemies of the Ten Hour Bill, places my character, and that of my fellow witnesses, in jeopardy. Our veracity may be impeached *in the dark*—but we can demand no clue by which to detect the interested and specious slanderer, over whom the constitution of your Commission most injuriously spreads the thick veil of secrecy. Our Evidence before the Select Committee was given in the presence of Enemies who cross examined us in the severest manner, and it is all printed, all published, all open to the closest scrutiny, and if we have dealt falsely, or set down aught in malice, we are justly liable to detection. Whereas, by the Constitution of your Commission, the greatest glory of British Judicial Administration is set aside in favour of the Secrecy of a Spanish Inquisition. I assert, that to establish such a principle is virtually to destroy every constitutional security for honesty in Witnesses, and for the protection of character. It operates as a Bonus to malice, slander, imposition, and misrepresentation.

2. *I protest as a Christian Man, and as a Minister of the Church of England.*

The God whom I desire to serve is "no respecter of persons," and has told you as well as me by the mouth of Solomon, "*It is not good to have respect of persons in judgment.*" Now it was palpably "respect of persons," of Rich Capitalists and their influence in Parliament which induced the ministry to sue out a Royal Commission, sanctioned by an insignificant majority of one or two in the House of Commons, to adopt a method for the trial of the cause of the rich, diametrically opposite in Constitution and character to that, which they—yes the self same parties adopted for the trial of the cause of the Poor. *I Protest as a Christian Man*;—

Because that Divine Redeemer and Lawgiver, who rebuked even his own disciples, when they would have kept the children from him—who pronounced twelve hours occupation to be a day's work for men—would never have suffered any Rich Capitalist of that day to have asserted his *right* because he was rich, to work children longer than their Parents, depriving them of health, moral improvement and youthful recreation. No, Sirs, had such a right been asserted by the chiefest of all the Pharisees, neither his sleek, sanctimonious visage—his many prayers—his ostentatious alms-deeds, his broad phylacteries, nor his hoard of Gold would have obtained for him a "Commission" to redeem his respectability—to receive his evidence *in secret*, or to delay for an hour the release of those helpless ones whom the Saviour owned and blessed as a peculiarly beloved portion of his kingdom below.

As a Minister of the Church of England, I conceive it my duty to maintain the cause of the oppressed and the poor, and I regard this favorite system of *Commissions*, now so generally adopted, as so many parts of a Dexterous Conspiracy, which certain Political Philosophers are under plotting, the effect of which is, to establish the domination of wealth, and the degradation of industrious Poverty. I feel, too, that the interests of Christianity itself are betrayed, into the hands of unreasonable and wicked men, by the Judas-like conduct of many of its professors, whose capital is embarked in the Factory System, whose lips salute our altars with apparent devotion—who raise their hands in her sanctuary as if to adore, but who make them fall with tyrannous weight upon the children of the needy. Whether such bitter foes of the true Religion of Christ are shrouded in a Priestly Mantle, or dwell in those Mansions and are surrounded by those parks and lawns which the over laboured infant has enabled them to procure, my Ministerial duty to my Country is the same; and whether I regard its general prosperity its social happiness or its religious advantage, I am bound to rebuke and oppose them.

I believe, the oppression of the Rich—of those especially who hypocritically assume a Christian profession, has done more to injure Christianity than all that Voltaire or Pain ever produced.

14

3. *I further Protest against this Commission in the capacity of a Religious Instructor of Youth.*

The present System of Factory Labour generally precludes the possibility of sufficient Religious or common instruction; and any limitation which involves more than 13 hours occupation (which is involved in a Ten Hour Bill) will be an intolerable Evil. I am disgusted to hear from the same quarters a great cry of exultation that "the School-master is abroad" and a greater and more sincere cry against a Ten Hour Bill. The avowed object of those who obtained the appointment of the Commission, being to set aside that benevolent measure. I recognize in you, their Representatives, and not those of our Gracious Sovereign, who has too kind a heart and too honest a mind, knowingly to authorize the object of those interested and obdurate men, to whose influence you are indebted for your appointment.

As Public Men, you are open to public Remark. Of your PRIVATE *Characters I have no knowledge, of your Motives I am no judge. I have only to wish that your next appointment may not be unconstitutional in its character, and not opposed to the interests of Religion and Humanity in its object.*

I am, Gentlemen, with all submission, yours faithfully,

G. S. BULL.

Byerley, June 4th, 1833.

P.S. *The 4th of June is associated from my earliest recollections with the memory of George III, who I am sure would have wished every Factory Child in his Dominions to have* TIME *to read his Bible.*

APPENDIX B

At a General Meeting of the Lancashire Central Short Time Committee, held at the house of Mr Thomas Wilkinson, Red Lion Inn, Manchester, on Tuesday evening, 8 June 1847, the following resolutions were unanimously adopted.

1. That this Committee feel deeply thankful to the disposer of all good gifts, for the glorious success which has attended their efforts to ameliorate the condition of the women and children employed in factories, and sincerely congratulate their fellow-labourers in the good work on the peaceful and constitutional character of the agitation, as well as the triumphant manner in which the Ten Hours' Bill has passed the British Parliament.

2. That the hearty thanks of this Committee are due, and are hereby gratefully tendered on behalf of the working people of Lancashire, to the Right Honourable Lord Ashley, for his zealous and efficient services in this sacred cause, during a period of fourteen years of constant, consistent, and exemplary perseverance, to improve the moral, religious, and mental condition of the factory workers by endeavouring to obtain for them leisure hours to be devoted to that purpose; and especially for the zeal and activity he has displayed during the present session of Parliament.

3. That the best thanks of this Committee are also due to John Fielden, Esq., M.P., for the honest, consistent, and straightforward conduct which he has ever pursued on behalf of his poorer fellow-countrymen; and especially for his exertions during the present session of Parliament in bringing the agitation for the Ten Hours' Bill to a successful issue.

4. That this Committee tender their heartfelt thanks to the Right Honourable the Earl of Ellesmere and Lord Faversham, for their zealous exertions in conducting the Ten Hours' Bill safely through the House of Lords.

5. That this Committee are deeply grateful and tender their best thanks to J. Brotherton, Esq., M.P., H. A. Aglionby, Esq., M.P., C. Hindley, Esq., M.P., and all those members who spoke and voted in favour of this measure during its progress in the House of Commons.

6. That this Committee are deeply impressed with the gratitude they owe to the Duke of Richmond, the Bishops of Oxford, London, and St. Davids, and all the peers who spoke and voted in favour of the Ten Hours' Bill.

7. That this Committee offer their most hearty congratulations and sincere thanks to John Wood, Richard Oastler, W. Walker, Thomas Fielden, and Joseph Gregory, Esqrs., and to the Rev. G. S. Bull, for their support of this cause in times when it was unpopular to be ranked amongst its advocates; and also to all its friends and supporters out of Parliament.

8. That this Committee view with extreme satisfaction the past support of the clergy of the Established Church, as well as of those ministers of religion of all denominations who were ever found amongst the supporters of this measure, and sincerely hope that they will live to see realised the happy results which we believe were the aim and object of all their pious labours in this cause.

9. That we heartily tender our best thanks to Mr. M. Fletcher, surgeon, of Bury and all the medical men throughout this county who supported the Ten Hours' Bill.

10. That the most hearty thanks of this Committee are due and are hereby given to the delegates, who have been in London promoting the measure, during the present session, for their zeal and persevering efforts to obtain an efficient Ten Hours' Bill.

11. That this Committee tender their best thanks to Mr. Philip Grant, for his efficient services during 21 years of difficulty and trial in this cause, and especially for the close attention he has paid to the promotion of the measure in London, during the present session of Parliament.

PAUL HARGREAVES, Chairman.

From The Ten Hours' Advocate, 12 June 1847.

BIBLIOGRAPHICAL NOTE

THERE is no space here to give a list of all the contemporary publications dealing with the events outlined in this book and the subsequent developments. Almost all of them are to be found in the Bibliography in Professor Driver's *Tory-Radical*. The three histories of the Movement written by contemporaries are out of print. They are: *The Ten Hours Bill: The History of Factory Legislation* (Philip Grant), *The History of the Factory Movement* (Samuel Kydd), and *Oastler and Factory Movement* (W. R. Croft).

White Slavery, quoted frequently in this book, is the collection made by Richard Oastler himself and now divided between the libraries of London University and of Columbia University, New York.

The novel by Mrs Frances Trollope, *Martin Armstrong*—now a collector's piece—is based upon her observation of the textile areas and her conversations with people concerned. Bull was amongst them. He figures in the book, thinly disguised as "Parson Bell of Fairly".

J. C. G.

INDEX

ACKROYD, W. A., (manufacturer, of Otley, near Bradford), 17, 33

Adams, Jane, 172, 173

Agnew, Sir Andrew, 82

Akroyd family (manufacturers of Halifax), 11, 33, 190

Almeley, 193

Althorp Act, 115f, 120, 123, 133, 145, 147f, 151

Althorp, Lord, (later Earl Spencer), 59f, 98, 110, 115, 119, 123, 135

America, 6, 144f

Armstrong, J., (Vicar of Wallsend), 188

Arnold, Dr, 132

Ashley, Lord, (later Seventh Earl of Shaftesbury): M.P. for Dorset, 82; agrees to present Ten Hours Bill, 82; tribute to Sadler, 83; gives notice of motion in Commons, 84; praised by Doherty, 112; willing to forego "personal punishment clause", 113; defeats Althorp on a matter of procedure, 113; defeated by Althorp on major issue, letter to Oastler, 115; temporarily superseded by Hindley, 150; persuades Hindley to withdraw his Ten Hours Bill, 154; place in the Movement, 82, 178, 197

Ashton, 151, 154

Ashworth, Henry, (manufacturer, of Turton, near Bolton), 170

BAINES, EDWARD, (Editor, *The Leeds Mercury*), 16, 18, 19, 20, 33, 52, 73ff, 116, 133, 143

Baines, Edward, Jr, (Junior Editor, *The Leeds Mercury*), 18, 73ff, 149

Balme, Matthew, vii, 147, 189

Bardsley, Dr, 34

Baxter, Richard, 179

Birmingham, 191, 193

Birstall, 133

Bishops: attitude to Reform Bill, 7, 34, 68; attitude to Factory reform, 118, 130; attitude to New Poor Law, 173

Blackburn, 116, 154

Blackstone, Lord, 174

Boddington, J. C., 20, 149, 180f

Bowling, xiii, 2, 10, 35, 42, 48, 63, 130, 147, 191

Bradford, 2, 10, 17, 25, 31, 108, 110, 147, 172, 182, 189; 1831 Meeting, 20f; Bull's letter to the inhabitants of Bowling and Bradford, 36–43; Bull campaigns there 1832, 26, 48; Bull's account of moral and social conditions, 64ff; Reform Parliamentary Election, 69; 1833 Conference, 80f, 84, 86; Petition to Parliament, 93; protests against Factory Commission, 98, 107, 128; meeting protesting against the Althorp Act, 118; opening of John Wood's school, 147; National Regeneration Society meetings